PENGUIN BO

MURDERERS AND OT

'As an autobiography it is as idiosyncratic as one would hope from this
writer, for it allows us to make our own discoveries through a series of
highly personal journeys and crusades. These involve his family and
parents – and the significant journeys he has made literally to
Australia, Russia, Singapore and South Africa where, in search of his
roots, the book is at its most moving' – Michael Codron in the
Evening Standard

'Mortimer always [writes] with such clarity and elegance. He also has
the actor's gift for timing ... I roared out loud several times as I read
this book, either because the portraits of Tony Richardson or David
Niven are so visibly right, or because the stories are so outlandish ...
his writing [is] both hilarious and warm' – Brian Masters in the
Mail on Sunday

'A pleasure to read' – Judge Stephen Tumin in the *Sunday Express*

'I laughed out loud at John Mortimer's reminiscences' – P. D. James
in the *Daily Mail* Books of the Year

'Both in the courts and in the world of entertainment, Mortimer ...
graces all that he touches with industrious good humour '
– Frederic Raphael in the *Sunday Times*

ABOUT THE AUTHOR

John Mortimer is a playwright, novelist and former practising barrister. During the war he worked with the Crown Film Unit and published a number of novels before turning to theatre. He has written many film scripts, radio and television plays, including *A Voyage Round My Father*, the Rumpole plays, which won him the British Academy Writer of the Year Award, and the adaptation of Evelyn Waugh's *Brideshead Revisited*. Penguin publish his many collections of Rumpole stories; two volumes of his plays; his acclaimed autobiography *Clinging to the Wreckage;* and *In Character* and *Character Parts*, which contain interviews with some of the most famous men and women of our time. His novels include *Summer's Lease, Paradise Postponed,* its sequel, *Titmuss Regained* (all of which have been made into successful television series), *Charade* and *Dunster*.

John Mortimer lives with his wife and their two daughters in what was once his father's house in the Chilterns.

JOHN MORTIMER

Murderers and Other Friends

Another Part of Life

PENGUIN BOOKS

PENGUIN BOOKS

Published by the Penguin Group
Penguin Books Ltd, 27 Wrights Lane, London W8 5TZ, England
Penguin Books USA Inc., 375 Hudson Street, New York, New York 10014, USA
Penguin Books Australia Ltd, Ringwood, Victoria, Australia
Penguin Books Canada Ltd, 10 Alcorn Avenue, Toronto, Ontario, Canada M4V 3B2
Penguin Books (NZ) Ltd, 182–190 Wairau Road, Auckland 10, New Zealand

Penguin Books Ltd, Registered Offices: Harmondsworth, Middlesex, England

First published by Viking 1994
Published in Penguin Books 1995
1 3 5 7 9 10 8 6 4 2

The publishers would like to thank
John Murray (Publishers) Ltd for permission to quote from 'Myfanwy' and 'Christmas', both
published in *Collected Poems* by John Betjeman; The Hogarth Press with Princeton University Press
for permission to quote from 'Waiting for the Barbarians' from *Collected Poems* by C. P. Cavafy,
translated by Edmund Keeley and Philip Sherrard, edited by George Savidis; Warner Chappell
Music Ltd, London W1Y 3FA/International Music Publications Ltd for permission to quote from
'I'm Putting All My Eggs in One Basket' and 'Top Hat, White Tie and Tails' by Irving Berlin
(both songs used by permission of Irving Berlin Music Company administered by Williamson
Music); Faber and Faber Ltd with Random House, Inc. for permission to quote from 'New Year's
Letter' and 'The Novelist' from *Collected Poems* by W. H. Auden, edited by Edward Mendelson,
and from *The Dyer's Hand* by W. H. Auden

Printed in England by Clays Ltd, St Ives plc

For Penny

Illustrations

Castle Howard visited: with Laurence Olivier, Charles Sturridge (director) and Derek Granger (producer)

With John Gielgud: chain-smoking, bubbling with reminiscences, and eighty-five years old on the set of *Summer's Lease*

Penny with Rosie

Rosie and I, both under the weather

In the grounds of the Novodevichy Convent with Henrietta Dobryakova and Emily

John Piper with a face like a cardinal and a taste for drinking a good deal of red wine with everything

Myfanwy Piper: John Betjeman wrote a poem about her fortunate bicycle

With Neil Kinnock and Barbara Castle: she's eloquent, scornful and unfashionably optimistic

In Tbilisi with the ghost of Stalin and a glass of Georgian red

Rosie, nine years old with large eyes and an indomitable will

Emily has learnt to speak beautiful lines in a language I can't understand

Sally: if the world's divided into patients and nurses, she's one of the great nurses

Jeremy, gentler and calmer than his sisters

My Aunt Gertie known to the Zulu community as Umuthimkulu, The Great Tree or The One Who Offers Shade

The children act us (*left to right*): Emma Hodge as Anna Ford, Tom Ward as Katie Boxer, Emily as Rosie, Claire Boxer as me, Katie Boxer as Tom Ward, Rosie as Penny

As a general rule, people, even the wicked, are much more naive and simple-hearted than we suppose. And we ourselves are, too.

Dostoevsky, *The Brothers Karamazov*

I

I am running down the cold, marble corridors of the Law Courts to do some case I haven't prepared; in fact I know nothing whatever about it. Not only have I no idea what to say, I am inappropriately dressed. I am wearing a bright blue shirt, bought some years before for a summer holiday, and shorts, or I am in pyjamas. I turn up the collar of the shirt so that it may look as though it were of the stiff and stand-up variety. Someone I pass gives me a pair of crumpled white bands, which I try to tie round my neck, but I can't undo, or do up, the knot. I borrow a wig which I perch on my head. I haven't shaved for several days. When I get to the glass-panelled door of the courtroom it's locked and I rattle it uselessly. Inside I can see nothing but darkness.

In the years since I stopped being a barrister I have had this dream less often, but it still returns two or three times a year. One day the glass door will be unlocked and I will walk into the dark courtroom to be called on to argue from a brief I haven't read, on instructions I have never clearly understood.

I don't know how many lives you get. Not counting immortality, maybe two. Tolstoy, trying desperately for a third, dropped dead at Astapovo railway station. I had a new life, unlooked-for and no doubt undeserved happiness. Yet I was still in my childhood home, in my parents' house, trying to keep their garden in the station of life to which it had grown accustomed, and exercising my father's

I

profession, although in courts he never visited, doing cases which he would have considered just as down market as my mother would have thought the pool which we have implanted at the end of the lawn. To make up for this, we have acquired more woods and a meadow, uncultivated for a hundred years, which are inhabited by strange snails, the Duke of Burgundy's fritillary butterfly and a number of orchids, one of which has to be guarded, when in flower, by a man from the nature reserve, who lives next to it in a tent and protects it from ruthless and predatory botanists.

The ghost of my father is a hard one to banish and I still see him down the long borders, feeling for the flowers in his blindness. He is dressed in an ancient tweed suit, darned at the knee where it has worn thin, and an unusual straw hat tinged with blue. He is seated beside my mother on a low, three-legged stool with broad feet to prevent it sinking into the soft earth.

His presence lingers also in his chambers, Number One, Dr Johnson's Buildings in the Temple. His room seemed part of our home. I used to go there with my mother when I was a child and the clerks would give us tea and chocolate biscuits as we waited for him to be freed from some sensational divorce case. The room was dark, never very tidy; some of the chairs were broken and the leather bindings on many of the law reports were powdering into dust. When I came home for the school holidays I found my father sitting there in a black jacket and striped trousers, wearing white spats over his boots in the summer, grey ones in the winter, massaging his sightless eyes and listening to my mother reading out the histories of broken marriages. 'Is it the boy?' he would ask, and when my mother confirmed the fact he gave me a great shout of welcome. I thought, with gratitude, of how he had never patronized me, always treated me as an equal, and on our long walks had introduced me to the writers he loved and left me with a great store of pleasure for the rest of my life. It was the room I had taken girls to during the war, when my mother and father spent their nights in the country, and we had helped ourselves to the vintage port stored with dusty briefs in the cellar, listened to distant bombs and, occasionally, made love.

The middle-aged, middle-class Englishman in the thirties had a licence to shout, and my father used his to the full. His rages were legendary, Lear-like and uncontrolled. They were never about his blindness – his temper was as bad before he lost his sight – but were brought on by soft-boiled eggs, cold plates or being kept waiting for anything. He frequently complained that he was surrounded by cretins, but I find myself missing his storms of anger which ceased as suddenly, and as unreasonably, as they had begun.

I am looking at a picture painted by my mother. It's of Paris rooftops, greys and blues, in the early morning or at the end of the day, chimney-pots emerging from, or vanishing into, the mist. She must have painted it in 1912, when she was teaching art at Versailles, and it was accepted by the Paris Salon. She'd been to Birmingham School of Art and there she was, in the Paris of Matisse and Picasso and Modigliani, of whom she knew nothing at the time. She had her whole life before her; how was she to guess that she'd end up reading the dubious evidence in divorce cases aloud to a blind husband in a train? How could she know that, after a number of disappointments and miscarriages, she would give birth to a son who, perhaps, never showed his love for her sufficiently?

She had given up painting by the time I was born, although sometimes, sitting by the fire in the evenings, she made drawings of my father and me. She took me to art galleries when I was very young and I remember looking at Van Gogh's yellow chair with his pipe on it. I thought it dull and clumsy but I pretended to like it, not only to please her but to appear grown up. She had large, dark eyes, and was in her late thirties by the time she produced a living child. She often wore a blue brooch which I imagined was pinned into her flesh, and I thought it typical of her that she bore

3

the pain of it without complaint. When I was sent away to boarding-school – exiled, it seemed to me, for some crime I didn't know I had committed – I blamed her and not my father. He was, I thought, like all men, including me, naturally selfish and didn't want to be bothered by a child all the year round. When I told my mother I wanted to come home she smiled tolerantly and went off to help my father get dressed.

My father and I formed an alliance from which my mother was thoughtlessly excluded. She was never asked if execution had been done on Cawdor, his favourite question to me. We went on long walks, had tea together in distant farmhouses, played word games and went through the Sherlock Holmes stories. She stayed at home and cooked meals we weren't slow to criticize. Once she offered to join in the one-actor plays I did at home, painted a beard and a moustache on her face with a stick of dark brown make-up and took the thankless part of Tubal to my Shylock. The make-up was unnecessary because my father saw neither of us. I felt grateful to her for her trouble but I should have said so louder and more often. I know that I should.

During his frequent bouts of fury my father shouted at her, not at me. As a child I protested but I could, I think, have done more to protect her, because my father's rage was grossly inflated and easily punctured. No one could blame her for taking him more seriously than he deserved. Once she left home and he was distraught. She came back after an hour, carrying a pair of whited antlers she had picked up in Stonor Park. He was on his knees, begging her forgiveness and she helped him up, anxious that he shouldn't appear pathetic and ridiculous in my eyes. Although I never told her, I think it was then I realized that most women are better, calmer and more civilized than most men – a view I have never forsaken, despite occasional evidence to the contrary. I am unable, for instance, to understand the fuss about women priests. Given the record of many men priests, from the Borgia pope downwards, it seems to me that women are best qualified to celebrate Mass and hand out forgiveness. For this reason I have always welcomed women on juries. They are less prejudiced than men and not spurred on by guilt at their own delinquencies to punish others. My views on this subject were not shared by my clients in the dock, who usually felt that a woman's place was in the home and not out robbing banks or judging bank robbers.

Although gentle and blushing easily, my mother was a stronger character than my father. After Versailles she saw an advertisement for a girls' school in South Africa, a kind of colonial attempt to establish Roedean in the Natal midlands, and wrote off for the job. She must have been brave, a thin, big-eyed girl from Leamington Spa, to set off on the long sea voyage to an unknown land, recently torn apart by the Boer War. Eighty years later I was to set off to find traces of her teaching there and I read the pieces she wrote in the school magazine, calling for high standards in the practice of art: 'We must be very stern judges of our own productions, always careful to realize the difference between what we do and what we would do, and each time more anxious to get nearer to our own idea of perfection.'

I had visited my father's room as a child and made use of it as a teenager during the war. When I became a barrister I went there to work for him, drafting paragraphs of cruelty and intolerable behaviour in his divorce petitions or advising on the evidence to be called in his contested will cases. As the years passed and I began to acquire his practice, he spent more and more time in the country, receiving news of the herbaceous border, and I sat alone at his desk, noting briefs, giving opinions (it's your decisions they pay for, not your doubts, my father told me), and writing novels and stories whenever I got the chance.

I thought of leaving the bar in the 1960s, when I'd had two plays on in the West End of London and it occurred to me that I could do without the support of adultery in Ruislip, the question of who flung the toast rack in 1952, or the unnecessary inquiry into why a happy, active love affair subsided into a miserable marriage. I told this to Charlie, my clerk, a shrewd operator who starred in farces put on by his amateur group, and he perfectly understood the lure of show business. But although he had been dead for five years, my father's shadow hadn't lost its power. I felt I wasn't ready to leave his room. I became a Queen's Counsel, as my father had never done, put on the silk stockings and knee-breeches and tailed coat that he had never worn, and was prepared, for the next fifteen years, to continue his career and take it into dark areas of the law where he had never ventured. My legal life changed dramatically. I did my first jury trial and no longer had to woo single judges whose likes and dislikes I had come to know by heart. I began to learn about fingerprints, bloodstains and police verbals. Crime came, at first, gently, with disputes over small quantities of cannabis at Bow Street, the level of alcohol in the blood of my clerk's brother as he sat in a parked car, affrays between mini-cab drivers, and the defence of a likeable ox of a man known as the Bull of Waltham Cross. He trained trotting ponies and, among his other activities, took part in bare-fist boxing matches in the manner of the pugilists of the Regency, fighting by night on deserted airfields and empty football grounds. In gangland wars, so the prosecution alleged, he used to be sent in first, like a kind of battering-ram.

And then the time came when I got to know murderers.

2

A barrister, an experienced and effective defender in criminal trials on a good day, rises to his feet in the Old Bailey. This is not a good day. His life is in tatters. A mental storm, long threatened by gathering black clouds of depression, is about to burst inside his head. He has had a liquid lunch in the pub across the road and, although a large and weighty man, he sways and creaks like a tree in a high wind. It's a quarter past two in the afternoon and he feels a strong disposition to sleep overcome him.

'Members of the jury' – his voice is deep and comes softly at first, the half-audible hint of approaching thunder – 'this is the point in the case at which I am supposed to make a reasoned and persuasive speech on behalf of the accused. That will be followed by an unbiased summing-up from the learned judge, and you will then retire and come to a just decision. But' – here comes a great sigh and then a louder, clearer burst of thunder – 'as I am far too drunk to make a reasoned and persuasive speech, and as the judge has never given an unbiased summing-up in his entire career, and as you look far too stupid to come to a just verdict, I shall sit down.' He does so and, happy at last, closes his eyes.

That happened but not, thank God, to me. The barrister retired and a retrial was ordered for his client. Beneath all the suave, assured, perhaps pompous, behaviour of advocates in murder cases there is a haunted insecurity, a dread of forgetting to ask a question or, worse still, asking too many and so destroying the future of the client in the dock, who is also giving a more or less convincing performance of quiet confidence and who has become, for the short period of the trial, your dependant and, in some strange way, your friend.

It's not, I suppose, what you would call true friendship. I mean, people on trial for murder are not the sort you'd want to go on holiday with, or ask to be godparents to your children, or confide in when plagued by doubt and insecurity. The friendship only lasts for a short time, a few weeks or however long the trial takes. When the trial is over, you say goodbye to them in the cells and they are still full of the adrenalin which kept them going throughout the case – as actors are still in a high mood after the curtain falls on a play in which they have starred. If you have shared a success, the relationship is also over and they will stare straight through you, even though you meet again in the most respectable circumstances, on the terrace of the House of Commons, for example, or in the Crush Bar at Covent Garden. They no longer depend on you, try to impress or even entertain you. When they are out of danger they want to believe you never existed. Those accused of murder are at the best fair-weather, or rather ill-weather, friends.

What the defending counsel learns – a useful lesson when dealing with all types of friend – is to refrain from judgement. There are plenty of people whose business it is to perform this unpleasant function: judges, juries and, perhaps, God. The defender's task is to listen and suspend disbelief.

Filson Young, writing in the Notable British Trials series about Dr Crippen, a murderer who impressed everyone with his politeness and modesty, said that it was 'what we have in common with a criminal, rather than the subtle insanity which differentiates him from us, that makes us view with such a lively interest a human being who has wandered into these tragic and fatal fields'. The lively interest almost always falls short of understanding. One of my greatest friends, at Oxford and for many years after, was a pacifist, a Greek scholar, a lover of Mozart and a country doctor. He ended his life, after killing his mistress, by committing suicide. I can only think of him as a friend, as a murderer I cannot understand him at all.

To defend in a murder trial is an unpredictable business; cases can be won or lost because they happen to come on before a certain judge, or because of the random selection of the jury, or because the defendant is likeable or apparently unpleasant. Some trials go well from the start, others seem to attract ill fortune and blunders. Sometimes the luck can change in a most unnerving manner, as it did in the case of a young man whom I'll call Jimmy O'Neill, although that wasn't his name. He was accused not only of murder, but of writing a letter to the devil in his victim's blood.

Jimmy O'Neill was small, Irish and very young. He looked like an office boy in some huge, bureaucratic department where the work was dull and he saw little of the daylight. He lived around Earls Court in a flat which he shared with a male friend. In his spare time Jimmy read the works of Dennis Wheatley who wrote about satanism and black magic. The night he started on his journey to the dock in Number Two Court down the Old Bailey, he came back to the bed in which he slept with his flatmate and his flatmate's girlfriend. He announced that he had killed a man, washed his hands and hidden the Malayan dagger which he often carried. His friend seemed to show no great interest in this revelation. In the morning Jimmy was sitting up in bed smoking and no one referred to what had happened the night before.

Charles Wistey was good-looking, young and well connected. Somewhere or other his family contained a Lord. He had been having dinner with the girl he planned to marry; they had parted in the restaurant and he was on his way home by himself when he was stabbed to death in the portico of a Victorian house in Earls Court. The police made inquiries in the neighbourhood; Jimmy

9

realized they were after him but was too frightened to give himself up. He was eventually found and charged with murder; there was no doubt he had stabbed Charles Wistey with the dagger.

Detective stories ask 'who dunit?' In most murders that question is quickly answered and the trial attempts to discover 'why dunit?' Did the customer in the dock intend to kill or do serious harm, did he or she act in self-defence, was there provocation, was it all an accident or the result of a diseased mind? These are questions fingerprints and bloodstains cannot answer; they require the jury to perform the difficult act of getting inside the skull of someone who may or may not be a murderer.

Jimmy's account, I was not particularly delighted to learn, was one well known in criminal courts as 'the Guardsman's Defence'. I suppose it came from the days when humble guardsmen were sexually assaulted by officers and gentlemen and protected their honour too energetically. Charles Wistey had, it seemed, propositioned the pale, young Jimmy O'Neill in the street and pursued him into the portico of the house and had him cornered. Jimmy's statement described him pulling out the knife he often carried, holding it in front of him and shouting, 'Get off, you dirty man!' Undeterred, Wistey advanced remorselessly and ran himself on to the dagger in the way an antique Roman fell upon his sword. As a general rule it's unwise to attack the character of the deceased, who cannot, after all, answer back. In Jimmy's case we were alleging that a young man of 'good' family, engaged to be married, was a homosexual rapist – without the support of any evidence at all. We would be in for a bumpy ride before Carl Aarvold, the gruff but decent Recorder of London, who was chairman of the Wimbledon tennis matches and had a long, and no doubt weary, experience of 'the Guardsman's Defence'. There was, however, one singular fact. Earls Court, then an area well known for gay pick-ups, was nowhere near the route Wistey would have taken from the West End restaurant to his home.

*

The day starts with a lonely breakfast in the café opposite the Old Bailey, a site where Londoners once paid a great deal for a window to watch the executions outside Newgate Prison. I am surrounded by anonymous people, talking quietly about the day ahead; they may be jurors, witnesses, villains or police officers. Then I go up to the robing room and put on the fancy costume: the winged collar and the bands, the Tom Jones tailed coat and the silk gown. In this very robing room I once saw an elderly ex-Solicitor-General slip my wallet into his jacket pocket. I go out carrying my wig and my brief. My next stop is the cells, down in the basement.

I pass the old, scratched, kicked oak door, carved with the names of forgotten criminals, the last remnant of Newgate, and the prison officer lets me into the cells. These men always seem to be drinking mugs of tea and eating doorstep sandwiches. They have a prison pallor and are overweight. Then I am let into the interview room where Jimmy is already taking cigarettes off my solicitor, Paul Laity. Paul is short, thickset, plods about looking like a farmer and has a fund of filthy reminiscences about his life in the Navy. He comes from Cornwall and goes beagling, walking vast distances in the company of hunting dogs. He has a great determination to win cases and will not forgive me if I fail to ask a question. He will have one brilliant idea which will be an enormous help to us. I also have a junior barrister named Peter who is consistently entertaining, can mimic all the judges and discuss politics and the theatre with great insight. He will be able to view the case with an amused detachment neither Paul nor I can manage. At the moment he is being entertaining somewhere else. This is the small squad I have to do my best to command, and from whom I must try to hide my doubts and fears.

The visit to the client in the cells is less to gain information than to calm his fears and give him a confidence which you may not feel. Jimmy has to trust me but I have no such duty. I must merely suspend my disbelief about him. I am there to put his case as well as it can be put and never to judge him. I know he won't tell me much more about the facts of the stabbing which, like all traumatic events, have been buried in some dark corner of his mind and he doesn't want to disinter them. I also remember that Sir Patrick Hastings, a great advocate, would never see a client in a murder, in case, overwhelmed by his dominating and Irish charm, they might pour out their hearts to him and confess.

So we watch Jimmy, looking paler and younger than ever, buoyed up by the excitement of the great day which has come at last. We smoke Paul's cigarettes and talk about the weather and conditions on remand in Brixton, both horrible. Then Jimmy tells me that his letter to the devil, which began 'Hail, Lucifer' and contained the Lord's Prayer in reverse, was written, not in his victim's blood, as the prosecution's expert would testify, but in his own. I know that my job, for the next few days, is not to prove Jimmy innocent but to demonstrate that the prosecution evidence is not entirely convincing.

Now I am in court. The prosecutor is an elegant lawyer who wears a bowler hat with a curly brim, striped shirts with stiff white collars and takes holidays on Greek islands. The jury looks solid and working-class with one Irishman (is this a hopeful sign?) and a shy Kensington lady who seems strangely out of place. The judge is silent, almost motionless. Nobody looks surprised as the prosecutor flourishes the dagger and deciphers the blood-stained letter to the Prince of Darkness. Peter, my junior, has appeared and is looking round the court with quiet amusement. At lunch-time, in the pub, he will give the prosecutor's opening speech a severe mimicking. Two clerks of the court, sitting below the judge, have dropped into a light doze. The pathologist gives evidence and we examine the dagger with detached interest, as though we were passing each other clues from the crossword puzzle. We have met in many such trials and always enjoyed friendly conversations across the court. At least he agrees that the wound is not inconsistent with our story. The judge snorts loudly, like an old boar awakening, and asks some questions. They are very fair. I remember defending an elderly husband who had killed his terminally ill wife. 'You have undertaken a task,' Judge Aarvold told him, 'which only the Almighty performs and that with reluctance. Go now and sin no more.' I wonder if there is any chance of him telling Jimmy to go and sin no more, and decide that, even if he doesn't, I like this judge very much.

Jimmy's flatmate gives evidence. He is thin, long-haired, elegant and now married to a Swedish girl. He seems an unlikely friend for the pallid young Irishman. He says he couldn't believe it when Jimmy said he'd killed someone, and didn't remember if he was laughing or crying when he said it. One court clerk, now awake, wakes up the other who can't face the reality of life in court and is soon off again. The judge starts to yawn and clerk number one keeps awake by closely watching everyone's movements. Courts are not the quiet, peaceful places you see in movies: a stream of people are coming in and out, whispering, passing notes and dashing off to other cases. Now, the wakeful clerk concentrates on making telephone calls. As I realize the prosecution wants to prove Jimmy gay and therefore unlikely to resist the deceased person's advances (as though a heterosexual girl would be bound to accept all would-be lovers), I ask his flatmate about a disease he and Jimmy caught from the same woman. He looks at his shoes and admits the truth of this suggestion. Then we go to lunch in the pub where Paul reads a prediction of doom in Jimmy's horoscope and Peter tells me he hates being led.

In the afternoon we get Jimmy's sister, a sensible Irish nurse who seems undisturbed by the proceedings. She says her brother is a perfectly normal young man. A friend from the Lebanon gives evidence and says he had teased Jimmy for being 'queer'. 'And was it because he wasn't that you felt it safe to tease him?' I ask a distinctly risky question and am rewarded by an undeserved yes. Paul, who is writing feverishly, mutters, 'Good question!' Peter is whispering something highly entertaining to the junior counsel for the prosecution. We get a youngish doctor who puts on a bowler hat to take the oath and says that he examined Jimmy in prison and came to the conclusion that he had been 'buggered frequently'. 'You are an examiner of the back passage?' The judge is making a note in which he is not inclined to mince words. I remember the book on forensic evidence which says that area of the body can be distended for many reasons. People sometimes put strange things up themselves; for instance, in various recorded cases, a tin of Brasso, a boot brush, or a small bust of Napoleon III. It can also be distended by chronic constipation. The judge takes down the evidence about Napoleon III without a smile and then looks at the doctor in some bewilderment. I feel I have done my best with the medical evidence and sit down sweating and thinking of a hot bath and clean clothes. When the day ends Jimmy is in a mood of exhilaration and thinks things are going 'brilliantly'. Paul says he's going to see a haemotologist and work on the case most of the night. He hopes to have something for me by lunch-time tomorrow. Peter gives us an imitation of the doctor in the witness-box.

The next morning the court is crowded. There is a party of schoolgirls and a contingent from the Women's Institute. The judge is friendly, the jury look anxious and attentive; the prosecutor winks at me from time to time, remembering our blue movie sessions in Scotland Yard. Nothing has gone seriously wrong and, although I had another nightmare about turning up in court in my pyjamas, I am feeling relaxed. And then a large, jovially upper-class doctor appears in the witness-box and says he is a friend of the Wistey family and had been asked by them to keep an eye on young Charlie in London. He says the dead man had a low IQ and was emphatically not homosexual. I feel that this medic and the judge are going to get on well together and start a polite, low-key cross-examination. 'When you say Wistey was sexually immature, does that mean he was at the homosexual stage?' I ask a question which is politically incorrect but might be forensically effective. The doctor will have none of this and embarks on a long lecture about the nature of homosexuality which is distinctly

14

unhelpful to our case. Hoping to stop his flow I sit down, to be fixed with a glare from Paul, who looks at me as though I were the first sign of blight on the potato crop. 'Why didn't you suggest that Master Charlie wouldn't have admitted to being gay to his upper-crust friends?' he hissed at me. I smile in a way which I hope indicates I had thought of that question and, after careful considera-tion, rejected it.

By lunch-time Paul has forgiven me. We go to an Italian restaurant and, among the breadsticks and beside the plates of spaghetti carbonara, he gives me notes he has made about the blood in which Jimmy wrote his letter to the devil. I absorb a glass or two of Chianti and a crash course in haemotology. I realize with intense gratitude that I have a solicitor who may help win the case.

The forensic expert looks like an anonymous housewife with glasses and a high, monotonous voice with whistling s sounds. She has formidable qualifications and handles all the exhibits with elaborate care, putting the dagger back into its sheath as though it were a valuable antique. It is to her that I have to put the body of instant learning I have got from Paul in the restaurant not half an hour before. I embark on the subject of the classification of blood: 'All our red corpuscles are the same. What varies are the agglutin-ogens which must fit in with the appropriate agglutinin as a lock fits its own key, and causes the red cells to clump together like bunches of grapes. These varying types of lock can divide human blood into four groups, which have been named A, B, O and AB.' An advocate must be able to take an instant lesson in any subject and at least sound knowledgeable when cross-examining an expert who has studied it for years. So far, the witness agrees. Then I put Paul's great thesis. The deceased's blood was of the common O variety. Jimmy's is of the slightly more rare A. Now, when the blood on the letter was tested it was classified as O and it was assumed that it had been written after the murder because it was in the victim's blood. But if, in fact, Jimmy had written it months before in his *own* blood, the passage of time could have caused the antigens to fade and the blood would have become very hard to classify. So the letter might not have been the devilish work of a murderer performing black magic with his victim's blood, but the act of a schoolboyish young man who pricked his own finger to do something he had read about in the works of Dennis Wheatley. The judge is wide awake and looming forward as though in the Centre Court at Wimbledon. The expert, for whom I now feel a surge of love and admiration, admits the possibility of what I am suggesting. What may turn out to be a match point has been won by Paul Laity.

The prosecution case is over and I'm opening the defence to the jury. I want them to perform an act of imagination. What would it be like to be an eighteen-year-old Irish boy who'd had a few drinks and was cornered by a bigger, taller, more athletic, better-nourished and sexually ravenous young man late on a wet night in the Earls Court area? The prosecutor has always called my client O'Neill. I call him Jimmy. I can tell his story for him but the moment comes, all too soon, when he has to tell it for himself. He leaves the safety of the dock for the dangerous witness-box. I take him through his evidence and then sit down. He's alone now, beyond my help, facing a prosecutor who's no longer smiling or winking at me but attacking Jimmy in a well-judged simulation of controlled outrage. It's all lies, isn't it, the story of an accidental death and a sexual attack? Jimmy turns out, rather to my surprise, to be an intelligent witness, perhaps too intelligent. He can see the rocks ahead. He sticks to his story, although some strange facts emerge. He wrote the letter in blood to frighten a girl he didn't like, but it seems to have frightened her not at all. He says he'd never heard of buggery until he got to England and then 'a queer told me'. He appears strangely innocent and prudish and doesn't know that the word 'come' means to have an orgasm. He says he made his statement to the police in a hurry because he wanted his cherry-coloured corduroy trousers back. He told some lies in it in order not to involve the friends he'd told about the killing. 'You lied to save your friends. Didn't you also lie to save yourself?' The prosecutor sits down, well satisfied, without waiting for the answer.

The defence is always at its highest point at the end of the prosecution case, at its lowest after the accused has given evidence. Jimmy hasn't made any obvious mistakes, in fact he's done rather well, but we've got no evidence to support the story of violent soliciting by night. There's plenty of evidence against Jimmy, none at all against Charles Wistey. And then Paul, who's been outside the court, comes back in a state of high excitement with a piece of paper in his hand. This is what can be said, he tells me, by a surprise witness, a *deus ex machina* who has arrived from nowhere and wants to give evidence. 'For God's sake,' Paul whispers deafeningly, 'get him into the witness-box before the bugger changes his mind!'

Our unlooked-for, unhoped-for witness turns out to be a model of credibility, a medical student about to do his finals and also engaged to be married. He'd read about our case in the *Daily Mirror* and decided to come and tell the court about his own experience. He'd been walking home late at night in Earls Court when a well-built, upper-class young man solicited him, pursued him into a doorway and urgently demanded sex. He's able to recognize the photograph of Wistey. No, he has no doubt about it at all. The advocate is frequently taken by surprise in the course of a case and has to hide the fact; it's particularly unnerving to discover that your client may have been telling nothing but the truth.

The final speech has always been the part I most enjoyed. You don't have to flatter the judge or risk unexpected answers from witnesses. You can form a relationship, a very temporary friendship even, with twelve people you hope to persuade to uncertainty. You can choose those members of the jury you feel are sympathetic and build up their confidence, or you can concentrate on those who have sat po-faced and disapproving and hope to convert them, or at least make them smile. It's also the best part because the end is in sight, the blessed moment when you've done all you can and the responsibility is no longer yours. I try to make them remember that Jimmy O'Neill's life will be changed for ever by what they decide, long after everyone else in court has forgotten what his case was all about.

And now the deep, growling voice comes from the bench, fair, moderate, still somewhat puzzled. 'This is a strange, unfamiliar world to us, members of the jury,' the judge tells them, as though Earls Court were in darkest Africa, thousands of miles from the tennis at Wimbledon. Jimmy is listening, pale and intense, as the judge dismisses the suggestion that he was buggered and accepts that Wistey pursued him with lecherous intent. 'That young man was on the prowl in Earls Court,' he says. It's twenty to twelve when he finishes, the jury file out in solemn silence and Paul and I go up to the Old Bailey canteen to wait and drink coffee.

This is the worst part. You can't concentrate or think of anything else. Peter arrives smiling and asks if the case is all over. The woman behind the tea urns is shouting at a deaf man because he failed to send someone a birthday card. The clerk who spent most of his time asleep in court comes up to our table. 'Your defence of that young man. Bloody top hole!' he says. 'If I were in charge I'd acquit immediately. And I say that from my extremely humble position.' I decide I don't like this work, and yet some inherited aptitude, or listening to ancestral voices, has kept me at it far too long.

We drink coffee until it feels as though it's running out of our ears and then we go to lunch in the pub. Doing nothing makes it the longest, the suspense makes it the most exhausting, day of the trial. At three o'clock in the afternoon the jury come back. 'Will your foreman please stand.' The clerk of the court is now wide awake and quietly excited. I hold my breath and stare at the ceiling, a gambler waiting for the roulette wheel to slow down and the ball to stop rattling. Jimmy, who has learnt chess from one of the screws during the long wait, seems entirely calm as the jury acquit him of murder and find him guilty of manslaughter by a majority of ten to two. I make the sort of mitigation speech, the appeal to mercy, which I have never been particularly good at and Jimmy stands, saying he's sorry for the family of the deceased gentleman. Judge Aarvold, talking sadly about the dangers of drinking and carrying knives, gives him four years, which like so many things in life is probably worse than he'd hoped for but better than he'd feared. Of course I never see him again.

And that, so far as I can recall, is how it was living through a murder trial. Years later I put some element of Jimmy O'Neill's trial into a Rumpole story, so fact became fiction. On another strange occasion a fictional murder ended up as fact. I wanted Rumpole to appear at a court martial and, as I had never been engaged in such a proceeding, I went off to the British Army in Germany to see how it worked. I was shown great hospitality by the Judge Advocate's office and taken to see the trial of a young guardsman accused of smoking a cannabis cigarette. An interesting point of law arose because the only evidence of what was in the cigarette was what he said at the time, and he might have been boasting or lying or just having everyone on. I learnt the procedure of a court martial and then I came home to write my Rumpole story.

It was called 'The Bright Seraphim' and it concerned a court martial for murder in a guards regiment. I started the story with what I thought was a dramatic image: a British sergeant-major is lying, stabbed through the heart, outside a disco in a small German town. The bloodstains were not immediately visible as, instead of his uniform, the sergeant was wearing a long, bright-red evening-gown. The story was written and, in due course, televised.

Years later I was invited to dinner with the Queen's Guard in Germany. It was an extremely pleasant occasion organized by an assistant adjutant whose name was Delia. Before dinner she suggested I might like to have a drink in the Sergeants Mess. One of the sergeants looked over his pint and said, 'Were you ever out with the army in Germany before?' 'Oh, yes,' I told them, 'I came out to see a court martial. It was quite an interesting case, actually. A young guardsman was accused of smoking cannabis and the only evidence against him was that he said it was a joint.'

'That wasn't the case!' An older, no doubt more important, sergeant corrected me. 'You came over here because of that murder we had. You know, the one where a sergeant-major was found stabbed outside a disco? And him wearing some tart's red evening-dress.'

3

I'm giving a talk at lunch-time. It's not especially well attended, but a man has come to interview me for a radio programme. He sits in the front row, an elderly, untidy person with a haversack full of documents. After the talk he takes me up in a creaking, coffin-like lift to an empty office. He produces an old tape-recorder which is about the size of a portable wireless in the days when they were substantial instruments. He strikes it with his fist and its red light flickers and then glows sullenly. By way of warm-up he tells me the following story. His grandfather used to act in melodrama at the old Lyric, Hammersmith, and played star roles. At the end of one of these performances he was holding an actress playing his wife, recently dead. 'My wife is dead in my arms', was the line this old actor had to sob out to the front of the house. 'What shall I doo — oo?' A voice from the gallery answered, 'Screw her while she's still warm!' For some reason this story endeared my interviewer to me but he managed to chill our relationship by delving into the haversack and bringing out a battered typescript. 'And this' — he flourished it proudly — 'is what they're going to say about you on the radio on the day you die. I thought it would be great fun if you read it out during our interview. It starts: "John Mortimer was —".' I stopped him there. Why? Because I might be in danger of believing it? Or because I prefer not to dwell on thoughts of death?

Another part of life started for me with Penny, more than twenty-three years younger but considerably more sensible than I. We met at a New Year's Eve party. Our wedding might be considered unromantic by some. I was in the middle of a trial when a member of the jury asked if he might have a day off because his mother-in-law had died and he wanted to attend the funeral. I then rang Penny and said we were having a free day because of the juryman's mother-in-law. Might it be possible to book the Harrow Road register office on the date of the funeral, which also happened to be my birthday and we were having a party? It was free and we were married.

It was the start of the seventies, the vanished age of flower power and headbands, Nehru jackets and Afghan waistcoats, protests against the Vietnam War and posters in bed-sitting rooms advising their occupants, who had no intention of fighting anyone, to Make Love Not War. It was a time when no one young thought they would have the least difficulty finding a job, and that society would inevitably become more tolerant, liberal and humane.

It was also a time for numberless underground magazines. These publications, printed in pink on darker pink paper, or in green on green, were full of rude cartoons and vaguely anti-establishment opinions. They were also hard to decipher and enjoyed the smallest of circulations. Richard Neville started such a magazine called *Oz* when he was a student in Australia. He and *Oz* came to England and in due course a 'Schoolkids' edition was published, which had apparently been largely written by children and young people. It contained attacks both on the Vietnam War and school dinners and a cartoon in which Rupert Bear, the somewhat boring hero of a respectable children's comic strip, was depicted in a high state of sexual excitement. There followed a lengthy trial at the Old Bailey in which the editors were charged with corrupting the morals of young people, the offence which led to Socrates drinking hemlock. A large number of doctors and psychiatrists gave evidence and made lengthy speeches. At the end, the *Oz* editors were convicted on certain charges and sent to prison, to be released a few days later by the Court of Appeal which overruled all but one minor conviction.

During the *Oz* case Penny sat below the dock, a slim girl with an unmistakably swollen stomach. When the trial was over, we went to stay with Tony Richardson. He had directed John Osborne's plays, *Look Back in Anger* and *The Entertainer*, at the Royal Court Theatre and had made, it was said, a million pounds – a sum which made us gasp with amazement – out of *Tom Jones*. He invited us to the South of France to discuss writing a film. When we arrived, he took us to lunch at a restaurant on a gay beach near St Tropez where heterosexual couples, particularly when one of them was young, wearing a bikini and very pregnant, were looked upon with as much approval as a couple of Sikhs entering the Club Bar in the heyday of the British Raj. This was the first of a long series of visits to Tony's house, his cluster of houses, his hamlet, his village, hidden away among the cork trees on a hillside near La Garde Freinet. However described, it was a place of undoubted magic and he ruled it with the absolute and arbitrary power of Prospero, producing – to deter the ever-present threat of boredom – tempests, quarrels, misalliances, scandals, seductions and betrayals, which only occasionally won through to the happy ending of Shakespeare's last play.

Tony was a tall, angular man whose long limbs were curiously uncoordinated; but he was resolutely, if not always successfully, athletic. He only learnt to swim in middle life and, although he spent more hours practising on the tennis court than Nastase before Wimbledon, he was easily beaten by a one-armed player who had to throw the ball into the air and then grab his racket from between his legs when he served. Tony spoke in a curious nasal drawl, much imitated by his friends and acquaintances, and specialized, as had my father, in saying outrageous things which you would have been unwise to take seriously. Once, when Penny was seeing me off at the airport on some misguided trip to Hollywood, he said to her, 'I suppose you hope the plane crashes, don't you, darling, and you'll be left a nice rich little widow?'

His normal expression was one of amused contempt but he was capable of great enthusiasm. When he was richly entertained, usually at some disaster, he would double up and massage his thighs with bony fingers, gulping with laughter. He was also extraordinarily generous. The long table, set out for lunch in front of the house, where the cook and the cleaning lady and a crowd of children all sat down with Nureyev, Jeanne Moreau, Lee Radziwill or John Gielgud, never seemed to be laid for fewer than twenty people. He once, while filming in Australia, lent his house to a dress designer who ran up a debt of ten thousand pounds on Tony's account at the St Tropez grocer's. He paid it without a murmur and only regretted doing so when he tried to telephone the couturier on some quite different subject and his calls were never returned. For all his appearance of lofty cynicism his children adored him, he was loyal to his friends and he managed to produce, in the house he lived in, a curiously potent magic.

The place was called Le Nid du Duc after an owl that must have made its nest there. I suppose it's the smell I remember most: the pungent scent of log fires, coffee, herbs, lavender and cooking. The group of houses, straggling down the wooded hillside towards the big swimming-pool Tony had built with the proceeds of directing a Mr Potato Chip commercial, were dominated by the main farmhouse which was wonderfully untidy. In the living-room, the cushions, the sofa and the chairs had been chewed by a large number of whippets, thin and adventurous as their master, who would travel vast distances through the woods and return, exhausted, to sleep by the fire. Last night's half-empty wine glasses, cards scattered after the game of bridge which Tony played with great daring and withering contempt for his opponents and partners, and pages of half-read and rejected scripts, littered the place. Doves fluttered around the house until one day Tony issued an imperious order that they should be slaughtered and served up to us at lunch. They proved to have been more enjoyable alive.

I had heard stories of guests being asked by Tony to have dinner in the village on chosen nights so that 'we can all talk about you' but nothing like that happened when we were staying. He did, however, greatly enjoy dramas. If things were getting a little slow and if Prospero were to experience moments of boredom, his servant – major-domo, butler or chief steward – could be guaranteed to provide an entertaining diversion. Jean-Pierre was by no means a Caliban. He was small and dark, with a face like some angelic youth in the background of an Italian painting. Tony, who had found him scratching a living as a pavement artist in Toulon, gave him a home, a car and a job well suited to his talents. At times he was unreliable, being what Tony described darkly as 'on the sauce'. He would occasionally expose himself to the children, who were completely unimpressed by what he had to show them and would urge him, in a bored manner, to put it away. However, he was ready and willing to make love to persons of either sex in order to provide much-needed excitement. When one upper-crust married lady was changing for dinner, he emerged unexpectedly from under the bed and was, apparently, received with enthusiasm. He was often charming, frequently entertaining, although he hated having to bring in the groceries and the wine in a wheelbarrow after one of Tony's gigantic shopping sprees. On such occasions he would tell us what a *con* the *patron* was. Once he was removed to prison in Draguignan for some motoring offence, where he played cards all day and said he had never been so happy.

Jean-Pierre's end came with far too much drama. He quarrelled violently with his girlfriend and Tony found him in possession of a loaded automatic rifle, which he had bought quite easily in Cogolin. The *patron*, like some gaunt hero in a western, walked down the main street of La Garde Freinet to hand this weapon in to the police. Jean-Pierre soon replaced the gun, and, after another scene with his girlfriend in Toulon, shot her and then himself. She escaped with a superficial wound but he died, slowly and painfully. He was, without doubt, melancholy, dangerous and unbalanced. But during those early Easters and brilliant summers he had seemed essential to the spirit of the place. When he had gone the great days of Le Nid du Duc were over, as surely as the sound of axes marked the destruction of the Cherry Orchard.

Tony's hamlet was not a perfect place to work; there were, as you will already have guessed, far too many distractions. One day I was trying to write in the garden when a white cockatoo, which had been off on some private adventure, flew down the wooded valley, alighted on my table and, taking a few delicate steps forward, shat all over my script. I tried not to take the hint. In those days Natasha, now a star, as were Tony and her mother Vanessa Redgrave, was under ten and her sister Joely a couple of years younger. Natasha was always not only an extremely talented actress but businesslike and probably the most sensible character around Le Nid du Duc. Tony would encourage frequent theatrical productions, although his only part in them was to supervise the lighting. It was Natasha who would walk among the guests calling out, 'Ring! Ring! Time for everyone to come to rehearsal!' We evolved a play about Saint Tropez, after which the doves (then still alive) were released from dustbins to the strains of the Hallelujah Chorus, causing an effect so exciting that Dominic Elwes, who had been suffering from a bout of impotence, recovered his full powers. Unhappily Mr Elwes had talked too freely to the press about the murder of the Lucan children's nanny and, having been sent to Coventry by Lord Lucan's friends, he committed suicide.

We also performed *Gypsy* with the young Natasha as Mama Rosa, Joely as Gypsy, and Penny performing in the chorus with Helen Osborne, Jacqueline Rufus Isaacs and a transvestite from Milan. When these productions were over, we composed reviews of them in the manner of Harold Hobson and Ken Tynan, the dramatic critics of the period. The notices had to be dreadful; Tony would not have been amused by success.

Mealtimes often produced dramas and could be discussed and analysed in detail afterwards. There was an elderly economist, often on the telephone in the café in La Garde Freinet advising Harold Wilson on the British economy, who would turn up at Le Nid du Duc in extremely baggy shorts. The grass around the lunch table was always scattered with rubbish, bones abandoned by the dogs and bits of dead animals. Seated opposite the economist, a girl grasped a chicken's severed claw between her toes and inserted it, gently and cunningly, up his voluminous shorts. When the yellow leg was in position she scratched his private parts with it. This entertained her neighbours and caused the flattered victim to believe, with delight, that the elderly lady at his side was making a pass at him. After this, Tony was able to massage his thighs, choke with laughter and feel that the day had not been entirely wasted.

One night a French movie actress whose beauty I had long admired was invited to dinner. The evening was uneventful, Tony was bored and we went to bed early. At breakfast, much to our surprise, he was in a mood of bubbling delight. At about two in the morning, it seemed, the exquisite actress had thrown a glass ashtray at her boyfriend's head and he had to be taken to the hospital in St Tropez to receive several stitches. 'The marvellous part was,' Tony told us, 'he said she usually held on to the things she hit him with, but this time she let go and it was much worse.'

I was first invited down to discuss a film version of *I Claudius* and *Claudius the God*, books which I have always admired. Then Tony decided to do them as a stage play and 'go for broke' by bringing it straight into the West End. I wrote what I thought was a chamber piece with parts doubled by a fairly small cast of actors. Tony kept on getting new ideas. He stripped the cork trees of bark which he had painted blue to make armour for the Ancient Britons. He decided that the set should consist entirely of 'bleachers', the sort of steps which are erected for an audience at sporting events or presidential inaugurations. He said that the spaces between the steps should correspond to those in front of South

American temples where 'little Inca priests had to jump up and down'. He invited the leading players to Le Nid du Duc where they drank champagne and rehearsed round the pool. These rehearsals were an unmitigated delight.

I was surprised, when we got to London, to find that the full cast consisted of about thirty actors and many of my lines had been transferred to characters for whom I hadn't intended them. However, the rehearsals continued to look promising, kept alive by Tony's endless enthusiasm and flow of invention. He gave a party at his house in London before the first night, at which I sat on a sofa between Jo Grimond, the former leader of the Liberal Party, and Robert Graves, who was immensely handsome, with the sort of head you might expect to find on a Greek statue or a Roman coin. There was a lull in the conversation and then Graves said, 'Of course Jesus Christ lived to the age of eighty, went to China and discovered spaghetti.'

'In which Gospel,' Jo Grimond was puzzled, 'do we learn that Jesus Christ discovered spaghetti?'

'In no Gospel.' Graves was smiling. 'It's simply a matter of common knowledge.'

Jo Grimond was wise enough to ask no further questions on that subject, but when the legendary writer said, 'Keats wasn't a great poet. He couldn't be because he was not a gent,' Grimond uttered another mild protest. 'I didn't think you had to be a gent, to be a great poet.'

'There, sir,' Graves told him firmly, 'you are wrong!'

I broke another prolonged silence by asking what Robert Graves had done in the last war. Was he, perhaps, in some secret service? We all knew, from *Goodbye to All That*, of his experiences in the First World War.

'In the last war,' he said, quite without boasting, 'I won the Battle of Anzio. Shall I tell you how I did it?' Jo Grimond said he thought we'd be very glad to know.

'Well, I was bicycling round the island of Jersey,' Graves told us, 'and I met an officer from my old regiment. I asked him what he was doing and he said he was off to fight the Eyeties at the Battle of Anzio. So I said if he'd give me time to ride round a little more I'd come back to him, in say half an hour, and tell him my plan for defeating the Eyeties.'

'And did you?'

'Oh, yes. I rode around and thought it all out and then I came back. My officer was still there and I said to him, "Look here, I've thought out a perfect plan. Let me tell you the secret of the Eyeties. They cannot stand the sound of a woman in labour. If he hears the sound of a woman in labour your average Eyetie will run a mile. So all you have to do is to go down to Queen Charlotte's Hospital and record the cries of women in labour. Then play them on your gramophones on the beaches and every Eyetie soldier will run a mile." Well, he did and they did, and that is exactly how we won the Battle of Anzio.'

Robert Graves also told me that the play was bound to be a huge success. I said I was very relieved to hear it. 'Of course it will be,' he said. 'But to remove all possible doubt I've brought a magic stone, a small piece of meteorite, which will do the trick for us.' He produced a fragment of rock and I looked at it with respect.

'What do you have to do,' I asked, 'to make sure it brings us good notices?'

'I just have to say to it, "Magic stone, do your stuff!"'

I have no doubt that he gave his stone the appropriate instructions but, on our first night, it disobeyed orders. In spite of an excellent performance by David Warner as Claudius, much energetic leaping up and down the bleachers and all the excitement of Tony's staging, the magic didn't work. 'We didn't win,' Tony said at the first-night party held in a boat on the Thames. He spoke with that excitement and genuine delight which disaster always brought him. 'I could feel the play sinking beyond hope in that red-plush sea of stalls. We used to have nights like that at the Court. We went down with all hands!' The production lost about

£20,000, which seemed an enormous amount at the time, but there was no word of protest or blame from Tony and we remained firm friends.

At his best, with the Osborne plays and the film of *A Taste of Honey*, Tony Richardson was a magnificent director. In his later work, such as *The Charge of the Light Brigade*, there were moments of great visual beauty and a weakness of narrative line. His talent was for inspiring actors and writers, generating enthusiasm and producing the feeling of excitement and danger which is essential to all dramatic enterprises. He should have stayed in the theatre and made British films, for his courage and sense of irony and physical ineptitude were the very British characteristics of the son of a North Country chemist and Mayor of Bolton. Unfortunately, I think, he came to the conclusion that England was a curiously backward country, living in the past. In America, he would tell us with amazement, they have deep-freezers and cordless telephones and washing-machines, and plumbers came almost before you'd put down the telephone. In vain we told him that all these devices were readily obtainable in England and it was hard to get a tap mended in Los Angeles. He bought a house in the Hollywood hills, with a view almost as spectacular as the country behind St Tropez. It was typical of Tony that there were found, on his American domain, the dead bodies of a couple in a Cadillac, buried in a landslide.

The English do best as visitors to Hollywood; if you're there all the time you're not thought of as hard to get and therefore not worth getting. Tony continued to live in Los Angeles like the prince of some small and magical country, and no doubt he made money, as you can in the movie business, preparing endless pictures which never got to the screen. When I saw him last he had given me detailed instructions as to where to stand outside the Beverly Hills Hotel for his car to pick me up. He looked older, even thinner, with the grey, close-cropped hair and the high, autocratic voice of an elderly general. He commiserated with me on the banality of having a novel in the bestseller list and then he brightened up and told me about the disasters in France, the forest fires and the broken marriages, and the weird behaviour of that summer's visitors. Life was dangerous and absurd and totally enjoyable.

At the heart of Tony, as at the heart of Prospero, there was mystery. Were these magicians proud of producing happiness, or were they victims of their own power to manipulate other people's lives? Both loved their daughters; I am not sure how much they loved anyone else. Both were at their best when they had a whole enchanted island to themselves. I imagine that when Prospero got back to Milan and his dukedom he was difficult at other people's dinner parties. Tony Richardson was also a tricky guest; off his territory he seemed to shrink, became silent and discontented. Even when he was at home, in Los Angeles or the South of France, much of his life remained concealed. He left few traces of his presence and spent little time unpacking. It was hard to discover in which of his many bedrooms he slept, or with whom. When Aids arrived, the dark, demanding, uninvited guest, he ignored it, refused to mention or remember its name and offered it no publicity. He died in Hollywood, cared for and attended by the daughters who loved him and whom he loved silently and whose success he greeted with pride.

4

There are occasional exceptions to the rule that the advocate must, in the years after the trial, become invisible and blotted from the memory of his client in the way that violent crimes or near-fatal accidents are expunged. Sometimes you are remembered. In my early criminal days I defended an Irishman (was he Catholic or Protestant?) who was accused of dealing in arms from the safety of a sweater shop in North London. All that I remember clearly, and always have remembered, was a question and answer during the police interview with my client in the cells. It went something like this: SUPERINTENDENT: *Now, Neil, tell us where the guns are.* NEIL: *Sure, Superintendent, the only gun I've got is between my legs and it gets me into terrible trouble with my wife, Bridget.*

I am standing in a Belfast bookshop. A tall, grey-haired, softly spoken and entirely respectable-looking lady asks me to sign a book for her two sons who are both practising lawyers. She is very happy about this, she tells me, and about the beautiful house she has in the Mountains of Mourne. So I inscribe the book to her sons, who have names like Peter and Peregrine. As I do so, she smiles and says, 'Neil died ten years ago. I'm sure you remember the case you did for him?' I realize that I am, at last, talking to Bridget, who was constantly troubled by her husband's gun.

I can still see the bracken houses I built on the common with the gardener's daughter and the children of the chair-leg maker next door. I can smell the white mice ceaselessly proliferating in the garage. I can shiver at the memory of the icy walk down to the earth-closet by the vegetable patch and stub my toe against the stone hot-water bottle in the cold bed. I know exactly how it felt to be sitting alone on a radiator, unwrapping the blue bag of salt and shaking it into a packet of crisps, my eyes pricking with tears, apparently abandoned by my parents in the first week at prep school. I can see the pages of the books I read then – *Beau Geste* and *Beau Sabreur* – and smell the floor polish and the blankets as I knelt beside my bed singing an old Fred Astaire number under my breath: 'I'm putting all my eggs in one basket, I'm betting everything I've got on you,' because I didn't know what to pray for. This heightened perception occurs in childhood and old age; in one because it's all happening for the first time and in the other because you may soon have to say goodbye. Like childhood, old age is irresponsible, reckless and foolhardy. Children and old people have everything to gain and nothing much to lose. It's middle-age which is cursed by the desperate need to cling to some finger-hold halfway up the mountain, to conform, not to cause trouble, to behave well, and it is, perhaps mercifully, the period which becomes blurred in the memory, the time when you did nothing more difficult than survive.

When I'd started in the schizoid business of being a writer who had barristering as a day job, and was never entirely certain what to do when I grew up, the Inns of Court were run like a rather backward public school, with barristers calling each other by their surnames, only stopping short of referring to their younger brothers as Elkins Minor. When my first plays were on, and my photograph appeared in the *Daily Express*, I was fined a dozen bottles of champagne for receiving such vulgar and unprofessional publicity. Judges had that licence to be bad-tempered, which my father claimed in shops, restaurants or on Paddington Station. Police evidence, however improbably the verbals were phrased, was received like Holy Writ and any suggestion that policemen might not be telling the truth was treated as blasphemy. I remember one judge, who had served for a long time in the colonies, telling an Old Bailey jury that they had heard the evidence of a 'white policeman', which they would surely have to accept in every detail. In those days homosexuals over twenty-one were imprisoned, robbers flogged and murderers hanged. I was told of one judge who apparently enjoyed passing such sentences. He would whisper in baby-talk to his marshal (the young barrister appointed to listen to his jokes, sharpen his pencils and look up his law) about the prisoner during the course of the trial, using such phrases as, 'Is oo a naughty little liar, is oo then?' or 'I'se going to give oo something which will teach oo a lesson!' From this period of our legal history, things could only get better.

It's fashionable to look back on the sixties and seventies with ferocious disapproval; this was the period surely when youth took to drugs, when the decent values of family life were destroyed and teachers stopped making children learn to spell and set them to modelling new towns out of yoghurt pots and cotton wool. In fact, the sixties saw a move towards a slightly more humane society. The death penalty finally went, adult homosexual men weren't answerable for what they did in private, and literary merit had become a defence to a charge of obscenity in Roy Jenkins's Act, a piece of legislation which caused us all a good deal of gentle amusement. No doubt many mistakes were made during those years, but it was a time when we became more tolerant of each other's peculiarities and judges, for the most part, cut out the rages and the baby-talk.

Emily, the first child of the second chance, was born just after the *Oz* trial. I was defending a publication called the *Little Red School Book*, which described Marxism and contraception and was, without difficulty, condemned as obscene, when Penny began to haemorrhage dangerously and was hardly consoled when the cleaning lady told her she was not to worry because it wasn't her life's blood she was losing but her 'other blood'. She had just the strength to ring the doctor who closed his surgery and followed the screaming ambulance to Queen Charlotte's Hospital where they had some difficulty searching for a still available vein.

I got a message, pulled off my wig and fled the court, greatly to the annoyance of the judge, one of the old school, who thought the possible death of a wife of little importance compared with a lengthy discussion of the enormity of mentioning Marxism and French letters in a book which might fall into the hands of schoolchildren.

With no help from me the lifeblood was staunched and restored. Emily grew up with scraps of my father's immortality about her, fond of words, jokes, puns and quotations, able to get her own way by a judicious mixture of outrage and charm. In the year before she went to university, she was studying Russian in Moscow, where she fell in love with a poet, improbably called Denis, who knew no English. One night Denis led her across Red Square, held her hand in the moonlight, and said, in Russian, 'It's such an honour to be walking across Red Square with a girl whose father defended the Sex Pistols.' I had forgotten this part of my life, but my mind went back to a record called *Never Mind the Bollocks*, which was accused of having an indecent title unfit for public display in record shops. I met only one of the Pistols, but I remember him as having greenish teeth and wearing a sola topi. I thought it best to keep him well away from the provincial Magistrates Court, where the trial was to take place. We called a clergyman from the local university who was also a lexicographer. He told the magistrates that the word bollocks might well have been used to describe the rigging of an eighteenth-century man-of-war. They nodded wisely, appeared to accept this definition, and the record was then inflicted on the public. This case wasn't my proudest achievement at the bar, but somehow its fame lasted in Russia for twenty years.

Sometimes the early seventies deserved their present reputation for silliness; and the cases seemed unable to live up to the knee-breeches, the tailed coat, and the solemn oath of a Queen's Counsel taken in the House of Lords. I remember coming back to the room that had been my father's after lunch one day. I was about to sink into the client's chair when I saw that it was occupied by an open suitcase in which a number of battery-controlled penises of alarming dimensions whirred disconsolately or flashed on faint lights when I disturbed them. I telephoned, in some distress, down to the clerk's room and I found that this was part of a consignment of sex aids which had been confiscated by the customs at a North Country airport and classified as illegal immigrants. My task was to make them available to such British subjects as wished to enjoy their mechanical company.

As I drove up the motorway in the muddy wake of speeding trucks and container lorries, I racked my brains for some sort of convincing defence for my ingenious little clients and their would-be importer. My mind was still a blank when I reached a grim Magistrates Court, parked the car and went in to find the questioned articles lying on the exhibits' table, occasionally whirring in a pathetic and hopeless sort of way. I took my seat and, as I had been appointed as one of Her Majesty's Counsel, learned in the law, I wished that the Queen would offer me a better class of work.

And then fate, or whatever merciful power looks after defence barristers bankrupt of ideas, came to my aid. I heard the magistrates approach down the corridor and some of the footsteps were distinctly uneven. When the chairman of the bench arrived I saw an elderly man with a stiff and undoubtedly artificial leg. When I was asked to defend the embarrassing exhibits I put forward a legal argument which I hoped would appeal to that particular tribunal. 'Some of us,' I said, 'stand in need of artificial limbs. Others cannot maintain our erections. There is no reason, either in logic or in law, why some should be helped by mechanical devices and others left to suffer. Furthermore' – and here I moved to the more respectable part of my submission – 'these little fellows were made in Denmark. The Treaty of Rome was signed to ensure unrestricted distribution of goods among Common Market members. It's far better, surely, that the Danes should make and export such articles as these. If we forbid their import there might well spring up, in this fair part of England, a cottage industry for the manufacture of mechanical genitalia. I ask the question, of course, rhetorically but would that be the socially desirable outcome of this difficult and anxious case?' I sank back in my seat, exhausted. The chairman of the bench conferred briefly with his colleagues and announced that they found all the exhibits 'totally acceptable'.

Such cases were among the foolish things that happened in a forgotten age, before unemployment and Aids and the breakup of nations into murderous tribes left us no time to mind about the bollocks at all.

Advocates are meant to have some sixth sense which enables them to have an immediate insight into the characters of witnesses, detect liars and recognize secret sympathizers. In fact, first appearances are frequently misleading, and so it was in the case of a juryman in the Free Wales Army trial, another strange engagement during my early years as a QC.

The Public Order Act makes it illegal for a private army to gather, or drill, or wear uniforms in order to subvert the government, or cause people to fear that that is its intention. This was what it was alleged the Free Wales Army had done when half a dozen or so men with varying political beliefs, and a wide range of levels of intelligence, were put on trial at Swansea Assizes. It was not long before the Prince of Wales was to be installed in Caernarvon Castle, wearing a uniform specially designed for him by Lord Snowdon, and kneeling in front of his mother. Dire rumours were abroad suggesting that the Welsh freedom-fighters planned to fly a radio-controlled helicopter full of pig shit over the historic ceremony; its automatic doors would open and the load would be deposited on the royal group. I don't believe that this fell scheme was ever within the capacity of the army, any more than its other plan of fixing magnetic mines on to Welsh dogs, who would leap at attacking English tanks, stick to them and explode. All the same, the judge seemed anxious to keep the case going until Charles had safely assumed the mantle of the Black Prince. In an effort to show no partiality for England or Wales, the powers that were had chosen a Scottish judge to try the case. Each morning the court was carefully searched for bombs, and when it was declared safe the judge would enter nervously, while the defendants sang some stirring anthem in the Welsh language.

I was very grateful to the army for introducing me to the beauty of the Gower peninsula, where I lived for many weeks. In the evening the Welsh barristers would entertain us, often singing, to the tune of 'Bread of Heaven', the words:

> Bread from Morganses,
> Beef from Evanses,
> Beer from the Royal Oak!

'Oh, John,' said one old Welsh QC late at night, 'tell me honestly. With our beer and our singing shall our profession *ever* die?' While Welshmen were prepared to plan military insurrection in the hills, I didn't think it would.

The fatal misinterpretation of a juryman's character happened to me at the start of the trial. In those distant days you were allowed to challenge a number of jurors without giving any reason. That right has now been removed from the defence, wrongly, I think, because you should be tried by a collection of people who at least look like your peers; after all the prosecution can 'stand by' as many jurors as it pleases. I had instructions from my clients to challenge any potential juryman who was wearing a collar and tie or carrying the *Daily Telegraph*. When one of nature's bank managers, showing these outward and visible signs of respectability, appeared in the jury-box and was about to take the oath, I climbed to my feet and was on the point of sending him packing. 'Don't challenge him!' an urgent Welsh whisper came from somewhere behind my left shoulder. 'He's winking at the boys in the dock!' Three weeks later the bank manager was still winking. The truth of the matter was that he had a nervous tic.

Most of the police officers by whom we were surrounded were named Dai, but in the manner of the Welsh (Jones the Milk or Williams the Post) the nature of their work was added to their name, so we had Dai Exhibits, Dai Scene of the Crime and Dai Book and Pencil (who supervised the parking arrangements). I wanted to call the officer who said he'd found fuse wire in my client's possession, and when I asked who he would be I was told, I suppose in a spirit of harmless fun, 'Oh, you want Dai Plant.' Another officer, perhaps Dai Exhibits, produced what he alleged to be a Free Wales Army jacket, a sort of battledress top covered with various shields and badges. I took him through these decorations.

'Officer, please tell the jury, is that the badge of the Westminster Bank Rowing Club (let's say)?' 'Yes, it is.' 'And is that the insignia of the Swansea Ramblers' Association?' 'Yes.' 'And on that shoulder, the Bowling Club Supporters badge?' 'It would seem to be.' 'And that, the Cardiff Choral Group?' 'Yes.' 'And what about that little golliwog on the right arm, is that a badge for those who have collected enough labels from jars of marmalade?' 'It might well be.' 'Then tell the jury, officer, why do you call it a Free Wales Army jacket? Why not call it a golliwog marmalade jacket?' I won a little laughter in court, and it seemed to have been one of my more successful cross-examinations. But when the case was over, a number of dubious characters were seen coming from the public gallery and all of them were wearing golliwog badges. To this day I don't know if the politically incorrect device had any sinister significance.

At the end of the trial I stayed away from the Welsh lawyers' singsong to compose a final speech. It seemed that the essence of the charge was that the public had been put in fear by the Free Wales Army's activity. I was prepared to argue that no sane person could have been in the least alarmed by the military manoeuvres of the little handful of men in the dock. I relied on the fact that they all had high-sounding titles; in fact, they were all commanding officers with no men to command.

'"There lived a king, as I've 'been told,"' I quoted from *The Gondoliers*,

> 'In the wonder-working days of old,
> To the top of every tree
> Promoted everybody . . .
> When everyone is somebodee,
> Then no one's anybody!'

Therefore, there was no one of any real importance in the Free Wales Army. This argument, frail as it may look now in print, seemed to appeal greatly to the jury and the judge, who might have starred as Tessa or Fiametta at some distant prep school, and clearly enjoyed the Gilbertian joke. However, I was interrupted by violent protests from the dock. Our clients were outraged by my suggestion that the Free Wales Army was not a formidable and alarming fighting-force, and I was instructed to abandon this line of argument. After I had done so, they received quite modest sentences and the dreaded helicopter never flew over Caernarvon Castle. I had discovered that the object of the accused in political trials was not acquittal but martyrdom, and my failure seemed to be a matter of all-round satisfaction.

Among the barristers who also became friends during my legal life was Jeremy Hutchinson. He is tall and apparently languid, although he was ferociously hard-working at the bar. His father had married into the Bloomsbury Group and Jeremy would address the juries from Dagenham or Brent Cross in the high and plaintive tones which might be heard in any drawing-room where Lytton

Strachey or Virginia Woolf were holding forth on the pathos in Shakespeare's sonnets or the vulgarity of Arnold Bennett. 'Can you imagine, members of the jury,' he would say, 'this poor, poor man? Taken to the police station. And asked questions. Over and over again. For simply hours! Can't you understand why this poor, poor man, treated like that, would say simply *anything*. Just to get home. Away from the *boredom* of it all!' Curiously enough, the jury were entranced with this mandarin eloquence and Jeremy had a high degree of success. He was junior counsel to Gerald Gardiner in the Lady Chatterley case, the prosecution of the publisher of D.H. Lawrence's novel in which words, used by many people in their daily lives, caused a great stir when they were first seen between the covers of a book. Later Jeremy successfully defended a book called *The Mouth and Oral Sex*. He was much helped in this case by the judge, who, after Margaret Drabble had given evidence as to the merits of the work in question, unwisely asked her, 'Why is it important to read about oral sex now? We've managed to get on for a couple of thousand years without it.' When Miss Drabble appeared taken aback by this thought, he said, 'Witness! Answer the question.' To which she replied, 'I'm sorry, your Lordship. I was just trying to remember the relevant lines in Ovid.' After this, it was said someone in court was heard to murmur, not altogether inaudibly, 'Poor, poor his Lordship. Gone without oral sex for two thousand years.'

Jeremy had a habit of referring to the judge, or the prosecutor, as 'the poor old darling' if they did anything particularly unpleasant, and this was a figure of speech I never forgot. He came from the strange old days and had been one of the marshals to the judge who indulged in baby-talk. Now we meet occasionally, have lunch and tell each other what a joy it is not to be barristers any longer. He was a great defender and, as a one-time husband of Peggy Ashcroft and former vice-chairman of the Arts Council, brought a much-needed breath of civilization to the Old Bailey.

*

I first met Ann Mallalieu when she had just left Cambridge, where she was the first woman President of the Union. She's blonde and beautiful and, when she was called to the bar, I led her in a number of trials. I believe the jury thought that if a nice girl like her was on my side my case couldn't be all that bad. We went to Birmingham together and spent some time defending the seller of a work unattractively entitled *The Return of the Enema Bag Rapist*. Ann's father and uncle were both Labour ministers, and she added this dubious book to the presents in her father's Christmas stocking.

When I first met Tim Cassel he was a prosecutor whom I found full of charm. He dropped his case against the projectionist in a blue movie cinema I was defending when I told him of my client's excellent war record. Tim's father was an elegant barrister and judge who tended to speak in Victorian upper-class Cockney, saying things like, 'Me poor old eyes ain't strong enough to read the document what you gave me.' He was once trying a burglar who had handcuffed a householder before robbing him. Judge Cassel insisted on demonstrating the way these handcuffs worked by putting them on his own wrists, and he brushed aside the prosecuting counsel's frequent attempts to dissuade him. When he was helplessly manacled, the judge allowed the prosecutor to explain that the police never recovered the key to the handcuffs. Tim's father had to be led off the bench and the local ironmonger was sent for.

Ann was made a Labour peeress by Neil Kinnock and Tim's political views make Mrs Thatcher look like a member of the Workers' Revolutionary Party. Fierce political arguments seem to add excitement and passion to their marriage. Ann gets up at around four in the morning in their house across the hills from us, delivers a few lambs, drives to London, and after a day in court makes for the House of Lords, where the sight of her cheers the elderly Conservative peers enormously.

Geoff Robertson is a more radical barrister. He is an Australian and was a Rhodes Scholar with Bill Clinton, which shouldn't, however, be held against him. When he was at Oxford he came to help in the *Oz* trial because he had known Richard Neville at university. He looked up the law, worked tirelessly and had many good ideas, although perhaps his judgement left him when he decided we ought to call Marty Feldman. The fact that we won the *Oz* appeal was, in a large part, due to Geoff's industry. He was soon called to the bar, came into my chambers and acted, for years, as my junior in a number of curious and sometimes sensational cases. He was always cheerful, looked boyish and sat behind me, shouting brilliant ideas at my back while the judge fired destructive comments at my face. Often I felt like slipping out from between them and putting them in direct touch with each other. Geoff is a much better lawyer than I could ever be and he supplied the legal arguments. In return I think I handed on to him my father's secret of the art of cross-examination which must, he used to say, never be confused with examining crossly. It should be used to lead the witness, gently and with courtesy, through a number of propositions with which he has to agree until he has no alternative but to say yes to the final and, you hope, the fatal question.

I have been accused, mostly by women, of having few men friends, and it's true that my idea of hell would be an eternal, black tie, all male dinner of chartered accountants. An English middle-class education has made me allergic to sport and my only interest, when forced to take part in any sort of game, is to lose it as quickly as possible in order that it may be over. I have a fear, implanted in my childhood, of locker-rooms and the smell of sweaty gym shoes and I believe that exercise is a serious health risk. I am therefore cut off from many masculine preserves and my men friends are often people I work with: directors, actors and a very few lawyers, of whom Geoff is the one with whom I went through most triumphs and disasters.

We went down to Brixton Prison together when we acted for John Stonehouse, a Labour minister who staged a fairly convincing

43

death by drowning, leaving his clothes in a pile on a Florida beach in order to defraud an insurance company. He was arrested in Australia because he was suspected of being Lord Lucan, the vanished aristocrat wanted for murder. We got Mr Stonehouse bail and then he decided to conduct his own case, with disastrous results.

Geoff and I had some gruelling, as well as hilarious, times together. I was known to vomit in the lavatory before arguing cases in the Court of Appeal or the House of Lords, and Geoffrey, for all his legal brilliance, would suffer prolonged bouts of nervous indigestion.

Once we defended a large, mournful man who was accused of issuing death threats to a rich South African. He did this by ordering a succession of funeral cortèges to call at the South African's house. Nothing could have been more unnerving than having a black-clad undertaker knock at the door in the dawn mist and announce that the hearse was waiting. Our client advertised in *Time Out* for a number of helpers and a young girl student, among others, applied. She was also in the dock. Many years later I was handing out bursaries to young playwrights in the committee room of a television company. A woman appeared who had written an excellent play about life in prison. I looked at her for a long time and then I remembered where I had last seen her: it was in the dock at the Old Bailey where she was sitting next to my lugubrious client, the sender of funerals.

As defenders, we naturally found ourselves on the side of books and films which the prosecution was trying to ban. That didn't mean that we found these works particularly attractive; it's not necessary, when defending an alleged murderer, to believe that the best way to end an unhappy marriage is with a kitchen knife in the stomach. Prosecutors who seek to keep the purity of our national life unsullied can be similarly detached. Geoff and I did a long case about some questioned publication or other against a particularly jovial prosecutor who would push his way past my middle-aged knees every morning and chirrup, 'Give us a kiss, darling,' as I sat gloomily preparing my work for the day. I used to write in a number of notebooks which had dark circles printed on their covers. In his final speech to the jury this prosecutor was saying, 'And if this sort of publication is allowed, youth will be corrupted, authority will be undermined, family life will be in peril and civilization, as we know it, will grind to a halt.' Then, glancing down at my notebook, he muttered, 'Arseholes all over your notebook, darling!', and went on with his peroration. The truth is that the defenders of public morality are not always all that they seem to be.

Geoff has gone on to enjoy an extremely successful practice, forcing the government to disgorge 'secret' documents in a case which revealed official connivance at the sale of material which might be used for making arms in Iraq, and saving the lives of a large number of prisoners kept in horrible conditions on death row in Caribbean countries. Few defenders can have had such triumphant results.

When I was a barrister we used to spend weeks discovering if those accused were guilty, something which often became perfectly obvious in the first half hour, and about twenty minutes deciding what to do with them. Prison was the usual solution, and one which required the least thought. No one had any faith in prison. The judges didn't believe they reformed anyone and, though it would keep offenders out of circulation for a while, they would be shovelled back into the community more hardened, brutalized and dangerous than ever. Politicians are fond of saying no one commits crimes in prison, but of course they do: daily offences ranging from murder and rape to drug-dealing and aggravated assault. The problem is that the British public is extraordinarily penal-minded. We once stood second to Turkey in the league of those European countries who gaoled the highest proportion of their citizens. Now we have done even better: Britain is top of the imprisonment stakes. Thinking that it's what is expected of them, some judges and most vote-hungry politicians are anxious to oblige, and young and old, serious or petty criminals, and a large proportion of those who haven't been convicted of anything at all, are banged up in stinking and dangerous Victorian slums. Recently a mother of young children was given a custodial sentence for failing to pay her television licence. One hundred and fifty years after the publication of *A Christmas Carol*, we need a Dickens to open our eyes to poverty, homelessness and the building of prisons in which children and young people, to whom no other future is being offered, may be locked away to take more advanced courses at universities of crime.

I have been working lately with the Howard League for Penal Reform which became concerned about the number of fifteen-year-old boys, children by anyone's standard, who had hanged themselves in custody and while awaiting trial. We accordingly went, as a small delegation, to the then Home Secretary, a smiling man, whose slicked-down hair was known in parliamentary circles as 'self-basting'. He received us with great affability as he sat surrounded by his parliamentary secretary and his civil servants. He greeted me by asking if I'd seen any good operas lately. I did my best to explain that we hadn't come about operas but about boys hanging themselves.

'Of course you have!' Then came a chorus from the politicians assembled which went something like this: 'And we think you're doing a grand job!', 'We've got the greatest possible admiration for your campaign', 'You and the Howard League, you just keep up the good work.' The Home Office, it seemed, was right behind us, so I made bold to ask why it didn't do something about it.

'Well, there it is. We're really helpless. The sentencing classes, that is the judges, keep sending these chaps to prison and the local authorities won't spend any money on homes for them. So what can we do? Something, perhaps, in two or three years' time. Meanwhile, you carry on protesting. We think you're doing absolutely splendidly.'

The problem was, they explained, that it costs such a terrible lot of money, about £20,000, to make a secure place in a council home for a boy. I then suggested a tariff be put up in all magistrates courts: £20,000 for a secure place, so much less a week for community service, so much less for bail. 'Then,' I said, 'you could reform the prisons on strict monetarist principles.' This suggestion caused delighted laughter all round. '*You* honestly think that? Well, that is *quite* hilarious, coming from you! Are you becoming a Thatcherite, John?' The meeting ended in great merriment. As we left, I thought I'd rather have heard them say, 'Good luck to them. We'd love all the little buggers to hang themselves.' That might, at least, have been honest. As it was, I felt an extreme frustration which was only slightly alleviated when I put a version of the incident into a Rumpole. Later we called on an Opposition spokesman who wondered how many votes there were in preventing children hanging themselves.

Things have not improved since then. The present Home Secretary, in order to put even more distance between us and the field in the Euro Penal Cup, has ordered six new prisons and declines any sort of conversation at all with the Howard League for Penal Reform.

Of course there are dangerous criminals who shouldn't ever be let out of prison, but there are also many people who should never have been sent there in the first place, and many others who are there to have their criminal tendencies confirmed and perpetuated. Experience in other countries has shown that reducing the prison population may mean reducing the crime rate. It's hard to persuade the British public of this.

Watching what the Home Office called the sentencing classes, and discussing the treatment of offenders, it seems to me that what we fear most are the criminal tendencies in ourselves. We are terrified, no doubt with good cause, of our baser instincts. Fear leads to a passionate belief in the righteousness of punishment. Shakespeare, who understood most things, understood this when, in *King Lear*, he wrote of the beadle flogging the whore: 'Strip thine own back. Thou hotly lusts to use her in that kind For which thou whip'st her' and of the judge railing at the simple thief: 'Hark in thine ear: change places and, handy-dandy, which is the justice, which the thief?' How much, I wonder, are our bursting prisons due to our own irremovable feelings of guilt?

The Christian religion, which has otherwise brought us many blessings, has also taught us that we are born guilty; we are the stained products of the fall of man, corrupted by the fatal taste of the apple of knowledge, only to be freed by the gift of redemption. Will time redeem us? As our hair falls out and our fingernails are renewed, do we not become different people, innocent of the crimes of our youth? The last novel I wrote was called *Dunster*. I made an amalgamation of all the most decent and honourable men I knew and suggested that such a character might, in the faraway past, have been guilty of a war crime. The conflict between the two younger men in the book is whether such guilt has to be dragged out into the light of day for the purposes of punishment, or whether old sins, committed in the heat of battle, might be allowed to sleep in the shadows. I didn't provide an answer to this dilemma; it's the purpose of the novelist, as it is of the defending barrister, to go on asking awkward questions.

5

My father used to take us each year to what was then called the Shakespeare Memorial Theatre at Stratford-upon-Avon. There I saw the actors I most admired: Randle Ayrton, now an unknown name but an unforgettable Lear for me, and Donald Wolfit, gone down in history as an irredeemable ham, who was the actor who most easily, in those days, made me cry. In London, during the holidays, we also went regularly to the theatre, after prolonged dinners at the Trocadero. Perhaps it was my father's fault that I longed to be an actor, and then a dramatist, and finally caused his character to become submerged by a sea of leading players.

Ten years after my father's death I wrote a play about him and much of him departed into fiction. In *A Voyage Round My Father* I made up new dialogue for him and began to forget which words he had spoken in his lifetime and which I had given to his subsequent shadows. Most people keep their memories, and their fathers, mothers, husbands, wives and lovers, safely within them. For writers, such characters are redrawn, reconstructed and given away in books and plays; they leave and go for a while into the public domain, until they and their authors are forgotten. My father's spirit drifted into strange company.

He was excellently acted by Mark Dignam at the Greenwich Theatre. At the Haymarket he was performed by Alec Guinness, an actor of great subtlety who was extremely moving but perhaps

49

not sufficiently aggressive to encompass my father's rages. When Michael Codron, who put the play on in the West End, plucked up his courage to mention this, Guinness protested that he did, indeed, hit his egg very hard in the breakfast scene. After Alec Guinness left, my father was taken over by Michael Redgrave, then coming to the end of a distinguished career. He had difficulty in remembering his lines and wore a sort of hearing-aid into which they were repeated, together with stage directions, from the prompt corner. I was told that one night the hearing-aid picked up messages from radio taxis. Redgrave sat down on a sofa beside the actress who was playing my mother and said loudly, impressively and to her complete astonishment, 'I must now proceed immediately to Number Four Flask Walk.' I hope that this story is true.

Then there was, as they say, some film interest and a character, about as far removed from my father as my father was from Don Giovanni, was about to take up his clouded malacca walking stick and put on his hat. Rex Harrison was, undoubtedly, one of the best light comedy actors the world has seen. He had impeccable timing and a sort of highly charged, nervous and rapid delivery handed down from Seymour Hicks and Gerald Du Maurier, the stars of the Edwardian theatre. He also had, on the stage or in films, a quizzical and baffled charm which most people, and particularly women, found irresistible. He had once flirted with an earlier play of mine, but as he always avoided meeting me and the producer in restaurants I wasn't sure of his intentions and he ended up by turning us down. However, I thought his comedy well suited to the way I write and I lived in hope. Then an American producer announced that he was anxious to make a film of *A Voyage Round My Father* in which Rex Harrison had agreed to act.

Some actors of the old school fall into the error of thinking that the characters they play must be sympathetic. Actors of genius, such as Laurence Olivier and John Gielgud, know better and realize that the plum roles are given by writers to complete bastards, or at least to persons who are a considerable pain in the neck. Richard III comes on to the stage, seduces a grief-stricken widow over the coffin of the husband he has murdered, and then goes on to do in practically everyone in sight, including the Duke of Clarence and the little Princes in the Tower. But there was never a better part for an actor. Henry Irving did very well out of a murderer in *The Bells* and Charles Laughton can never be entirely separated from a sadistic sea captain. Rex Harrison, however, seemed not only anxious to appear, in drama as in life, as charming and sexy, he set out to minimize any characteristics which his many fans might find unacceptable in their adored Rex. In the early days of our acquaintance he was playing a homosexual but he was careful, he said, to make it clear that his character wasn't 'really gay'. In a Feydeau play I translated, the entire plot turns on the fact that a wife finds her husband incapable of making love and so jumps to the conclusion that he has exhausted himself with other women. When he played the character in a disastrous film version of *A Flea in Her Ear* Rex Harrison spent hours at the Boulogne studios explaining to me that his fans would not, of course, accept the absurd suggestion that their much-loved star was impotent and Monsieur Chandebise's incapacity was, at worst, a momentary hiccup.

When I was told that Rex was to play my father, in a film which opens with his being struck blind, I knew exactly what to expect. I visited him in his London house and he stood, dressed with his usual elegance, rubbing his forehead, his voice rising to that high note of comic petulance which was so effective in the song 'Why Can't a Woman be More Like a Man?' He made it clear that his public wouldn't accept the tragic fact that their hero was totally blind. 'I'm quite sure,' he told me, 'that he can see *shapes*.' It was in vain that I told him that my father couldn't lift the food to his mouth and my mother had to do it for him, that he couldn't cross a room without his hands outstretched and his knees knocking into the furniture, that after the retinas left the backs of his eyes, and despite his best efforts to deny his own helplessness, he had no idea of the size of his grandchildren unless he felt them carefully with his hands. Rex's mind was made up; he wasn't going to play a character who couldn't see shapes.

So filming began, for the first time, in the house, which became, not a home for my new family, but a set, a place where the walls were repainted, bookcases walled over and the garden, unable to act springtime in late autumn, filled with artificial flowers and that uncheckable growth of paper cups which shows that a film unit, with its incessant demands for meals, has been in occupation.

'Play one of the scenes in a conservatory,' the American producer said, breathless with enthusiasm. 'And consider the lighting, Rex. Can't you just see the lighting possibilities?' 'Oh, my God. Yes!' The Harrison voice went up an octave and he massaged his forehead in a light comedy version of amazement. My father never owned a conservatory but one was constructed, an elegant octagonal building set against a wall of the house, where it remained for many years, acting, for as long as it could, as a genuine plant house though now, as if reconciled to the fact that it had only been run up for a movie, it has gently collapsed.

Apart from the brilliantly nervous acting and the determination not to disappoint his admirers by playing the handicapped, there was a ruthless side to Rex. When a film was to be made of *My Fair Lady*, in which he had enjoyed an enormous success in the theatre, the producers, so the story goes, wanted another star to play Professor Higgins. The director, George Cukor, with commendable good sense and loyalty, battled for months against that decision and finally said that he would refuse to make the film if the leading role were not offered to Rex. The day of decision came and Rex Harrison, who knew exactly what was going on, was pacing up and down in his villa in Portofino, chain-smoking and waiting for a call from the producers. Then the telephone rang and a deep and distant Hollywood voice growled, 'Well, Rex. We've taken George's advice and we want to ask you to repeat your great stage performance in *My Fair Lady*.' It is rumoured that Rex was silent for a moment and then said, no doubt in his voice of comic bewilderment, 'Are you sure that George Cukor is quite the right director for us?' In the discussions before we started our filming, he was similarly disconcerting. The director, Alvin Rakoff, a Canadian, suggested we might profitably 'investigate the character of the mother'. 'That's the trouble with you bloody Americans,' Rex said with no touch of light comedy. 'You want to investigate everything. That's what's got you into all this trouble over Watergate.' This conversation occurred, if I remember, during dinner in a restaurant where he had ordered the most expensive wines, two bottles of Pichon Longueville. When the bill came, light comedy returned as he slapped his pockets, smiled helplessly and discovered that he had left all means of paying at home.

Rex Harrison was a man of many wives and lovers; my father, determinedly monogamous, said that 'Sex has been greatly overrated by the poets.' Rex Harrison sang 'I've Grown Accustomed to Her Face' and my father stayed with 'Pretty Little Polly Perkins of Paddington Green', and yet the actor's talent was enormous and the two might have merged into a convincing, even a moving, character. Fate and the harsh realities of show business decided otherwise. The producer, who had been speaking hopefully of 'lines of credit' and a 'garbled telex' from an American bank, suddenly discovered that he had no money. Rex Harrison never played his first scene as my father; the crew evacuated our house and garden and no signs of them were left, except the fragile conservatory, the paper cups and an unlikely tulip, blooming in the autumn, which turned out to be made of plastic.

In my childhood the theatre was dominated by actors who seemed to me twin gods, Gielgud and Olivier. John Gielgud was a perfect Hamlet: a handsome, sensitive, princely intellectual, cruel and gentle, witty and profound. I wrote up for his photograph and got back one of him wearing a hat at a rakish angle which I pinned to my wall beside those of Annabella and Greta Garbo. Olivier was always the most dangerous and physical of actors. His Hamlet was an Olympic athlete, leaping from a great height, sword in hand, to fall upon the king, like the angel of death, to avenge his father's murder. When he died, as Coriolanus, he rolled down an interminable flight of steps and almost into our laps as my father, mother and I sat amazed in our front-row stalls at the Old Vic. When he played the same part at Stratford after the war, he fell from a rostrum, spear carriers caught his ankles and he died swinging upside down in the manner of Mussolini. Olivier's clipped, staccato way of speaking the verse was then thought by critics to be greatly inferior to Gielgud's mellifluous tones, which I also preferred. Many years later traces of my Gielgud voice, my attempt at beautifully orchestrated pathos, would return when I was addressing the jury on behalf of some car thief or bank robber, although I doubt if it had much effect on the verdict.

Stories abound about the differences between these giants, but Gielgud seems to have produced nothing but devotion among all those who worked with him. Later, when he was no longer a prince but an elegant, witty, chain-smoking, wonderfully tactless old man, he played some parts I had written and I found him to be the only actor you'd wish to take to a desert island. Olivier had some reputation for ruthlessness. Alec Guinness played the Fool in his *Lear* and was surprised that he was the only one of the supporting cast to receive any attention from the critics. Wondering at this, he remembered that the Fool only enters with Lear and leaves the stage when the King does. Then he noticed that the lights went up a good many points every time Olivier came on to the stage and dimmed to a similar extent as he departed. The Fool was therefore the only character to share in the star's illumination, whereas Goneril, Regan, Edmund and Gloucester were left to stumble around in the dark.

I don't think that Olivier is to be blamed for these tricks; no doubt they've been part of the armoury of all the great actor-managers of the past. He has traced the secret of Shakespearian acting as whispers passed on from Burbage to Betterton, from Betterton to Garrick, from Garrick to Kean and Kean to Irving, on whose memory Olivier's generation was raised. His well-justified claim to be part of this great chain was mixed with a very theatrical humility, a good deal of laying of the hand on the heart and the announcement that he was, indeed, a miserable sinner and altogether unworthy of the honours and praises bestowed on him. He used to address the National Theatre board in the obsequious tones of Othello before the Senate, scarcely forbearing to call us, with a great deal of mock humility, 'my very noble and approved good masters'. He said that he got his timing, essential in playing tragedy, from great comics like Jack Benny and Bob Hope. He also admitted that when he played 'the Black One' ('by far the most exhausting, dear boy'), he thought of the pompous way in which Charlie Chaplin used long words and convoluted phrases – so his addresses to the board came from Othello by way of Chaplin. In spite of these moments of dramatic self-abnegation, he was a genuine old actor laddie at heart and his favourite stories were those that elderly pros might tell in the Last Gulp, the bar in the wings of the old Brighton Theatre Royal. He loved to remember the Gloucester who staggered on to the stage to be greeted by a cry of 'You're drunk!' from the gallery. 'You think *I'm* drunk?' the actor went down to the footlights and asked with great dignity. 'Just wait till you've seen the Duke of Buckingham!' He liked, even more, the story of the bankrupt touring company which was performing *Macbeth* when a man from the Electricity Board came to cut off the supply. Understanding that the matter was urgent, the stage-door keeper swathed himself in a cloak, put on a broad-brimmed hat and, coming on in the banquet scene, marched up to the unhappy king, who was about to see Banquo's ghost, and said, 'My Lord, an't please you. There is one without that, but for us placing upon his palm certain gold pieces within the instant, threateneth to douse yon glim!' The story, no doubt, went back to the dawn of the century, but Laurence Olivier loved it no less for that.

He was an instinctive actor and you could no more ask him to describe his performances than you could expect Picasso to let you in on the secret of how he painted a picture. They were not entirely unconsidered, however. In thinking of the way Oedipus screamed when he was blinded, he remembered reading about the way they trap ermine. Salt is put down on the ice, he said, and the small animal tries to lick it off so its tongue becomes frozen to the ground. He imagined the agony of being pinioned in that way and the result was Oedipus's terrible cry of pain, which rent the theatre. Unlike Gielgud, who retains much of himself, Olivier only became an actor when he put on a nose, a wig or an accent which was so carefully chosen that he could tell which side of Chicago it came from. During the production of *A Flea in Her Ear* at the National Theatre, he played the smallest part, the butler, and, although the lights didn't brighten at his entrances and dim at his exits, it was a similar exercise in attention grabbing, because, when he was on the stage, the audience couldn't look at anyone else. The great quality of Olivier's acting was danger and no one could be sure what the butler was going to get up to next.

He had battled against illness and scared away death. When the cures became even more dangerous than the disease, he went to Italy, dived off high rocks and swam great distances. The dark beauty of Romeo and Heathcliff had long gone when he came to do another film of *A Voyage Round My Father*. His features had become pinched, his hair thin and, with spectacles and a grey moustache, he looked like an ageing military man who had suffered severe fever in the tropics. But his eyes were still as magnetic as ever and his consonants still cut the dialogue like a knife. When he agreed to play the part, he asked me to read the entire script to him one evening in his house in Chelsea. I used to read aloud every night to my blind father: Browning, Wordsworth, Evelyn Waugh, the Sherlock Holmes stories, and even, as the time went on, chapters of a novel I was writing. I had never contemplated reading to the actor who was going to play my father's part. I suppose I did my best and when I had finished he said, with that fatal clarity, 'That was a bloody awful reading, dear boy, but never mind!'

What Olivier brought to the memory of my father was the danger, the genuine fear produced by an often sentimental man who could weep with laughter at absurd stories or happy endings but, left to wait for five minutes on the platform at Henley-on-Thames, could give a convincing imitation of King Lear abandoned to the storm.

So, for the second time, the lorries and the catering vans, the honey wagon (which contained the lavatories), the false flowers, the paper cups and the camera crew, the sound man (whom nobody consulted), the wardrobe and make-up caravans, came back to the house in the country. The books were again walled up and the conservatory repaired and repainted. Looking out of a window I saw myself as a small boy, carrying a bucket, and Olivier, wearing my father's clothes and my father's straw hat, going towards the border to drown the earwigs, which they would pretend had infested the artificial dahlias, a curious form of blood sport which I had long ago abandoned.

In the big bedroom, with the balcony that overlooks the garden, I had watched my father die in a bed which I now shared with a new wife. I stood among trailing cables, dazzled by lights, squashed in the doorway behind make-up girls and electricians, watching an actor perform my father's death. He stirred and said the line which I think my father had also prepared carefully: 'I'm always angry when I'm dying.' Then he stopped breathing, watched by me, sitting at his bedside in the handsome person of Alan Bates. It seemed to me then, it seems to me now, a metaphor of a writer's life. You live through a terrible and private experience which you reinvent for artificial lights and actors and then give it away in public. I don't know if I did justice to my father's memory when all that happened or whether I diminished it. I really do not know.

6

*T*he humdrum nature of much crime is a disappointment to judges, crime
*reporters and politicians, who like to give the impression that we are
living in a world lit by the flames of Hell, where good and evil do battle
for our souls and where we are bowed down by the weight of original sin.
England, in truth, has a lower murder rate than many, indeed most, countries
in the world, including peace-loving Canada. The great majority of crimes in
this country are committed without violence; when it comes to murder,
however, judges often let their imaginations run away with them and take
refuge in great literature. In those early days of crime, I had to defend a
dwarf who had stood on an empty packing-case for the purpose of striking his
tall, Irish landlord across the head with a length of lead piping. I should not,
in this age of enlightenment, refer to my client as a dwarf; he was, of course,
'a vertically challenged person'. He was also one of my less successful cases.
In sentencing him the judge, determined to be dramatic, said something I
found extraordinary and my client deeply wounding. 'You, vertically challenged person,' he said. Well, as a matter of fact, being a judge of the
politically unreconstructed sort, he said, 'You, dwarf, are a mixture between
Clytemnestra and Lady Macbeth.' To a vertically challenged male person
these harsh words seemed almost more painful than the mandatory sentence of
life imprisonment.*

Much has been written about the theatrical nature of trials but the
parallel is not exact. Boredom is a weapon you can use in court;

given sufficient endurance you can bore a judge into submission by going on until he's in real danger of missing his train to Hayward's Heath and is ready to submit. You can't, in any other form of drama, win over an audience with relentless tedium. Legal dialogue, however, is often as artificial as anything in Restoration comedy. Addressing judges, a barrister says: 'in my humble submission', 'with the very greatest respect', 'if I might be allowed to bring to your Lordship's attention an argument with which your Lordship, with your Lordship's great experience, will be entirely familiar'. What these ornate phrases mean is 'Keep quiet, you boring old fart, and listen to what I've got to say.' Judges not only make judge-like remarks, such as, 'Who is Kylie Minogue?' and 'What is a T-shirt?', they sum up to juries as though they believe that the twelve random citizens are commonsensical, worldly-wise members of the Garrick Club who got their moral code from a rather decent housemaster at Winchester. And the criminal (as well as the sentencing) classes take part in the performance and adopt the role of cheerful Cockney characters which they hope will entertain the jury.

To all of this artificiality must be added the British passion, no doubt the result of having produced the best in world drama, for dressing up. I defended an unstable character accused of having committed a murder, apparently motiveless, in a van which was sent round to accommodate chest X-rays. He was due to come to trial on the opening day of the Old Bailey session, so he was brought up from the cells and emerged mole-like in the dock, where he blinked at the ceremonial customary at such a time. A city dignitary, with what looked like an outsized fur muff on his head, was parading with a huge sword. After him came the Mayor, wearing lace and a three-cornered hat decorated with black ostrich feathers. He was followed by the judge, dressed in scarlet and ermine, who was carrying a nosegay of flowers designed to protect his delicate nostrils from the stench of Newgate Prison, which had closed about a hundred years before. Unhinged by this extraordinary spectacle my client cried out, 'The Day of Judgement is at hand!' and had to be removed to a criminal lunatic asylum.

So when I slid away from the final speeches of my learned friends, the summing-up and the verdict, to a rehearsal in a chilly youth club or drill hall, I felt I had escaped to a more rational world. Few people become criminally insane from watching plays, and even the most disastrous flop in the theatre doesn't carry with it a sentence of imprisonment. Moreover, I was moving from a world I often mistrusted to one I loved, from one which I knew I would choose to abandon in time to one I hope and pray I shall be allowed to inhabit until the day I die.

I did not, as a child, put on a small wig and address my mother and father as though they were a jury. I spent my holidays making model theatres, painting scenery, performing one-boy versions of Shakespeare's plays and of musicals to my, no doubt, embarrassed parents. All these efforts culminated, I suppose, in the production of *A Voyage Round My Father* at the start of the seventies. Three years later I wrote a play called *Collaborators*. A husband and wife try to keep a large household of children afloat on almost no money and collaborate on a script for an American producer whom they both, in their separate ways, exploit. Michael Codron liked the play and persuaded Glenda Jackson, John Wood and Joss Ackland to be in it. It was directed by Eric Thompson, who died ridiculously young, having fathered Emma who was to grow into a remarkable actress. I remember the rehearsals as being entirely happy. I was back in the excitement of an empty theatre, watching actors try out lines I'd written. I was still excited by the smell of plush seats and backstage corridors, and the dread approach of a first night when they let an audience in and nothing is ever quite the same again.

What I remember most clearly about the theatre at that time is the smell of coffee as I went up the narrow staircase to Peggy

Ramsay's office in Covent Garden. The door was open and Peggy was always talking on the telephone, often standing astride an electric fire with the heat blowing up her skirts. As a writer's agent she didn't so much woo managements as inform them, gently but firmly, what plays they were to put on. As she had no hesitation in rubbishing many of her authors' works, her seal of approval was universally respected. I once heard her answering the telephone to a manager who wanted to put on a play by an extremely famous writer out of whom Peggy had made so much money she had turned it into precious jewellery which she kept in shoeboxes under her bed. 'Do have a bit of sense,' she was telling this manager. 'You really don't want to put on a play by a boring, middlebrow, middle-of-the-road writer like him. Everyone's done him to death. For God's sake, be adventurous! Back the future! And do give me a ring when you've had an *interesting* idea.' She looked, at that time, like an extremely intelligent cockatoo, with bright reddish hair and protruding eyes behind glasses she constantly mislaid. No other agent has ever understood writers and writing so well, or been so kind to young playwrights during their struggle for existence. Her reward was that most of the dramatists of the seventies and eighties struggled up her narrow staircase, welcomed her to share their royalties and got called by someone else's name. There was a time, I remember, whenever she saw me she would say, 'Hallo, Mercer. Mortimer's fallen in love again and can't write a word.'

It was hard to discover the past history of Peggy Ramsay. She had, it seems, come from South Africa, where a pilot fell so much in love with her that he flew constantly over her house, dipping his wings by way of amorous salute. She married a husband who was a disappointment to her; 'couldn't do it, darling' was the way she put it. They came on a honeymoon to the Savoy Hotel in London. On the third or fourth day she told him she was going out shopping and would be back for tea. She never came back and so far as we knew he was still waiting for Peggy among the cucumber sandwiches. That afternoon she joined the Carl Rosa opera company and became, for a while, the most short-sighted Valkyrie of them all. She also committed the solecism of walking down the stream on which the swan was to float in *Lohengrin*. Despite this, she was promoted to small parts and, 'Darling,' she said, 'didn't the other girls in the chorus hate me for it!' Whether or not it was a great loss to the opera, she eventually left the Carl Rosa, ran the little Q theatre for a while and then two far-sighted writers decided to set her up as an agent in a couple of small rooms off St Martin's Lane. Her first client was Robert Bolt and from then on her future was assured.

When I had done my first short plays, *The Dock Brief* and *What Shall We Tell Caroline?*, Peggy had written to me. So the climb up the narrow staircase in Goodwin's Court began. I showed her everything I wrote, discussed all my plans for writing and for life. I always listened to what she told me, although now I can't remember any of the advice she gave. And Peggy's judgement was by no means infallible. When Peter Nichols presented her with *A Day in the Death of Joe Egg*, undoubtedly his finest play, she said, 'For God's sake, darling, put it away in a drawer and forget it.' And yet she was one of the few agents who loved writing with a passion which could overwhelm managers, theatre owners and even critics. Her enthusiasm pushed you on like a great gust of wind; her rages could be terrible. Her staff went in some fear of her and she once poured a pint of beer over the head of the late Caryl Brahms, novelist and writer of musicals. She was thought to have been in love with the small, rotund, French playwright Eugène Ionescu. She had as a lover, but rarely displayed, a quiet, gentle, English actor who wore double-breasted blazers and had appeared in many drawing-room comedies. She had an extraordinary eye for new writers and discovered and nourished Edward Bond, David Mercer and David Rudkin, as well as representing such hugely popular dramatists as Alan Ayckbourn. She was more responsible than anyone for the revival of British playwriting in the sixties and seventies. I could have found no one better to fan the flames of a long-neglected passion for the theatre.

Peggy was wonderful to her writers when they started out in the strange and fickle theatrical world. When I had my first plays on in the fifties she'd spend hours talking to me, improving the construction of scenes and buying me lunch. When my life was in turmoil she lent me her flat. Hardly a day passed without one of her phone calls, which always started at a high point of excitement and went on in a crescendo of plots and counterplots. As she never said, 'Hallo, how are you?' or used any such preliminaries, her words came drifting mysteriously across the air like Caliban's voices and I was never quite sure if I was the author she meant to ring up. 'Mercer,' she said once, her voice vibrant with excitement, 'Bolt wants to speak to you at once. What the hell have you done now, darling? Gone off with his wife?' 'But I'm not Mercer!' 'I know that, darling. Mercer's in a state and can't cope with his material.' 'But I hardly know Mrs Bolt.' 'Is *that* your story, darling? Then you'd better keep to it.' Suddenly her voice vanished, to trouble another writer and no doubt spread the gossip. When I rang Robert Bolt, it appeared he only wanted my legal advice for a friend who was going for a divorce; he had tried to explain this to Peggy, but she preferred her own version and was sticking to it. Life with Peggy was almost unbearably exciting when you were starting to write for the theatre.

Success brought about a noticeable decline in her interest in you. Considerable success might lead her to persuade managements to try to do something more novel than your plays, and when I had been married to Penny for some while her disappointed voice came unexpectedly and unannounced over the wires, 'You're not still with that little girl, are you? I never thought *that*'d last.'

Collaborators was set in a tall, North London house, where the children were offstage voices, insistent and, at times, threatening. The room was full of plastic basins of washing, nappies and knicker-linings, sodden bicky-pegs dangling on ribbons tied to

63

playpens – and the story was furnished with memories of living with six children and an unmanageable overdraft in the early days of my first marriage. Those were the times when I used to leave home after a terrible domestic row, sometimes torn about the shirt or scratched about the neck, the children were suffering from infectious diseases, the au pair girl had left home and I used to force the front door open against a great pile of bills. The overdraft was about to be stopped and the washing-machine repossessed. I would stagger into the street and find the car had been stolen. I would thumb a lift to my chambers in the Temple, sink behind my desk exhausted, and I was perfectly capable of advising sixty-year-old company directors on exactly how to conduct their married lives. 'You know what it's like,' the husband in *Collaborators* says, 'living with small children? It's like spending your days in a home for very old, incontinent Irish drunks! It's like life in a colony of hostile meths drinkers! They come swaying up to you with their dribble and their deep, hoarse cries and you smile – a smile of propitiation – and then they take a great swipe and smash the other candlestick.' And yet those menacing children, four step- and the two I had fathered, with their huge consumption of Farex and knicker-linings, became friends, companions, shrewd and sensible supporters. That house in Swiss Cottage, a small Victorian island lost in a sea of high-rise flats; those holidays in rented villas we couldn't possibly afford; those Christmases which required, if everyone was to give something to everyone else, around eighty-four presents, were from a past for which *Collaborators* was, no doubt, an inadequate obsequy. The notices were what is politely known as 'mixed'. Michael Billington, in a review in the *Guardian*, which was, on the whole, very favourable, said that I covered pain with jokes. I don't think that's an altogether bad thing to do and it is, at any rate, a part of my inheritance.

For as long as Glenda Jackson stayed in it, *Collaborators* did well at the box office. Penny and I went off to North Africa for a holiday, which, like the play, was not entirely successful. In the aeroplane we were told that Tunis was colder than London, and the hotel we stayed in was little more than a building site. On my birthday two boy waiters made me a rock-like and inedible cake and we drank Tunisian champagne, which seemed indistinguishable from Eno's Fruit Salts. Penny had found an English newspaper and we opened it eagerly to find an extremely hostile notice of *Collaborators*. I was half a century old, and in the years to come I would drift away from the theatre and climb Peggy Ramsay's stairs less often. I also became wary of opening newspapers.

It was during the run of *Collaborators* that we called on Rex Harrison in the South of France. I rang David Niven, who lived near Beaulieu, and told him that I was off to see Rex, a man to whom he didn't particularly warm. I hoped we might meet later for dinner. I then put down the phone, but minutes later it rang and I heard Rex's voice. 'Hallo, John. Rex here. Just want to tell you, before you get here, that you're a shit and you always have been. Have you got that perfectly clear? I didn't want to say you're a shit in front of the others. That was rather decent of me, wasn't it?' I was not only taken aback but somewhat wounded by this instant analysis of my character. It was, of course, just the sort of thing Rex would say − he who had called his agent's wife a 'clockwork cunt' because she thought a play he was in was a little too long. But did he, in all fairness, have a point? I was worrying about this when a gust of laughter came from the telephone in my hand. It was Niven who had been doing his Rex Harrison imitation.

I had met Niven years before when we were filming in Spain, doing a movie the main advantage of which was that we had met. His screen acting was always beautifully polished, deftly entertaining and, in such films as *Separate Tables*, touching. His greatest performances, however, were at restaurant tables, to an audience of a few friends, and his stories were beautifully performed and improved with repetition. In Spain we drank so much cheap

65

brandy that he called me Fundador, and he was delighted to find, in remote villages, tattered posters from his old Hollywood movies still sticking to the walls. In the Alhambra he became a little quiet, as though upstaged by a star as big as himself. His private performances, although irresistible, were never selfish; he had the talent Oscar Wilde was said to have had – of making everyone with him feel more alive, more entertaining than usual. When he visited us he would, if he arrived early, walk about the lanes for fear of boring us, for he was, despite his pleasure in his stardom, a modest man who would never make any great claims for his acting. His first wife, Primrose, had fallen down the stairs of a dark cellar in Hollywood during a game of hide-and-seek and died heartbreakingly young. Some of his jokes, I'm sure, were also to cover pain.

Now he was married to Hjordis, whom he called the 'beautiful Swede'. She had been a model, married to a rich husband, and he found her, for some reason, on the set of *Bonny Prince Charlie*. She sat by the pool making endless telephone calls. 'My ear is out to here!' she complained. 'Making all these telephone calls. What I need is a holiday!' I remember, because I was still at the cooking stage of my life, asking her if I could see the kitchen. With some difficulty Hjordis found the number of the kitchen – a place, it seemed, with which she was not familiar – rang it up and announced that a visit would not be possible. Niven took us out for drives and to small restaurants. Hjordis stayed at home, a martyr to the telephone.

So we listened to his ever-improving and ever more polished stories. We heard the long saga about the way his zip came undone when he was skiing down a Swiss slope and the icy wind froze his genitals: 'I looked down and saw this little Eton-blue acorn!' We enjoyed once more the way a bone flew out of an actress's corset and up his nose as he was embracing her on the New York stage, and we heard an entirely new one about the commercial for an underarm deodorant.

He had been asked to film this advertisement, but had steadfastly refused and when pressed had said he would do it only on three conditions. The first was that he should be paid a huge sum of money, the second that he could film it anywhere in the world he fancied and the third, and most important, was that the commercial should not be shown anywhere but in Japan. All these terms were agreed to. Niven chose to film outside the palace in Monte Carlo, no doubt because it was near home and perhaps in memory of his long-past but eternally memorable love affair with Princess Grace. He chose to play a sentry, sweating in a scarlet uniform and a busby, who is forced to give his armpit a generous spray of the magic deodorant. He then collected the money, went off to work in America and put the unpleasant incident out of his mind. When he came back to London he was walking into the Connaught Hotel, where he always stayed, with a number of friends and acquaintances when two large coaches drew up outside the hotel. From them emerged a huge party of Japanese who saw Niven and burst into high-pitched laughter, lifted their arms and dabbed at their armpits in hysterical mimicry.

We sailed through the harbour in a dinghy, slowly, with little wind. The rain, a permanent feature of holidays in the South of France, had stopped suddenly. Niven was talking about the great days of Hollywood, when he had emerged from central casting, an unlikely Scotsman to succeed in the tinsel city. He had shared a house on the beach, which they called Cirrhosis by the Sea, with Errol Flynn. He had organized an elaborate practical joke which again involved Rex Harrison. Niven and Nigel Bruce hired a young hooker to pose as Bruce's virginal cousin from London, whom he had promised to look after, and then affected outrage when they caught Rex making love to her. He also described the embarrassing moment during the filming of *The Prisoner of Zenda* when they were riding into the city and his horse, eager as Harrison, reared up and mounted the mare ridden by Douglas Fairbanks Junior. And then, floating along the coast in a moment of silence, we saw a leaking boat, an abandoned wreck. 'You know what that is?' Niven said. 'That's Flynn's boat.' The great old days of Hollywood, the scandals and the fabled romances, were rotting at the quayside and about to disintegrate entirely.

My father's repeated question, 'Is execution done on Cawdor?', boomed out across the garden in my childhood, echoed down the years. It became a password. I was sent to stay with George Clune, a distant connection of my father's, who had been converted to Rome and played the organ in a Catholic church in Eastbourne. He used to weave such tunes as 'Pop Goes the Weasel' and 'My Old Man Said Follow the Van' into the music when the congregation assembled and dispersed. My father had told me to ask if Cawdor had been executed and when I did so George Clune folded me in his arms and welcomed me as though we were members of some secret society. So the words of Shakespeare became passwords or incantations. 'Who's the silent Irishman in *Hamlet*?' my father would ask me. Long usage had taught me the answer: 'He's the one the Prince of Denmark's talking to when he says, "Now could I do it, Pat. Now he is praying."'

So the plays were part of our daily lives, like the evidence in divorce cases and drowning earwigs and ITMA being switched on during dinner when my father was bored. I thought hardly at all about the man who wrote them, whose coloured effigy seemed unreal and doll-like over his tomb in the church at Stratford. But then, towards the end of the seventies, I got a strange invitation from Associated Television, the fiefdom of Lew Grade, whose agile little feet had once been planted in the variety show and the summer season. I was asked to write six television plays about the life of Shakespeare.

The first professor I asked said that everything known about the life of Shakespeare could be written on a postcard and you would still have room for the stamp. It seems he adopted no public personality, in which he was wise. Other great writers have not been so well advised. Dickens took on the role of a warm-hearted, devoted family man and, when it was discovered that he was cruel to his wife, secretive with his mistress and sometimes hard-hearted to his children, the perpetual pleasures of his books may, for some, have been diminished. Philip Larkin took on the part of a racist, male chauvinist bigot, thus disillusioning the many *Guardian* readers who had written dissertations on his excellent poetry. Evelyn Waugh entertained himself by acting a curmudgeonly country squire with an ear trumpet, and then the wind changed and he was stuck with it. John Osborne and Kingsley Amis, having been called, in some distant dawn of the world, angry young men, have opted to become cross old blimps and have performed their roles with considerable success. But Shakespeare, engaged full-time in writing parts for other people, was apparently unable to think up one for himself.

If he had committed a murder, like his friend Ben Jonson, we should have known a great deal more about him. If he had been a double agent, in trouble with the Privy Council, and a noted atheist who died with a dagger in his eye like Marlowe, we might have had a good deal more to go on. As it is, Shakespeare, who transcended all other writers, beat them all in keeping potential biographers guessing. In fact we know a great deal about him, quite enough to cover a whole packet of postcards, but it's mercifully dull. We have details of his law-suits, his property-buying, his will; the unsensational moments of a life spent keeping out of trouble. He was kind enough to give us some blank years, between leaving Stratford and turning up in the London theatre, during which time you can create your own Shakespeare: a lawyer's clerk, a soldier, a traveller to Italy, a tutor in an aristocratic household – what you will. It is clear that he was born the son of a semi-literate glovemaker, went to London to act, wrote plays with considerable success, was admired by Ben Jonson, known and revered by his fellow actors, Hemmings and Condell, and returned to New Place in Stratford to enjoy his money and die, perhaps on his birthday. He was either William Shakespeare or someone else with exactly the same name. What is perfectly obvious is that he wasn't Francis Bacon; he had nothing whatever in common with that cold-hearted, urbane, secretly corrupt judge whose scientific interests led him to die stuffing a goose with snow; and yet the penalty of writing anything at all about Shakespeare is to receive weekly propaganda from the Francis Bacon Society. Somewhere, in some dusty office, some dullard spends his life collecting evidence that there never was a Shakespeare. If a writer keeps out of trouble he can be denied all existence.

The best I could do was to invent six patently fictional stories about Shakespeare's life. This subject allows a wide degree of speculation because of the form of his art. The novelist is for ever present in his work, sometimes addressing us directly like Dickens, Trollope or Thackeray, sometimes causing every scene to vibrate with his peculiar sensitivity like Henry James or, following Flaubert's precept and being like God in his universe, everywhere present and nowhere visible. The playwright is only on stage when he is pretending to be someone else, lost in his characters, whose views shouldn't be too readily mistaken for his. So you can prove that Shakespeare was a liberal anarchist – 'handy-dandy, which is the justice, which the thief?', or a conservative devoted to law and order and the class structure – 'Take but degree away, untune that string, And, hark! what discord follows', a pre-Christian stoic – 'As flies to wanton boys, are we to the gods; They kill us for their sport', or a man with a touching belief in Christian mercy – 'Why, all the souls that were were forfeit once, And He that might the vantage best have took, Found out the remedy'. You can also spell a great variety of plots out of the sonnets, no doubt the nearest he came to autobiography. Did he love an aristocratic patron called Henry Wriothesley or, as Oscar Wilde thought, a boy actor called Willie Hughes? Did his fair, male lover sleep with his dark girl-friend or were there other causes for his bitterness and burning sense of ingratitude? Such historical questions are best approached by way of fiction.

Writing the Shakespeare stories was an enormous pleasure. It was interesting to see the great female roles acted by boys before all-male Shakespeare became fashionable. And I worked with Peter Wood, a director of truly Elizabethan flamboyance. He would sit in the control room surrounded by his props: silver jugs of coffee, bay rum after-shave, and an assortment of pills, admiring the beauty of his shot and congratulating himself. One day he looked at the screen and said, 'Peter, Peter, that's really sensational! You combine the eye of a Rembrandt with a magnificent narrative drive. But silly, silly, Peter, you forgot to cue the actors!' We built the Globe Theatre on the lot at Elstree and filled it with ground-lings. One very hot day they were alarmed when the director appeared on the stage wearing little but a pair of Y-fronts and a Mexican hat. 'You may think I'm a bastard now, but you'll learn what a bastard I really am before the day is out!' he bellowed at them through a bull horn. They took fright and began to trickle away to the town, where numerous customers in doublet and hose were spotted pushing trolleys through Tesco's. I have the greatest admiration for Peter Wood who taught me something of great value: an hour's drama on television, which might be thought of as a one-act play or a long short story, is greatly enriched if it has not one plot but two or, better still, three. I have always found plots hard to come by; all the same I stuck to Peter Wood's rule when I came to tell stories about my own character, not the Swan of Avon, but Rumpole of the Bailey.

7

I'm writing in a Moroccan hotel. It's February and in England the skies are grey, the ground frozen, the daffodils have poked up before their time but dare not open. Here, all sorts of flowers are out at the same time: roses, carnations, geraniums, hibiscus, arum lilies and bougainvillaea. The sun is shining, the trees are heavy in the orange groves and there are lemons clinging to the wall. The sky is bright blue and far away you can see snow on the Atlas Mountains. There are a number of elderly English people in this hotel; it's very quiet and a good place to work.

Last year Penny and I were here, watching the other guests, trying to work out their relationships, or speculate on their lives, which is the chief pleasure to be got from staying in hotels. There was an Englishman, frail and birdlike, wearing elderly but expensive clothes and a brown trilby hat. He was in the company of a thickset, crop-haired, moustached and tattooed man with a North Country accent, perhaps half his age, who might have been a bouncer or a PE instructor. We thought he was the old man's bodyguard. At dinner, we noticed, they did themselves extraordinarily well, ordering lobsters specially brought from Agadir and pink, French champagne. After a while they invited us to join them for dinner and we found out more. The older man was called Tony. Mike, who had the tattoos, was his cook, housekeeper, gardener, driver, companion and friend.

'Tony's only got about a month to live,' Mike said, as all four of us sat at dinner. 'It was just a little while ago I sent him in roast pheasant with all the trimmings: bread sauce, gravy, sprouts and game chips. Though I say it

72

myself, it was done perfect. Not at all dry, nice and moist, really appetizing. And Tony took one mouthful and he couldn't eat it. So I told him then, straight out, "Cancer of the oesophagus. That's you." He's not got long to go now. Of course, I suppose he could be kept alive a bit longer with all sorts of drugs and that. But we'd both much rather he went as he is now. I want to always think of him as he is. At his best.' And to this, Tony, who had heard the entire speech, nodded a gentle and smiling approval.

Tony told us more about himself. He'd been very rich: 'born with a silver spoon in my mouth'. Disgusted by the poverty in his part of England he stood, on a couple of occasions and unsuccessfully, as a Labour candidate. He'd been in the Army and took part in the retreat from France. He sat with his sergeant on the beach at Dunkirk while the Germans shelled them and the British did their best to leave in every available craft to cross the Channel. Tony and his sergeant ate the ham, drank the four-star brandy and smoked the Havana cigars which his mother had sent him for his twenty-first birthday. When they'd finished their picnic, the sergeant suggested that they'd better try and get back to England. They swam out and found that the small boats had been ordered not to take more than thirteen passengers. When an officer tried to pull rank and climb on board a motor boat which already had its full complement, an NCO shot him. Tony decided that they wouldn't chance their luck. He and his sergeant swam on until they came to a leaky Polish ship on which they eventually escaped. Later in the war, the sergeant died of wounds, leaving his young wife pregnant with Mike. Tony had helped support her and the child, kept in touch with Mike when he was employed as a sports organizer, and they were now inseparable companions. Tony knew that he hadn't long to go which is why they ordered lobster and pink champagne.

'But aren't you afraid of dying?' Penny, who was furthest from death, asked at the end of this story.

'Not really.' Tony was still smiling. 'I'm so looking forward to meeting Mummy again.'

Two or three weeks after we got home I had a letter from Tony telling me more about his experiences at Dunkirk. A month later we read his obituary in The Times.

Thoughts of death are always a diversion from life and, as the years pass, there is less and less time for them. What I meant to write about, sitting somewhere south of the Atlas Mountains, was the arrival of Rumpole in my life, almost twenty years ago.

I'd wanted to write about a detective, a Sherlock Holmes or a Maigret, to keep me alive in my old age. Then I thought of making him a criminal defender, in honour of the Old Bailey hacks I'd known and admired. I thought of giving him my father's uniform: a black jacket and waistcoat, striped trousers and cigar ash on the watch-chain, although I left out my father's spats. I added my father's habit of quoting poetry at inappropriate moments and I am proud, at least, to have brought snatches of Wordsworth to a large audience. I thought of giving him Jeremy Hutchinson's habit of calling impossible judges 'old darling', although he resembles Jeremy in no other way. Then, because I wanted Rumpole to have as hard a time at home as he had in court, I gave him a powerful wife whom he wouldn't call 'old darling'. I began by writing some odd speeches for him and found that as soon as he stepped on to the page, he began to speak in his own voice, which is undoubtedly the greatest favour a character can do for you.

Rumpole was also indebted to James Burge, another admirable advocate who freely applied the word 'darling' to the judiciary. He had defended Stephen Ward, who was offered up as a sacrificial victim during one of the British public's periodic and absurd fits of morality at the time of the Profumo affair. Ward had been Christine Keeler's friend and was accused, on inadequate evidence, of living on immoral earnings. He committed suicide during the trial, but James Burge, who was also badly treated by the judge, soldiered on and, some years later, we sat together defending some murderous football hooligans. Searching for an Arsenal supporter to stab and being unable to find one, they had killed a stranger on Charing Cross Station, who was, so far as anyone could discover, totally uninterested in the game and supported nobody. Looking at the sullen and threatening faces in the dock, James Burge whispered to me, 'I'm really an anarchist at heart but I don't think even my darling old Prince Peter Kropotkin would have approved of this lot!' So I called the first Rumpole play *My Darling Old Prince Peter Kropotkin*. Of course someone wondered whether the television audience would be familiar with Kropotkin's works and I changed it to *My Darling Old Jean-Jacques Rousseau*, a name which also failed to ring a bell in the world of television. Finally the director suggested *Rumpole of the Bailey* on the lines of *Trelawny of the 'Wells'* and so it has remained. However, I am grateful to James Burge for a line I'll never forget and I'm sure Rumpole, although he would have disapproved entirely of Stephen Ward and his way of life, would have defended him with equal energy and courage.

When I wrote that first story in the mid seventies, I didn't know who would play Rumpole. I thought Alastair Sim would be excellent in the part, but sadly Mr Sim was dead and unable to take it on. On a happy day for me, the producer, then Irene Shubik, and John Gorrie, the director, suggested Leo McKern. He liked the part and was the first to suggest that we should do more stories. Now, when Rumpole speaks in his own voice, it is always Leo's voice also.

Sometimes, a writer finds an actor who not only becomes the character he's invented, but adds to and enriches it. This happened with Michael Hordern in *Dock Brief* and David Threlfall when he became a snakelike Conservative cabinet minister in *Paradise Postponed* and *Titmuss Regained*. It happened at once and then always with Leo McKern in Rumpole. Leo comes from Sydney, and Australians are born with one great advantage: they have almost no respect for authority. Rumpole's disdain for pomposity, self-regard, and the soulless application of the letter of the law without regard for human values, came naturally to him. There is a story I heard in Australia about a barrister who carried on his practice in

75

one of the states where they still wear wigs and gowns, and have also taken over our myth that a barrister who gets up to address the court not in fancy dress is invisible. This Australian advocate got up, wigless, without a gown, in front of a judge he particularly disliked and said, 'Your Honour, I wish to make an application.' 'I can't see you, Mr Bleaks,' said the judge, no doubt enjoying what he regarded as the great tradition of the old country's bar. 'But, your Honour, in my humble submission . . .' 'It's no good, I simply can't see you.' 'Am I quite invisible, your Honour?' 'Utterly invisible to me, Mr Bleaks.' 'Are you quite sure, your Honour?' 'Absolutely sure, Mr Bleaks.' 'Then if you're quite sure, this is something I've been meaning to do for years.' Whereupon Mr Bleaks put his fingers to his nose and stuck out his tongue at the judge. I'm not suggesting that Rumpole would ever do this; his insults are, I hope, a little more subtle, but that fine spirit of disrespect is still somewhere deep inside him.

Leo has Rumpole's hatred of pretension. During the filming of *Ryan's Daughter*, while everyone was kept waiting for the perfectly composed shot, with the seagulls all flying in the right direction, he grew so disillusioned with show business that he decided to give it all up, went back to Australia and bought a rain forest. Luckily for me, he changed his mind and left again. He's forever uncertain as to which country he wants to live or die in. As he has a perfectly reasonable dislike of flying, he spends a great part of his life on small cargo ships, his motor car stored in the hold, chugging across the Indian Ocean. Sometimes, it seems, he's changed his mind before he's arrived at his destination. In his youth he fell in love with a young Australian actress whom he saw swinging on a wire as Peter Pan and he followed her to England. They are still married; she is still thin and beautiful and can rarely be seen eating or drinking. Here, he lost his Australian accent and played Shakespeare, proving beyond all doubt he could play anything. His Iago was so good that the theatre at Stratford grew nervous of him and offered him Friar Laurence, the daftest part in the entire canon, so he wisely walked out. He was memorable in *The Alchemist* and acted at the Old Vic with Donald Wolfit, who desperately tried to put him off by shouting at him in the wings.

Leo McKern arrives in the rehearsal room long before anyone else and can finish *The Times* crossword puzzle before the coffee is ready. He likes simple jokes and has been known to put his glass eye (he lost his real one in an industrial accident) in the middle of the Bolognese sauce on a plate of spaghetti so that it glowers up and alarms the waiter. He loves boats; he fell off his most recent one in the dark and spent a long time floating in a marina, calling out mayday to diners who took no notice, until he was rescued at last by two tearaways who had been racing stolen cars. He acts with his entire body, and, like many fairly bulky men, is extremely light on his feet, dives expertly from the highest board and dances in the most sprightly fashion. I know about his dancing because, when we were on location on a Mediterranean cruise ship, he sometimes led me out on to the dance floor in the Dolphin Saloon and performed the difficult feat of waltzing me around. He learns his many lines during rehearsal and only changes them minutely, often for the better and after careful consultation. He can turn in an instant from comedy to pathos or play both of them at the same time. His acting exists where I always hope my writing will be: about two feet above the ground, a little larger than life, but always taking off from reality. As an actor he is to be compared with the great screen giants, Laughton and Raimu, the old French movie star, who was shapeless, lovable and could make you laugh and cry. He's a very private man who avoids speeches, dinners and public appearances. Once he starts work, he is entirely professional, an inspiring leader of a company.

For a long time he was reluctant to start each new series because he didn't want to be 'just thought of as Rumpole', and, perhaps, over the last eighteen years, he should have found time for Falstaff and Lear. Lately, he seems to have become reconciled to the part, but I sometimes feel I have had to take on the burden of being Rumpole in reality. Quite recently, after I had had a painful argument with a marble bathroom floor and a treacherous Jacuzzi in Australia, and I was being pushed, lamed, through airports in a wheelchair apparently constructed for a child, the passers-by waved and called out, 'G'day, Rumpole!' I have to protest that I am not he; I lack his courage, his stoicism and the essential nobleness of his character. I am not sufficiently Spartan to support life in Froxbury Mansions with 'She Who Must Be Obeyed'. I am no more he than any of the fat middle-aged barristers you can find sitting in El Vino's in Fleet Street (known in the stories as Pommeroy's Wine Bar), drinking claret and dropping cigar ash down their waistcoats, claiming to be the original Rumpole. He may have echoes of my father, and of Jeremy Hutchinson and James Burge, he may say something about the law and the state of England with which I happen to agree, but I hope, if you watch him or read about him, you will discover, he is nobody but himself.

Conan Doyle is said to have grown tired of Sherlock Holmes, pushed him off the Reichenbach Falls, and only brought him back to life at the urgent request of the readers of the *Strand Magazine*. I haven't tired of the old barrister, and I think this is because you can take today's events – social workers snatching children for suspected devil worship, the Court of Appeal having to eat the words of previous judges, the suggested reforms of the legal profession or the slender difference between actors and barristers – and write a Rumpole story about them. Any matrimonial dispute fits easily in the Rumpole marriage and Penny says that when we have an argument she can see me remembering her lines in order to give them to Hilda.

I don't know if it's because he's so irredeemably English that Rumpole has become something of a cult figure in America. The Rumpole Society started in California and grew rapidly. The first meeting I went to took place in San Francisco's huge gas and electricity building. A mock-up of Pommeroy's had been built there and judges in 'She Who Must Be Obeyed' T-shirts were serving behind the bar. There is a minor character in *Rumpole* called Dodo Macintosh, who makes 'cheesy bits' for the Chambers' parties and the evening began with a blind tasting of Dodo Macintosh's 'cheesy bits'. Some time later there was a Hilda look-alike contest, and much discussion of Rumpole's address. As I write the books quite rapidly, I am always forgetting exactly where he lives.

Actors like Peter Bowles, Jonathan Coy, Patricia Hodge and Julian Curry have always been a joy to write for, continually demonstrating that British light-comedy acting is the best in the world. Then there was an argument between Thames Television and Irene Shubik, the original producer of *Rumpole*, who cast them. She wanted the next series postponed until it was resolved and I didn't. Later Jacqueline Davis came into my life, stayed there, and together we have produced over fifty hours of television, working together at times of excitement, satisfaction, frustration and despair, but never really wanting to work with anyone else.

We met at lunch in the early Rumpole days and Jacquie came into the restaurant, a beautiful woman in a white dress, with huge dark eyes and a gentle voice. She is inclined to lose things, drop her notebook, files and glasses and run her red Alpha-Romeo into walls, while thinking of the elegance of such a motor car. She's as prone to despair as I am, but often with me it's a device to achieve a result, and with her, a genuine emotion. Her kindness and generosity are endless and her charm can win the hearts of that most brutal and intractable of bodies, a film unit on location. She remembers everyone's birthdays, gets them cards and presents, and, given the slightest excuse for any sort of celebration, bakes an enormous cake. She's the most expert wrapper-up of gifts and, when she comes laden with them, it seems an act of vandalism to undo the paper.

She lives in a small house with two cats and there we have gone through crises in casting, rows with directors and all the usual television traumas without any serious disputes. At our first lunch she told me her strange family history.

Before the last war a beautiful girl (I have no doubt she was beautiful and Jacquie has a photograph which proves it) came to stay in a Clapham lodging-house. She departed suddenly, leaving behind her a small baby. The landlady, who had children of her own, behaved in a noble fashion, brought the child up, saw her educated until she found a job in advertising and then in television. The baby became Jacquie Davis. Although she called the landlady her mother, and still visits her grave, she was always, and understandably, anxious to find out who her real mother was. In this long quest she has found a half-brother, and three half-sisters living in Cornwall, the result of her mother's marriage to a Cornish policeman who worked in Soho. Given the fact that many people devote their time and energy to avoiding their relations, it's a great tribute to Jacquie's persistence that she has found so many. I don't know if she will discover more about her mother, but I can imagine how important it is to her to know. Meanwhile, those she works with, her friends and her friends' children, are her extended family.

I began this chapter sitting in a garden, writing about death. A few years ago I was at some book fair or other when up came the author who is now Lord Archer of Weston-super-Mare, bubbling with excitement. 'I've got a great idea for you,' he said. 'Kill Rumpole! It'll make a terrific story.' I don't know when Rumpole will die, but all good things come to an end. And I'll always remember the tattooed companion, the gentle Tony and the life which began with cigars on the beach at Dunkirk and ended after the last lobster had been ordered from Agadir.

8

I am driving my daughter Emily up to London to go to school on a Monday morning. She's wearing a red beret and blazer. As soon as we get on to the motorway she invites me to play Twenty Questions, and she says, 'It's animal.' 'Can you eat it?' 'No.' 'Has it got four legs?' 'No.' I ask many questions to all of which she answers, 'No.' We play many games but I never win. Then I discover the secret of her success. She isn't thinking of anything at all. I am expending great ingenuity asking questions to which there is absolutely no answer.

Although I was not brought up to be religious, and was neither christened nor confirmed (an unholy state which I kept quiet about at school, together with other secret sins), I have always had the greatest respect for a religion which asserted the importance of the individual soul. Believer or unbeliever, I am part of a Christian civilization, with a Christian ethic, a faith in the possibility of redemption and the forgiveness of sins. It also seems to me that total materialism is unbearably drab and that a faith that recognizes the importance of mystery is essential. I envy the Catholic novelists, Evelyn Waugh and Graham Greene and Muriel Spark, whose religion adds shape and weight to their stories; they start with an advantage over the writer who is merely a well-meaning member of the Atheists for Christ Society. I have a great affection for the Church of England, in spite of its insane act of self-destruction in emasculating the language of the Bible. I can't imagine England without cathedrals and village churches, and I'm perfectly happy sitting in the garden arguing with the vicar. My difficulties come with the idea of an all-powerful, all-loving God who not only allows the Holocaust and ethnic cleansing but permits children to die of leukaemia. When Macduff hears of his wife and children's murder, he asks, 'Did heaven look on / And would not take their part?' It's a question to which neither he nor I have received a satisfactory answer.

Of course the theologian, and the vicar in the garden, will say that God has given us free will, and won't interfere with our evil decisions. This is understandable as far as Macbeth's hired assassins, or the guards at the gas chamber are concerned, but their victims can't be said to have exercised their free will or had much choice in the matter. The agonized question becomes harder to answer when a sick child dies and there is no element of free will at all. The amount of help religious leaders gave me on these points was small. The Cardinal said, 'In this world I can't understand it. But that doesn't affect my belief . . . I can't put it to God at my level. Full understanding is never possible.' The Archbishop said, 'Jeremiah shook his fist at God and asked Him what He was about. I don't believe prayer is necessarily peaceful. It may mean arguing with God.' Malcolm Muggeridge, I think before he was received into the Catholic Church, said he thought of God as the Supreme Dramatist, the Great Shakespeare of the Skies, so naturally He wanted to write tragedies as well as comedies, to create villains as well as heroes. This seemed to me to be the most convincing explanation. A moving and significant illustration of this dilemma is the story of those rabbis who, in their hut in Belsen, put God on trial. After a prolonged hearing they found Him guilty and, this done, they went to prayer.

I have always felt proud of the fact that my father, in his blindness, didn't change his mind and turn to God. He found his consolations in himself, in his anger and laughter, in the huge anthology of poetry he had in his head, in avoiding visitors and occasionally mocking his son. But there's no doubt that it's in moments of personal agony that these questions about God fall to be decided, as well as in vicarage gardens and archbishops' palaces. The worst place to discuss them is probably down the Old Bailey, but that was where we had to debate matters of religion in the summer of 1977 when Denis Lemon, the editor of *Gay News*, was put on trial for blasphemy, a proceeding which most people thought had ended with the Inquisition.

Mr Lemon, a handsome, intense and rather mournful young man, published a poem by Professor James Kirkup, who had held important posts in the English departments of many universities, and won a number of awards for his poetry. The poem, which was short, spoke of the physical love of a Roman centurion for the body of Christ on the Cross. It also spoke of Christ as a practising homosexual. The circulation of *Gay News* was not large, nor did it seem likely to be read by an audience who would have been profoundly disturbed by it. An Anglican bishop had recently suggested that Jesus, who was what discreet obituarists refer to as 'unmarried', might have been a homosexual of the non-practising variety. Long before, in D.H. Lawrence's story, 'The Man Who Died', Christ was described as having survived the Crucifixion and making love to a girl for the first time. Much metaphysical poetry expresses love for Jesus in physical, even erotic, terms. In spite of all this, the poem didn't escape the eagle eye of Mrs Mary Whitehouse, who was ever on the lookout for material likely to cause her offence. A private prosecution was launched and Mr Lemon and his company, Gay News Ltd, were accused of blasphemous libel contrary to the Common Law of England. I was briefed to appear for Denis Lemon while my friend Geoff Robertson represented the company. Mrs Whitehouse was in daily attendance with a number of her supporters.

This was the first blasphemy case to be heard for over half a century and many lawyers took the view that the blasphemy laws no longer existed. No less an authority than Lord Denning had said in 1949: 'The offence of blasphemy is now a dead letter.'

The common law of blasphemy seems to have been born, after a prolonged period of gestation, at the end of the seventeeth century when a madman named Jeremy Taylor, who claimed to be Christ's younger brother, announced that religion was a cheat. The then Lord Chief Justice said that these words tended to the destruction of both religion and the state and Taylor, who had been committed to Bedlam, was also ordered to be set in the pillory with a card tied round his neck bearing the legend FOR BLASPHEMOUS WORDS AND THE SUBVERSION OF ALL GOVERNMENT. When the Anglican Church was established by the state, an attack on its beliefs, but on those of no other religious denomination, was held to be criminal. Trying a case in 1838 the judge said: 'If this is only a libel on the whole Roman Catholic Church, the defendant is entitled to be acquitted. A person may, without being liable to prosecution for it, attack Judaism or Mahometanism, or even any sect of the Christian religion, save the established religion of the country.' So Professor Kirkup could have written, and Mr Lemon could have published, whatever they liked concerning the Pope or Buddha. It was only the Church of England's Jesus who had to be protected.

In the early nineteenth century, the era of atheist French revolutionaries and Chartist riots, the political nature of the blasphemy laws became obvious. The publisher of Thomas Paine's *Rights of Man* was prosecuted for blasphemy, as was the bookseller who sold *Queen Mab*, Shelley being a passionate enemy of the government.

Later in the last century society became more tolerant and, with the arrival of Darwin and Huxley (Darwin, in my father's Bible, was much like Jesus and Huxley his John the Baptist), reasoned criticism of biblical infallibility had to be tolerated. In 1883 Lord Chief Justice Coleridge said that a mere denial of the truth of Christianity wasn't blasphemous, there must be a wilful intention

84

to 'pervert, mislead others by means of licentious and contumelious abuse'. These words seemed to offer us a defence, and we could argue that if the prosecution couldn't prove Denis Lemon and the magazine had such fell intentions they were entitled to be acquitted.

So we assembled, one summer day, in one of the more modern courts in the Old Bailey. I was there, Geoff was there, as was Mr Smyth, the intensely serious prosecutor. Mrs Whitehouse was there. The solicitor who went out and bought *Gay News* was there. Professor Kirkup, alas, was not there. He was far away, it was rumoured, standing in a sunbeam somewhere East of Suez, because the Professor was a distinguished orientalist and had a Chair in Tokyo. The jury were ready and willing to decide all the necessary questions of theology, religious sensitivity and poetic truth; no doubt they were expecting a fascinating and sensational case, something which would make a nice change from a theft in Tesco's or an indecent assault in the local cinema.

Sadly, the jury were to be disappointed. The normal excitement of an Old Bailey trial – the procession of unusual, unlikely or self-consciously normal people who parade as witnesses; the evidence which seems to favour now one side, now the other; the cut and thrust of cross-examination; the effort of the imagination needed to understand human passions or inhuman evil – all these were missing. The jury spent almost the whole trial in their room while we engaged in days of legal argument. We were trying to decide whether the law of blasphemy was alive or dead; if it might be contrary to the European Convention of Human Rights, which guarantees freedom of religion to its signatories; whether, as in all other cases of alleged obscene publication, literary merit was a defence and expert evidence could be called on the excellence or otherwise of Professor Kirkup's poem; and whether, as Lord Coleridge had said, the prosecutor had to prove an intention to pervert, insult and mislead others. For the sake, I suppose, of impartiality a Jewish judge had been selected. He was small, neat, invariably courteous and he smiled a good deal. He couldn't, in view of my client's name, resist the temptation of saying, during argument, that 'the answer was a lemon'. However, he wrote in his autobiography that he had been 'shocked and horrified' when he read the poem and wondered if, in these circumstances, he should try the case. Any doubts he may have had on this subject were manfully overcome and he described the *Gay News* case as the most irresistibly absorbing he ever tried. Whether it was an equally fascinating experience for Denis Lemon is another question entirely.

After many days when the jury sat in their room, knitting, filling in their pools or doing the crossword, the judge gently but firmly closed the door on all our possible defences. He found that the literary merit of the poem was quite immaterial, so the Professor might stand peacefully in his shaft of sunlight and no other poets or professors would be allowed to give evidence. And the intention of the poet or the editor mattered, said the judge, not at all, so there was no point in troubling the jury with their evidence. Bernard Levin and Margaret Drabble, lone and courageous, briefly gave evidence as to the character of *Gay News*. Otherwise all Geoff and I, and indeed the prosecutor, could do was to let the jury read the poem and then make speeches.

I think Geoff made the best speech and Mrs Whitehouse agreed. I made a long speech in which I ventured to suggest that the real attack on the magazine and the poem was against homosexuality, and I reminded the jury, probably ineffectively, of the sad day when Oscar Wilde was destroyed at the Old Bailey and the prostitutes danced in the streets for joy. I think it was somewhere around this point that the judge said, 'It may come as a relief to you during this rather sordid case, members of the jury, to know that England is two hundred and ten for three wickets in the Test Match' – or whatever the score was. I was so amazed by this gambit that I put the words in the mouth of his Honour Judge Bullingham, Rumpole's old opponent. When the judge later

The day job – the British passion for dressing up

My father's ghost proves hard to banish. The family at Turville Heath

My father bought my mother a picnic

He prepared to go into battle wearing pince-nez

After a number of miscarriages my mother gave birth to a son who,
perhaps, never showed his love for her sufficiently

Tony Richardson, a Prospero, with his daughter Natasha

Penny with Emily

Geoff Robertson celebrating. Few defenders can have had such triumphant results

My family taken over by actors: Laurence Olivier, Elizabeth Sellars,
Jane Asher, Alan Bates

Peggy Ramsay, the most short-sighted Valkyrie of them all

Niven: his greatest performances were to an audience of a few friends

With Jacquie Davis, an expert wrapper-up of gifts

In San Francisco, where aficionados display Rumpole number-plates

With Leo McKern. His acting exists where I always hope my writing will be

Following after Leo's breakfast

protested to me about this, I asked him how he could possibly think that he, so quiet and courteous, bore the slightest resemblance to the savage old Bullingham. At his request I wrote a letter to the newspapers denying that Bullingham was in any way based on the judge in the *Gay News* trial, a move which gave rise to much incorrect speculation that he was.

When we had finished our speeches the judge summed up. Looking back on it, he wrote: 'As for the summing-up itself, I can confidently assert that it was the best, by far, that I have ever given. I can say this without blushing because, throughout its preparation, and also when delivering it, I was half conscious of being guided by some superhuman inspiration.' Both his Lordship and the unseen spirit guiding his hand seemed very conscious of cheeks reddening with embarrassment, because at the end of the joint charge to the jury they were asked if they would read the poem aloud to an audience of Christians. 'And if you did, could you do it without blushing?' the judge said. The jury were also asked if they thought that God would like to be recognized in the context of such a poem as this. To consider these difficult questions, they retired at half past twelve and were back at half past three to ask if the prosecution had to prove that the poem tended to cause a breach of the peace. At twenty-five to four they returned wearily to their room.

I have always rather liked, even admired, Mary Whitehouse. She has considerable courage and sticks to her, at times, somewhat absurd views. While the jury were out in the *Gay News* trial, she stood with her adherents in a corridor outside the court and they could be seen, so I was told, praying to God for a guilty verdict. Whether there was a God who did not wish to be associated with Professor Kirkup's poem, and if there was, whether He had heard the final speeches for the defence or merely had Mrs Whitehouse's view of the matter to go on, I cannot tell but, no doubt to that fearless lady's satisfaction, her prayers were answered. Just after half past five the jury returned to court and found the defendants guilty by a majority of ten to two. Denis Lemon was given a suspended prison sentence of nine months and fined £500. Gay News Ltd was fined £1,000. The mad John Taylor, who believed he was the younger brother of 'Christ, the whoremaster', had not been set in the pillory by Lord Hale in 1677 for nothing. As Geoff said later, 'Between the ravings of a lunatic from Bedlam and the measured metaphors of a professor of poetry, the literal-minded law allowed no distinctions.'

We spent more days in the Court of Appeal going through the history of blasphemy, discussing Darwin, Shelley, and a Mr Gott, who, in 1922, wrote that Jesus looked like a clown riding on a donkey, and was sent to prison for it (although in a recent musical Christ was presented as a clown on the stage with impunity). We lost our appeal, although the court freed Denis Lemon from his prison sentence. In the fullness of time, when I was in faraway Singapore and contemplating leaving the bar, the House of Lords also confirmed the conviction. So, to the amazement of many, blasphemy remains a part of our law, although to the fury of many others it is a weapon which can only be used to protect the Church of England. The judge's summing-up has been approved in the highest courts and it remains a criminal offence to make Anglicans blush.

It may seem extraordinary that a widely respected and beloved religion, for which so many people have endured ridicule, persecution and even death, should still require a protection so archaic and curious as our blasphemy laws. We all hold precious beliefs, but unless they can stand against mockery and abuse they are worth little, and it is an insult to Anglicans to suggest that their beloved forms of worship need to be supported by a criminal sanction. I'm sure that the House of Lords were wrong not to adopt Lord Denning's opinion and pronounce the blasphemy laws a dead letter. By saying that the Church of England has a blasphemy law, they laid us open to those who ask why other religions should not have one also at a time when an alleged blasphemy by a distinguished author was met, not with a suspended term of imprisonment, but with a sentence of death.

It's 1990, thirteen years after the *Gay News* trial, and I have driven down the M4, skirted Slough by the Beaconsfield Road, turned right by the Do It All shop, and been lost in the rows of similar semi-detached houses, silent in the sunshine, fronted by sweetpeas and dahlias and Ford Consuls. I am in search of Dr Kalim Siddiqui, head of the Muslim Institute, enthusiastic supporter of the fatwa, the Iranian death sentence, on Salman Rushdie for the heinous crime of writing a novel, which was short-listed for the Booker Prize, in which some reference is made to the alleged sexual life of the prophet Mohammed. Somewhere, in some more or less safe house, the author is suffering his nineteenth month in hiding, guarded by the SAS at a cost of £1,000 a day to the British taxpayer.

After knocking on a strange door and disturbing an unknown Indian family, I telephone the Doctor and he arrives to rescue me in his car. He is a short, tubby, frequently laughing man with grey hair and a beard. He is wearing flannel trousers, a fawn cardigan and a blue shirt. He looks exactly what he has been: a character around Fleet Street, an ex-sub-editor of the *Guardian* and one-time dramatic critic of the *Kensington News*. He was no doubt well-liked, full of jokes, buying rounds of drinks for the journalists in the pub and sticking to orange juice himself.

'The Rumpole man!' His greeting is extremely cheerful. 'I should have come to Henley-on-Thames to see you!' And when he leads me into the headquarters of the Muslim Institute, a semi indistinguishable from his home next door, he is still laughing. 'Make yourself comfortable,' he says, and I sit among the box files, the books on Islam and notice Dr Siddiqui's British passport on the desk. 'Now, what would you like? We can offer you coffee. Gold Blend? Or tea? Here you have a choice of Earl Grey or PG Tips.'

After he has fetched the tea and biscuits he tells me about the death of his young son. He doesn't speak without feeling but with a fatalistic acceptance of tragedy and, at the end, he can't stop chuckling at the line of Siddiquis to be buried on British soil. I have come to discuss assassination and religious persecution, and it's time to set about trying to understand a man who could countenance a murder because of the publication of a book.

'Tell me about yourself.'

'Not too much to tell, really.'

'You worked on the *Kensington News*?'

'Oh, yes. The first time I had ever been in a theatre was as a dramatic critic. Then I worked on the *Wokingham Times*, the *Northern Echo*, the *Slough Express* and eight years on the *Guardian*. I love the brotherhood of journalists.'

'You've said you're a typical *Guardian* man.'

'Oh, yes. That's what I am.'

'You're not a Thatcherite?'

'Oh, no!' Dr Siddiqui laughs heartily at the idea. 'I have never voted except for the old Labour man Fenner Brockway, when he stood for Slough and he didn't get in. Who's my favourite British politician? I think Harold Wilson added greatly to the merriment, although he didn't achieve much.'

'In all your years in England, did you encounter any racial prejudice? Against you, I mean?'

'Little pinpricks, perhaps. Nothing serious. I am fair-skinned. I could be a Spaniard. Oh, I think one fellow called me a "bloody Pakistani".'

What have I discovered so far? A *Guardian* man who, unusually for one of that species, thinks irreligious writers should be put to death.

'What's the worst thing about *The Satanic Verses*, from your point of view?'

'Oh, dear.' Dr Siddiqui's cheerfulness leaves him and he sighs. 'I thought we were going to discuss more interesting matters than that! It is definitely the attack on the prophet's personal character.'

'Have you read the book?'

'Not from cover to cover.' Dr Siddiqui cheers up again. 'I have read a few pages. Funnily enough, I was in Iran when the book came out. I was waiting in the VIP lounge for my plane when a cabinet minister came up to me. He asked me about Rushdie and I told him what I knew. At lunch-time that day the Imam pronounced the fatwa. I don't know if it was due to me at all.'

'You believe that the Islamic law is laid down by God?'

'Of course. And the sentence for blasphemy or apostasy is death.'

'But isn't Christ part of the Islamic religion?'

'Oh, yes. He is a prophet. We have to believe in His virgin birth.'

'And is the sentence death if you don't?'

'Quite certainly!'

Making a mental note to advise the former Bishop of Durham to be careful when travelling to the Middle East, I ask, 'Then don't the Christian virtues of forgiveness of sins, mercy, loving your enemies, have any part in your religion?'

'No part at all!' Dr Siddiqui laughs happily again.

'Wouldn't you want to show forgiveness?'

'We can't do so. We have no choice.'

'Don't you regret that?'

'Not at all. In the West you have choice and look what it's brought you. Abortion. Rampant homosexuality. Mental illness. One-parent families. Aids!'

'Do you believe in hell?'

'Oh, yes. I tell you. I live in the fear of God every day.'

'You don't think He'll forgive your sins?'

'He might not.'

'What's hell like?'

'Oh, very hellish, I'm sure!'

'Worse than Slough?'

'No, no, I assure you' – he was laughing now, in spite of his fear of God – 'I have been very happy in Slough.'

Dr Siddiqui has asked a large audience of Manchester Muslims to raise their hands if they agreed with the fatwa; this they did with enthusiasm. He has been at meetings where his audience chanted 'Rushdie must die!' and 'Burn the book!'

'Going back to Salman Rushdie for a moment, can't you understand that your complete denial of free speech, your support of something as outrageous to us as a death threat for publishing words you disagree with, have damaged Islam in western eyes? And you've made your religion as terrifying to us as the Inquisition?'

'That may be so. But . . .' For once Dr Siddiqui is not smiling, he is at a loss for an answer and there is a silence.

'I suppose you're going to say it's God's will, and inevitable?'

'Yes. Inevitable, yes.' He seems grateful for my suggestion. 'That is it, of course.'

The concept of God has no doubt brought many benefits to the world but it's my belief that He should, if at all possible, be kept out of the criminal law.

Back in the theatre I had one more sign of possible intervention by an angry God. I had been standing on the steps of the cathedral in Siena, looking across at the entrance of the hospital. Families were crowding into it with food parcels for their sick relatives, and sightseers joined them, perhaps thinking that it was just another medieval palace to be visited. I imagined them, shepherded by their guides, straggling among the beds and looking up in awe at some painted ceiling where God's foot protruded from the clouds. So I invented a story about a visiting lecturer who fell off the British Council balcony during a cocktail party and, waking up in the hospital, and looking up at the ceiling painted with a celestial panorama, imagined he had died and been sent to heaven. He had written works on Byron and Baudelaire and thought of himself as a bit of a devil, a fascinating sinner to whom heaven was about as attractive as a Christian Science reading-room. He spends much of the play railing at the injustice of his lot. This short play was called

Mr Luby's Fear of Heaven and I wrote a companion piece about hell in which the Prince of Darkness turns up as a curate to a trendy South London vicar. This vicar takes the view that miracles are the sort of vulgar conjuring tricks which a deeply caring, rational and Socialist God wouldn't stoop to. To his anger and dismay, when the Bishop comes to dinner unexpectedly, the miracle of the feeding of the multitude takes place in his fridge. Anything mechanical that happens on the stage is a gamble: doors that are meant to open for quick flight stick, doors that are meant to be locked swing open, and audiences giggle with delight at these accidents and actors panic. For three weeks the vicar's fridge didn't fail to deliver a huge number of loaves and fishes. Then, one Saturday night with a full house, just as the miracle was about to occur, the fridge burst into flames. Was it a complete accident or had the unseen hand of the spirit who wrote the judge's summing-up in *R.* v. *Lemon and Gay News* been at work again?

9

How do we come by our political opinions? What is certain is that we don't take a calm, dispassionate look at the alternatives available and decide to become a little Socialist or a little Conservative as the result of mature deliberation. Like much else about us, such things are decided by the accidents of birth, the fall of the dice which gave us our homes, our parents and the moment of history when we first became aware of the world around us. It may also be that only children, and I was an only child, are less tolerant than others of received opinions, more likely to espouse unpopular causes or join rebellious groups.

Not that I rebelled greatly against my parents' ideas. My father was a lifelong Liberal. The great political moment in his lifetime was the landslide election in 1905 when Lloyd George, a Welsh solicitor, orator and devoted womanizer, achieved power, routed the House of Lords and became my father's unlikely hero. My mother had read *The Intelligent Woman's Guide to Socialism* and her ideas came from the writings of Ibsen, Shaw and H.G. Wells. I suppose she was an early feminist, although she behaved like the most devoted and self-sacrificing of wives.

I was born only five years after the 1914 war ended and the government conspicuously failed to provide homes for its heroes to live in. When I was dispatched to school some of the masters still suffered from shell-shock and battle fatigue, or had pieces of shrapnel lodged in them, causing them to fly into sudden and incalculable rages. We were preached to by parsons who were convinced that God was on our side in the Battle of the Somme and would no doubt come to our aid in the 'next Great Match'. I remembered a sermon which began 'This is the story of me and my batman Harry. And, of the two of us, Harry was no doubt the better man' and ended with some grisly episode in the trenches. One Armistice Day we had an outdoor service by the War Memorial, for which we all had to design posters showing gas attacks, heavy howitzers, primitive battles in the air (between Camels and Fokker Wolfs) and graves among Flanders poppies. The British Empire still reddened large portions of the globe, Kipling was much quoted (one of our school houses was called Gunga Din), and we were urged not to slick our hair down with butter because 'some of the native regiments did that and it went rancid in hot weather, causing an unpleasant odour on the parade-ground'. There was no harm, we were told, in a little water on the comb.

It always surprises me that the proponents of various causes – peace studies, political correctness or family values – should be so anxious that these ideas should be preached to schoolchildren. My experience is that any idea recommended by schoolteachers sends the pupils scurrying off in the opposite direction. Even a fairly mild amount of Conservative and imperial propaganda at school led me to an early interest in Socialism and a romantic notion of eventually escaping from England and joining the International Brigade in the Spanish Civil War. I read Auden, Orwell and Hemingway, and imagined myself bumping on a truck through the dusty orange groves or planning the defeat of Fascism with a company of poets in the cafés of Barcelona. Politics, in those days, seemed delightfully simple: the Fascists were evil; the victory of the left would herald peace, justice and the age of the Common Man, whoever he might turn out to be.

When I was at Harrow another war had started and the rights and wrongs of world politics seemed even simpler. The good,

Britain, France, Russia and America, were ranged against the evil, the Nazis and Fascists of Germany and Italy and the tyrants of Japan. From Harrow Hill, in the suburbs, we could see the fires of the Blitz lighting up London. We sat in the shelter, with our gas masks in cardboard boxes, and our housemaster switched on the wireless so we could hear Gracie Fields trilling 'Wish Me Luck As You Wave Me Goodbye' and J.B. Priestley promising better days when the war was over. Whether we would live that long was a question that only rarely crossed our minds.

At Harrow I experimented with various political beliefs. I became, for a short while, a one-boy Communist cell and received instructions from King Street. I greatly admired the anarchists in Andalusia, and found their creed particularly attractive in a school where there were strict rules about the number of jacket buttons you could undo at various stages of your career. I wrote up for anarchist literature but found, quite naturally, that it seemed to be a movement without leadership or a defined programme. I knew, however, that I would always be on the left of the political spectrum. Lord Byron's Turkish slippers and some of his manuscripts were in the school library. I spent some time by the tomb in the churchyard on which he lay to write poetry. He was the one Harrovian with whom I felt any deep sympathy, and he had made a maiden speech in the House of Lords in defence of the unemployed Nottingham stocking weavers, threatened with the death penalty for destroying the machines which were depriving them of work. A close association with the children of the British upper classes at Harrow caused me grave doubts about their ability to run the country. My political path was already determined.

Needless to say, I didn't get to Spain to fight the Fascists. I was an incompetent member of the Corps at Harrow and, at Oxford, found to be medically suspect, so I didn't even fight the Germans or the Japanese. I went from the isolated and privileged world of middle-class education into a propaganda film unit where my friends were carpenters, electricians and prop men, and when I went to meetings I was called not Mortimer, as at school, but Comrade and Brother. I don't think anyone who hasn't lived through those years can understand how different they were from the hopelessly divided and aimless Britain of today. Certainly men and women were dying abroad and in the Blitz, but there was an extraordinary feeling of unity, a common aim which was not only to win the war but to create a juster society after it was over. Now no one can talk of a juster society without being first asked how much it is going to cost and then greeted with almost universal derision.

The longing for fairer times was deep rooted, widespread and passed almost unnoticed. It grew as a result of Army Education and men and women on lonely stations having time to read. When the war in Europe ended, and the election came in 1945, everyone expected Churchill who had, after all, won the battle, to win. The Labour landslide was as great an unexpected victory as Lloyd George's triumph forty years before. It seemed that in the foreseeable future there would be no more unemployment or class divisions, and very few Conservatives. The Attlee government, which introduced a welfare state supported by all parties for many subsequent years, was the most creative and successful of this century. With the gently decreasing faith and optimism with which Graham Greene used to go to Mass, I have continued to vote Labour and have held opinions which now seem, I'm sorry to say, to have gone out of style.

Like the old actors, the politicians of those times were giants compared with their modern counterparts, now that political oratory has degenerated into meaningless sound bites. Nye Bevan could spellbind an audience, introduce the Health Service and turn up at parties of poets and art students. Ernest Bevin was the embodiment of British common sense. The old voice of the Labour Party is, perhaps, too seldom heard now; although you can hear it from Barbara Castle, Minister of Labour under Harold Wilson and rejected by Callaghan, who still brings back the sound of that

97

great government after the war, eloquent, scornful and unfashionably optimistic.

In the forties I was occupied with becoming a barrister, publishing my first novel, making a living for my first wife and various children and stepchildren, divorcing people, contesting wills and writing for anyone who offered to pay me. I contributed to women's magazines, wrote a history of costume for Moss Bros and captions for the Hall of Coal in the Festival of Britain. I had little time for political life. The Attlee government faded in the Age of Austerity, but the old-style paternalistic Conservatives did nothing to destroy the Welfare State and talked to union leaders over beer and sandwiches. I can never understand why this civilized method of government is now thought ludicrously inappropriate.

As I write, the Conservative government is entertaining the nation with a number of more or less ridiculous scandals which seem to forecast its political demise. The same thing happened in the early sixties, when the fact that a Minister of War was sharing a mistress with a Russian diplomat escalated in the most bizarre way and a leading politician offered to be medically examined to establish the fact that he wasn't the mysterious masked man who acted as a butler at orgiastic dinner parties. It also led to Harold Wilson's election as the second Labour Prime Minister since the war. His first government was one of considerable achievement; but when he was later returned to power, after Edward Heath had unwisely tried to tangle with the miners, a good deal of the sparkle seemed to go out of Labour politics. It was during that election, which he won by only a handful of votes, that I first met Mr Wilson.

Stanley Baker, an actor who played heavies, was in charge of Harold Wilson's television commercials and through him I met Marcia Williams, who, though much pilloried in *Private Eye*, had considerable charm and a sort of toothy allure. I was to help write some of Harold Wilson's speeches and, when we met, he seemed enormously cheerful, making a succession of jokes like a sardonic

North Country comedian. He had an encyclopaedic knowledge of the Labour voters in most of the wards north of Watford and, when he had discussed them with us, he asked Marcia to come with him when he was to have his 'photey' taken. I noticed that he kept his best cigars in his briefcase and always smoked a pipe in public. He said if he won the election he'd get the RAF to fly him back to London from his constituency 'in state'. I wrote a lot of things for him to say, tapping the old well of emotion, never entirely dried up, which had led me to the Labour Party during the war. I have to admit that he rewrote most of it, and since then I have only written for actors and done my best to make sure they don't change the lines.

When the election had been won and the RAF had presumably flown the Prime Minister back to Downing Street, Stanley Baker and I were rewarded by lunch at Number Ten, at which Marcia was present. Something was going on with the Russian fleet in the eastern Mediterranean and Archbishop Makarios, then the Prime Minister of Cyprus, had disappeared in a mysterious manner and his whereabouts were unknown. Before lunch Mr Wilson was saying that he supposed he ought to have sent a British destroyer but he had nothing in the area, and here he grinned at us all, but one small rowing-boat. The conversation turned to a Tory scare about Edward Short, an ex-headmaster and somewhat dull Labour minister, having a Swiss bank account. 'I don't believe Edward Short's ever been to Switzerland, except on a package tour,' Mr Wilson told us. 'I'm going to call for a full and impartial judicial inquiry. And what I mean by an impartial inquiry is that when I see my enemy with his balls hanging out and I have a hammer in my hand, I strike!' In time the matter of Edward Short's alleged Swiss bank account, like many better and more fascinating rumours, was flushed down the toilet of history.

At lunch he asked us about the state of the British film industry and said, 'And how *is* Sir Michael Balcon?' as though the great days of the Ealing comedies had never passed. When the coffee was served, the Prime Minister stood up, chuckling with delight, and made a surprise announcement. 'We all admire your skirt, Marcia,' he said, 'but now I want you all to meet a character who has a skirt which is much longer than yours.' At this point a pair of double doors was thrown open and there stood a man with a beard, a tall black hat, a floor-length cassock and a pectoral cross. 'Archbishop Makarios' – the Prime Minister was clearly delighted with this *coup de théâtre* – 'I'd like you to meet Stanley Baker and his colleague John Mortimer. You know, we've got the Archbishop into Claridges. The Foreign Office found him a pair of pyjamas; luckily he doesn't need a razor!' We left Downing Street having promised to tell none of the waiting journalists about the surprising appearance of the Archbishop, and that was about the last I had to do with high affairs of state.

10

The final departure from my father's life, the wrench I was not able to achieve when I stood and thought about it in his room in chambers, happened finally on the other side of the world. It occurred in that Reader's Digest of a city, linked by a causeway to the wilder shores of Malaysia, where they discuss making chewing-gum illegal, where Chinese families burn paper Mercedes, paper TV sets and paper video tapes to placate the spirits of the dead, and where Mr Lee Kuan Yew, who was allergic to opposition politicians, was prime minister for many years and thought that the words law and order were in the wrong position. Order has always seemed more important to Mr Lee than law.

My first trial in Singapore happened long before I took the Great Decision, however. It was the winter of discontent when a few gravediggers went on strike and the British public came to believe that, if you died under a Labour government, you had little or no chance of a decent burial and would probably be put out in a black plastic bag with the rubbish. I was going, I thought, to a tropical Old Bailey, a far-flung outpost of what was once the Empire, where they still wore wigs and gowns and said 'if your Lordship pleases', and no doubt had tiffin. I discovered that if you are fond of shopping and eating out, Singapore is the place for you. If your interests extend to politics you had better stay away. Mr Jeyaretnam could not control his political longings and refused to leave the country. As a consequence he was the subject of frequent and ferocious litigation which he endured with a courage which I found both magnificent and foolhardy.

Ben Jeyaretnam is a Tamil, a devout Christian who worships in Singapore's Anglican cathedral and took his Bible to comfort him in prison. He was married to an English solicitor and has two sons who both got Double Firsts at Cambridge. He is a grey-haired man with bright brown eyes and a look of resolute cheerfulness, even during the days of direst trouble. He has long mutton-chop whiskers which he strokes repeatedly, as other men might fiddle with executive toys or click worry-beads. He had been a government servant and sat as a judge. His political views are, as far as I could ascertain, those of a right-wing member of the Labour Party. Indeed, if he were in England, he might be a Liberal Democrat. He is opposed to Singapore's draconian laws which prescribe death for a number of offences, flogging for many more, and led not only to the long imprisonment of a woman playwright for expressing her opinions but to the surprising discovery that a tombstone could be guilty of sedition.

In 1971 Ben became the Secretary-General of the Workers Party, an organization which, in the 1968 elections, only fielded two candidates and gained no seats. Despite the government's unassailable position, and the minimal threat to its majority, the Workers Party was accused of being a subversive organization financed from Kuala Lumpur This allegation was made by a candidate for the government party, the PAP, a Mr Tay Boon Too. The Workers Party sued him for libel and lost the case; this was to have important repercussions many years later.

Ben Jeyaretnam stood in the 1976 election. His government opponent dwelt on the fact that he didn't speak Chinese and suggested he would be of no use to his constituents. Nevertheless he got 40 per cent of the votes and he was followed by enthusiastic crowds round the workers' flats who called out 'we want Jeya!' repeatedly. He became something of a hero for his opposition to the monolithic power of the government, and no doubt began to see himself as a statesman with a popular following, the Nehru or Nelson Mandela of Singapore. The government worked overtime to extinguish such hopes. During the campaign Ben had made some criticism of the Prime Minister and, after the votes had been counted and the inevitable conclusion reached, Mr Lee Kuan Yew issued a writ for libel against him. As Ben wrote later: 'Lee brought out a QC, Mr Robert Alexander, to appear for him at the trial. I therefore felt I had to get the services of a QC myself. Mr John Mortimer of *Rumpole of the Bailey* fame agreed to come out at a special fee.'

On my first visit the old Singapore hadn't been entirely obliterated or moved into high-rise shopping precincts. A little of Chinatown remained. The food stalls in parking lots and on street corners, where you could dine lavishly for a dollar on savoury Malaysian omelettes and spiced mutton soup, were still there. At Fatty's in Albert Street an almost circular Chinaman used to lay his tables in the middle of the road and serve delectable Cantonese cooking. When the traffic got busy, your table might be seized from under you and hurried inside the restaurant to prevent a collision between the sweet and sour fish and a battered pick-up truck.

Penny and I were taken to Bugis Street where, out of politeness to our hosts, who had recommended this delicacy, I sat nervously eating a grey, 'hundred-year-old', hard-boiled egg. It started to rain gently as a girl with long legs and the contemptuous expression of a *Vogue* model came towards us, stalking among the stray dogs and cats and the bubbling food stalls as though she were coming down the catwalk at Yves St Laurent. She sat with us and, when asked what she would have, growled, 'I wanna 7-Up!' in the deep voice of a stoker in the Merchant Navy. She told me that most of the models who hang out in Bugis Street had 'had the operation' in England. The 'Billy Boys' who had not been fundamentally changed were condemned by the order and law of Singapore to a side-street. The rain came down harder and we had to leave her and the hundred-year-old egg. Later I read a touching letter in the *Straits Times*: 'I am a secondary school student and,' the writer confessed, 'in the past whenever I saw a male transsexual, I would deliberately stare at him as if he was something strange. Now I realize that such people must suffer enough pain without more being inflicted by people like me. [Signed] "Sorry".'

Raffles Hotel had already become a place of nostalgic pilgrimage for package tours. A newly decorated bar had been erected on the spot where, it is said, the fearless headmaster of the Raffles institution shot a tiger under the billiard table. There is still a portrait of Noël Coward, looking unmistakably Mongolian, wearing a top hat several sizes too large which rests on his huge ears. Old men remembered the past glories of the place. 'We always tried to avoid talking to Somerset Maugham,' one of them told us. 'He was such a tremendously boring old bugger!'

It's dangerous to accept facts about Singapore at their face value, the place has always been capable of deception. The lion that gave its name to the island, when it was fought for by a Sumatran descendant of Alexander the Great, turned out to be a black-headed tiger. The tiger shot under the Raffles billiard table had escaped from a circus. The country that finds chewing-gum decadent can accommodate relaxed nightclubs and the peculiarities of Bugis Street. We stayed in a hotel where a youngish and perfectly active English QC, who had come out to do a case, had been found mysteriously drowned in the swimming-pool. We discovered that you could order haggis for dinner and, if you did so, it would be brought to your table by Malaysian waiters playing bagpipes and wearing kilts. When we ordered shark's fin soup I asked where, in Singapore, you found sharks. 'In the barristers' room at the High Court,' was the immediate reply.

*

Robert Alexander is now chairman of the National Westminster which, like all banks, is in need of his skills as an advocate. He is tall, speaks slowly, always looks faintly amused and was extremely effective in court. He had a great success doing some case about cricket for the Australian millionaire Kerry Packer. That, he said, was a 'fun' case. I'm not sure appearing for Mr Lee Kuan Yew was 'fun' for him and he may, I think, have been a little embar- rassed by the result. At that time I had not done much libel and I had to look up the law. I left the hotel early and travelled, on occasion, by tri-shaw with a man pedalling me and my load of books through the hot and steamy streets around dawn.

I'd work in the empty courtoom, under a huge revolving fan, sweating in a wig and gown, a tailed coat and a collar like a blunt execution. Just before the proceedings started my wife and my opponent arrived together. They'd been playing early morning tennis without a care in the world. I found this very hard. Ben sat behind me with his gentle English wife who kept him relatively calm throughout the proceedings. She was suffering from the cancer from which she died not long afterwards. When the Prime Minister went into the witness-box, he looked long and hard at the Jeyaretnams, then said he thought they would be good for 300,000 Singapore dollars worth of damages.

Mr Lee, a friend of Harold Wilson and a member of the Inner Temple, is extremely intelligent and got a double first at Cambridge. Mrs Lee, who is a solicitor, achieved this distinction even more quickly than her husband. He once lectured the civil service on the superiority of his educational qualifications to those of Harold Macmillan. He was a trades union lawyer who ap- peared for the bus workers in a lengthy and hotly contested dispute. In those days he could be recognized by the thermos of Chinese tea he always carried with him. He was now a prime minister, a remote figure who, so it was said, bathed twice a day, changed his shirt frequently, disliked America and cold drinks, and meticulously checked the temperature of any room he was in. Unlike most Far-

Eastern politicans, he has never been connected with any scandal.

The afternoon I spent with Mr Lee in court was a novel experience for both of us. I had never before cross-examined a prime minister in his own country, and I don't suppose he had ever been cross-examined by anyone. I won't say it was a pleasure, but it was among the most interesting hours I spent at the bar. Our case was extremely difficult. Ben had obviously spoken the words complained of and it was difficult to argue that they weren't defamatory, but we could say that it wasn't a case for heavy damages. As I started to cross-examine the Prime Minister, I remembered my father's advice and tried to get him to agree to as much as possible. Mr Lee was, was he not, a great believer in democracy? His country held regular elections. The point of an election was to allow all sorts of points of view to be expressed freely and without fear. Of course, public speakers at election time get overheated. Politicians perhaps exaggerate and use colourful language to describe their opponents. Mr Lee would understand that, wouldn't he? As a democrat, surely, he wouldn't want it otherwise? Mr Jeyaretnam's words hadn't done him the slightest harm, had they? He went on to win the election by what it would be almost an insult to call a landslide majority. Surely he wasn't out for anything so mercenary and undignified as damages? Would it not be quite unseemly for the prime minister of a democratic republic to grub for money? This, so far as I can remember, was my general line with Mr Lee. I believe he found it a little difficult to deal with and, if it didn't impress the enigmatic Chinese judge, at least it seemed to be going down well with the foreign press. When I sat down, Bob Alexander wrote me a note: 'You would spend many years, and travel to many courts, before you had such an entertaining afternoon.' I felt very proud, although confident of defeat.

'There's a man called Neil on the telephone, and he says I'm to tell you Gunga Din.'

I was in the bath, washing away the sweated labour of a day in the Singapore High Court, when Penny answered the telephone. What was this, some coded message from the Workers Party? A spy from the British High Commission warning me not to endanger our diplomatic relations with Lee Kuan Yew. Then I remembered Gunga Din, a north Oxford villa into which my prep school dormitories overflowed. You had to walk across to it in the dark from School House after supper. Desmond Neil had inhabited Gunga Din and when I acted Richard II in the school play, the only unqualified success I've enjoyed, Desmond had been the Duke of York: 'See, see, King Richard doth himself appear, As doth the blushing, discontented sun' was what he had to say. Many years had passed since this production, but clearly the experience was fresh in our minds. Desmond Neil was now someone very important in a huge beer and soft drinks company with tentacles all over the Far East. He invited us to dinner, so we got dressed and went down to the hotel bar to await his arrival.

'Been on a salvage job. Haven't got pissed or had a white woman for three months.' The man seated unsteadily on the barstool beside us had, as I remember, ginger hair and flaming cheeks. He also had a look which was not only lean and hungry, but positively desperate. 'Can you imagine?' he asked me with considerable hostility. 'What it's like not to have had a fucking white woman for three months?'

'You've been at sea?' I tried to sound understanding.

'Fucking sea captain. Salvage. That's my business. You might as well be in sodding gaol.'

To my immense relief, I saw an elegant figure in a white suit bearing down on us. This, I profoundly hoped, was Desmond Neil, forty years on. 'I'm sorry,' I said to the sea captain. 'We're being taken out for dinner. Best of luck.'

'Ah, John. How good to see you! And you must be Penny. I've booked a table,' Desmond Neil greeted us. 'Not a fucking white woman!' the sea captain was muttering, when Desmond interrupted him. 'We'd better get going. Plenty to drink when we get there. Oh, and do bring your friend.'

'That's very good of you, sir. Thank you very much.' The sea captain was delighted to accept the invitation. So we all sank into the back of a long white Mercedes, driven by a uniformed chauffeur to whom Desmond spoke in Mandarin. Then he showed us a photograph of himself and E.P. Thompson, the author of *The Making of the British Working Class*, as small boys on a football field. This was rapidly followed by pictures of them both in the present. 'Don't you think,' Desmond said, showing these to the sea captain, 'I've worn a great deal better than Palmer Thompson?'

'Poor bugger!' The sea captain looked at the great historian and CND protester with sympathy. 'Probably hasn't had a white woman for years.'

Dinner passed like a strange dream. The Chinese restaurant on top of a tower rotated slowly, giving us ever-changing views of the harbour. The centre part of the table also revolved, offering us a feast of dishes, a great deal of sake and many bottles of Chinese beer. Throughout this banquet, Desmond would ask questions like 'What happened to the Mitchison boys?' 'What a tragedy about Bill Mann! Did you keep up with him?' 'Or was it Winchester that Peter Tranchell went to?' With perfect courtesy he always included the sea captain in these inquiries but his unexpected, ever more intoxicated guest could only mutter, 'Any chance of a white woman around here, or are they all Chinks?' In the end he helped himself to a dish full of a sauce called Dragon's Blood, went a deep shade of purple which clashed with his ginger hair, hit himself in the chest and cried out, 'Fucking hot food they give a bloke round here!', while Desmond was asking if Mr Rety, known to us as Rats, was still teaching dancing at the Dragon School. On our way back to the hotel the white Mercedes took us on a tour of the city, during which the sea captain fell into a deep and deafening sleep. 'Interesting fellow,' Desmond Neil whispered, 'have you known him long?'

'Only about two hours,' I had to admit, 'but it seems longer.' When we stopped at the hotel, the sea captain woke with a start and staggered off into the night. I hope he found some sort of comfort. Desmond Neil never asked about him again and was always a kind host in Singapore.

When I got to court next morning I discovered that Ben Jeyaretnam had sent a letter to a newspaper suggesting £5,000 damages for something written in a report of the trial. My line that damages for libel were not a thing that any sensible politician should stoop to claim was therefore somewhat weakened. My cross-examination of Mr Lee was not as effective as it had been the day before.

During my first Singapore trial one of the lawyers helping us was Mrs Murugason who wore a wig and gown and a diamond in her nose. Every morning, when asked, 'How are you, Mrs Muru?', she would smile at me and say, 'Very bright and perky, thank you, sir.' We had some time off towards the end of the case and I told her I was thinking of going to Bangkok to write my speech. 'Good idea, sir. And Mrs Mortimer?' 'She's coming with me, of course.' 'Oh no!' Mrs Muru shook her head. 'Coals to Newcastle, dear sir. Coals to Newcastle!' Despite this warning, Penny and I went off together, were duly solicited together and declined the invitations. I wrote the best speech I could in the Somerset Maugham wing of the hotel and on a boat going down the river. I handed a copy in to the enigmatic judge who, no doubt, read it carefully before he found in favour of the Prime Minister and awarded him 130,000 Singapore dollars, or about £35,000, by way of costs and damages. Ben Jeyaretnam sold his house, made certain economies and managed to pursue his perilous political career. Of my performance, he wrote: 'Mr John Mortimer's oratory at the trial won the admiration of many Singaporeans, but did not win my case.'

At that time, he had only put his toe into the sea which would engulf him and bring me back to Singapore where I would finally fall out of love with my legal career.

II

Publishing books and expressing any sort of opinion lead to many letters from strangers. Often they enclose bulky manuscripts or ask for advice on how to get into television. Because of my legal past they question me on points of law and wish me to right complicated wrongs. They send piles of documents, photographs of cracked kitchen walls or unsatisfactory partners, press cuttings of unjust court proceedings. Sometimes literature and the law are mixed in these requests. One woman wrote: 'We thought you'd like to know that our sister has just murdered our mother. Do you think this could be written up into a good play for television?' Sometimes they are saddened by what I have said and send me books on how to acquire religious faith. Often they are kind, sometimes not. A correspondent who disagreed with something I had said about free speech ended his letter: 'And I hope you die slowly of a painful cancer. Yours sincerely, A well-wisher.' About once in every two or three months I get a letter from a woman I have never met. She tells me a lot about people unknown to me. 'How Nell and Dave looked daggers when they saw us laughing together in the corner at Heather's place!', or, 'Julie couldn't get over how tired and out of sorts you looked and suggested Pam had been giving you a hard time over that business of the car.' These letters are unsigned, very neatly written and I have never answered them, as she sends no address. When they come, I look at the envelopes with dread, wondering where I've been or what sort of impression I created among so many unknown acquaintances.

So it seems I have a fictional life which I only learn about in occasional letters. Much of my time has been spent on fiction, and some of it trying to analyse and explain the deceptive nature of art and literature to not entirely sympathetic judges and Courts of Appeal when books went on trial. Courts often found it hard to separate the views of authors from their invented characters. For instance, when he wrote:

> Come, you spirits
> That tend on mortal thoughts, unsex me here,
> And fill me from the crown to the toe top-full
> Of direst cruelty. Make thick my blood;
> Stop up th'access and passage to remorse,
> That no compunctious visitings of nature
> Shake my fell purpose.

the author was expressing Lady Macbeth's thoughts and not his own. Indeed, there's no reason to deduce, from anything in the play, that Shakespeare approved of the murder of house-guests, any more than in *Richard III* he licenses political assassination. Yet, in the *Lady Chatterley's Lover* trial, for instance, it was assumed that every time the gamekeeper opened his mouth it was D.H. Lawrence speaking. It was always very difficult to get courts to separate authors from their characters, even if, as was clearly not the case with Mellors, they were characters the author disliked.

It was also hard to explain the state of mind of the audience. The courts seemed to assume that if the readers or viewers were submitted to some description of villainy, sexual indulgence or violent cruelty they would immediately rush out and try it for themselves. Yet millions of unadventurous men on commuter trains read the James Bond stories without feeling licensed to kill or sleep with sultry mistresses on Caribbean islands; even more millions of law-abiding citizens read Agatha Christie without the slightest temptation to stab the heiress in the library.

'Art is not life,' Auden wrote, 'and cannot be / A midwife

to society.' The blurred connections between art and life, their effect on each other, and the distinction between truthful art and mere pretence, were the subjects of discussion in a number of legal cases. The argument became even more complicated when the works themselves were calculated to deceive. The tricks in art that come off appear magical, the failures vulgar frauds. No one in their senses confuses art with reality or thinks they enter a gallery to look at actual sunflowers or live, naked women picnicking on the grass; what they are seeing is an idea of the world presented by a conjuror. But when artists borrow other people's ideas, or pinch their brand of trickery, they get branded as forgers and are occasionally prosecuted. The concept of forgery would be impossible had not money, in considerable sums, become inappropriately mixed up with the world of art.

There's no doubt that the art world welcomes forgeries. The wisest practitioners don't simply produce a drawing and call it a Rembrandt; they take a suitable drawing they have done to an art expert and ask for his informed opinion. Everyone likes to be present at an important discovery and the expert will no doubt say, 'Blow me down! I think this is a Rembrandt!' or words to like effect. The drawing then goes off and takes on a life of its own and art houses and museums will often protest that it's genuine however often, or however convincingly, the forger confesses. And yet how harmful is this delusion? The flattered lover may be genuinely delighted by his mistress's faked orgasm and the actor by insincere praise of his performance. The art lover may be deeply moved by a drawing, beautifully executed, in authentic ink on period paper, by a talented art student in Camden Town, which he has every reason to believe is by Rubens.

This line of thought is not easy to follow, and pursuing it is like walking down an endless passageway lined with mirrors which reflect and often distort each other's images. The argument is a difficult one to conduct before an Old Bailey judge who learns, to his apparent distress, that Marcel Duchamp, by the simple act of signing a urinal R. Mutt, sold it for more money than the judge was likely to earn from a year of toil at murder, robbery and grievous bodily harm.

It all started when the National Portrait Gallery mounted an exhibition of work by a hitherto unknown nineteenth-century photographer named Francis Hetling. The pictures, which were mainly of Victorian beggar children and street waifs, were described as ravishing; the exhibition was an undoubted success and a set of ten prints was later sold to an art dealer who seemed well pleased with his purchase. Unhappily, the National Portait Gallery was visited by a mother who recognized a pool-eyed child, who stood dirty, barefoot and shivering, clutching a shawl around her in the doorway of some Victorian slum dwelling, as the daughter she had driven that morning to school in Battersea.

Francis Hetling, although posthumously recognized by the National Portrait Gallery, turned out never to have been born. The 'ravishing' pictures were the work of Howard Grey, a photographer of Clapham, and Graham Ovenden, a painter of the ruralist movement, a sect devoted to living in the countryside and listening to the works of Sir Edward Elgar. Graham Ovenden was far the more interesting of the two. He was a brilliant artist whose genius was rated by none more highly than himself. One of the questioned photographs turned out not to be a photograph at all but a super-realistic drawing by Ovenden himself, thus adding bewilderingly to the layers of deception. When the judge looked predictably incredulous on being told this, Ovenden dashed off another convincing photographic drawing to add to his bewilderment.

It was Grey who had taken the photograph of the Victorian slum child. In fact she had been wearing an old T-shirt, was asked to rub dirt on her face and body, posed against a chimney-stack on the roof of his studio and was paid £35 for the session. Ovenden said that he had found Grey in a depressed mood, down on his luck, and wanted to encourage him and prove that his work was as good as that of any of the great Victorians. He put the photographs through various processes, in some cases drawing them and then photographing the drawings. He attributed the Hetlings as coming from the collection of Graham Ovenden and eventually agreed to give the art dealer some of the prints, but didn't take money for them directly. Instead he asked the dealer to buy some of his own works for the same value. Our defence, readily agreed to by Mr Ovenden, was that he was such a consummate artist that the photographs were far more valuable if he had had a hand in them than if they had been the work of Francis Hetling, an obscure Victorian, who had no real existence anyway. So, to debate questions which have puzzled art historians, confused connoisseurs and bedevilled critics down the centuries, we went down to discuss it all in front of an Old Bailey jury. 'Works of art,' I remember suggesting, 'can't be approached in the same way as frozen carrots,' and yet how should they be valued? Peter Blake, a friend of Ovenden's and, at that time, a fellow ruralist, sat in the public gallery throughout the trial. It further puzzled the judge to discover that Mr Blake only had to sign a postcard, say a sepia-tinted view of the promenade at Torquay, to increase its value astronomically.

Graham Ovenden, small, bearded, blessed with every talent except modesty, explained a letter of apparent apology he had written to the art dealer by saying, 'Great men humble themselves,' and fended off other attacks by agreeing with a smile that, 'Great men sometimes do things like that.' He did nothing to simplify life and art for the benefit of the court. Charles Lawson was a thoroughly decent judge with a ramrod straight back, a complexion the colour of vintage claret, a ready smile and a considerable amount of common sense. Given a charge of gross indecency in the Superloo at Euston Station he was in complete charge of the proceedings, saying, on one occasion, that my client, who was called Titus Brown, had 'the best name for a bugger I've ever heard'. On questions of aesthetics he was far less happy. When the prosecuting counsel suggested to Ovenden that a Van Gogh would be a good picture whoever had painted it, my client said, correctly, that there he was on dangerous ground and went off into a long catalogue of the pictures that are 'of the school of' or 'in the manner of' or simply 'after' great artists. The judge was clearly lost and the shorthand writer became too confused to continue her note of the evidence. The prosecutor then held up a photograph by Lewis Carroll, another specialist in portraits of young girls. Ovenden agreed that it was a valuable work of art. But when it was suggested that the Hetlings had no value, Ovenden was able to tell him that he was quite wrong. It seemed that once the Hetlings were known to be Ovendens they were worth more than the art dealer had paid for them.

The judge summed up the trial as 'one of the most interesting and unusual in the whole of my judicial experience and in my career at the bar'. At the start of the proceedings he had offered the jury a fascinating and entertaining case, but by the end of it they must have been in a state of utter confusion. I don't know exactly how they reached their verdict but they acquitted both defendants of conspiracy to defraud. They couldn't agree if Ovenden had obtained money by deception and the prosecution accepted the judge's hint and offered no further evidence. Ovenden had successfully pulled the leg of the National Portrait Gallery, fooled the art experts who failed to recognize some of the Victorian photographs as contemporary drawings, and led an unsuspecting judge and jury far away from the simple facts of fraud and theft into the swamps of aesthetics. I remember one moment with particular joy. I presented an art expert with what was said to be a Victorian photograph, by Julia Margaret Cameron, of a nineteenth-century staging of King Arthur at dinner with his Knights of the Round Table. When I asked him to look very carefully at the little knight seated on Sir Lancelot's right, he had to admit, blushing modestly, that it was himself in fancy-dress. In the world of art nothing is entirely credible and the camera lies with considerable ingenuity.

Recently I wrote, and Jacquie and our company produced, a series of television plays about life in an art auction house. For the production we took over a huge, and no longer used, old people's home somewhere south of London airport, which smelled strongly of urine and was full of rusting Zimmer frames and cranking-up bathroom equipment. We redecorated it, hung it with dark red wallpaper and a man, delicately applying paint with feathers, made the convincing marble archways. On the walls hung paintings of dubious authenticity found in stores of prop-suppliers or hired from owners who made extravagant and unconvincing claims for them. The old people's home was disguised as a smart auction house named Klinsky's and fake catalogues advertised the sale of a so-called Raphael that was put together in the art department. Each story dealt with a work of art which might or might not be genuine. To tell these stories, we ordered up an allegory Bronzino never painted and had an alternative salt cellar, which might pass for the work of Benvenuto Cellini, created for us in the Silver Vaults. The end result was, I hope, an expensive but moderately successful con-trick about the everlastingly deceptive world of art.

Something strange happened that proves not only the potency of the most spurious art but the reckless intoxication induced by auctions. At the end of shooting we gave a party for the unit in the Klinsky's set and decided to hold a sale of the props for charity. Admittedly a number of Harvey Wallbangers and Tequila Slammers had been consumed, but the bidding for what everyone knew perfectly well were complete fakes rose to dizzy heights. I can faintly remember paying a good deal of money for a pretended drawing by Juan Gris that I knew the young man who wore his gold-embroidered cap back to front had run up in the art department.

Then the work was finished. We left the old people's home and the local authority, who owned it, wanted us to restore it to the state in which we had found it. So we stripped off the damask paper, obliterated the marble and an elderly carpenter was strongly tempted to pee up against the walls.

12

My mother was always careful to mark the difference between her standards of what was acceptable and my less steadfast opinions. In the year the war ended, in the year of the great Labour landslide, Brideshead Revisited was published and I read it with admiration and misty-eyed nostalgia for an Oxford which, like the Drones Club, never existed on land or sea. I was twenty-three, pulling out Labour voters in my father's ancient Morris Oxford, but so intoxicated by Brideshead that I even suggested to my mother that there might be something romantic about the aristocracy, some magical charm surrounding the monarchy. 'You don't mean,' my mother was laughing as she was to do when I told her I'd been made a part-time judge, 'those people in Buckingham Palace? Really, do try not to be silly!' So she put on her veil and, carrying a device which pumped smoke into the hive to make the bees drowsy, went off to take the honey. Despite the veil, the gloves and the smoke, she was frequently stung, a fate about which she never complained at all.

More than thirty years later I was rung up by Derek Grainger at Granada Television and asked if I'd like to adapt Brideshead. Of course I would. Evelyn Waugh is one of the half-dozen writers to whom I owe most. His early books, Decline and Fall and Vile Bodies, seem perfect and A Handful of Dust a bitter masterpiece. Brideshead is perhaps too lush, too in awe of baroque architecture and the upper classes, to achieve the comic purity of his greatest work. But the fierceness of the religion gives the book its hard centre. I sat down to the job with great pleasure. Although Waugh was a true blue Tory and I'm a champagne Socialist, although he was a devout Catholic and I'm an atheist for Christ, I thought I could preserve the true spirit of his writing.

Only two things caused me embarrassment. One is the scene in which the narrator has dinner with the awful Rex Mottram in Paris. Waugh relishes Rex's failure to understand the correct way of eating caviare, or the proper manner of drinking brandy (*not* out of a great balloon-shaped glass, for God's sake!). This type of snobbery seems to me truly vulgar. The other difficult time for me came when Charles Ryder heroically helps to break the General Strike. Deeply shocked, I tried to keep him as far from the General Strike as possible. I enjoyed writing the religious scenes very much; anyone who is prepared to sacrifice their happiness for a belief deserves sympathy and respect, and the end of the book is genuinely moving.

A great danger in adapting books for film or television is that you lose the voice of the most important character, the author. Take Dickens out of *Bleak House* and you're left with little but dramatic scenes and eccentric characters. Remove P.G. Wodehouse from the Jeeves stories and you have only some rather thin farcical situations. *Brideshead* is narrated by Charles Ryder. Quite early on we decided to keep his narration and the director Charles Sturridge added a great deal more of it from the book. In that way Evelyn Waugh remained where he should have been, in the centre of the story. This and the length of a television series, which can be far more literary than a film, gave, I think, the audience the feeling of having lived through a book. Almost everything in the scripts came from *Brideshead* and I was careful to keep the dreadful passage in which Charles Ryder says he 'made free of her [Lady Julia's] narrow loins' to show that Waugh could write as badly as any of us if he set his mind to it.

'We were at the head of a valley and below us, half a mile distant, grey and gold amid a screen of boskage, shone the dome and columns of an old house.' Castle Howard was chosen to act as Brideshead and George Howard, its bulky owner, appeared, frequently wearing a voluminous kaftan and saying, 'Let's get down to make-up. That's where the fun begins!' The huge production, thirteen hours of viewing, delayed by strikes and a change of director, would be impossible today, when the so-called reforms of commercial television which took place in the Thatcher years have wrecked the system. The success of *Brideshead* was interesting. The book came out at the end of the war and it was hugely popular. In the grey dawn of the eighties, a materialistic, selfish and soulless decade, when we were governed by the Rex Mottrams of the world, it was again a great success. Everyone believed that, at some distant time, there must have been Arcadia. In an interview for the *Paris Review* Waugh said of the book that it was 'very much a child of its time. Had it not been written when it was, at a very bad time when there was nothing to eat, it would have been a different book. The fact that it is rich in evocative description, in glutinous writing, is a direct result of the privations and austerity of the times.'

He also wrote, in one of his letters, that he didn't think that more than seven Americans would ever enjoy this book. Since it was made, the series has been revived frequently in America, where devotees gather for *Brideshead* parties and stay up all night to watch the whole series. No doubt to the acute discomfort of Waugh, in whatever sort of Catholic heaven he now occupies, Lord Sebastian look-alike contests have been organized in San Francisco and fair-haired young men are to be seen carrying their teddy bears down to the Marina.

At its best, adaptation is carpentry. The torment and the excitement, the agony and the delight, come from catching an idea, as Henry James said, 'by the tail' and, god-like, creating characters and sending them on their destined way, allowing them the luxury of a little free will.

Brideshead came on television near the time of the Laurence Olivier version of *A Voyage Round My Father*. In both he gave magnificent performances and in both he performed death-bed scenes I had written for him. When he played my father, he had a great deal of difficulty in remembering his lines. We would get to eight takes and end up in despair; but when this apparently stumbling performance was edited, acting of great truthfulness and power emerged. Later I adapted a story by John Fowles called *The Ebony Tower* in which Laurence played a rascally old painter who lives with two beautiful and sometimes naked girls in an enchanted French forest. By then his grasp of the lines had failed entirely, so my words were written on large sheets of paper and hung from the trees like Orlando's second-rate love poetry in the Forest of Arden. In one scene the director asked Sir Laurence when he would start speaking. 'I shall first speak,' he replied with great dignity, 'when I approach the dialogue.'

I have always hated things coming out. Getting ideas, waiting for the arrival of plots, is breathtakingly difficult; writing is, by and large, a daily pleasure, provided you can convince yourself no one else is ever going to read it. Interfering with the preparation of a play or a television series is entertaining and it calls for great political skills to get your own way about the casting. You can enjoy the importance attached by actors to a writer until the rehearsals are over, the umbilical cord is cut and they and the play go off to live a life of their own. However, the process of watching people filming is about as exciting as watching your fingernails grow. Among a film unit on location a writer has no real function, feels like a spare prick at a wedding and is always standing on a cable or, worse still, in the shot; although boring and quite unnecessary, the process is neither painful nor alarming. The bad times come when the work pushes its nose out of doors, the audience is let in, the book is in the shops, the final speech has been delivered and there's absolutely nothing you can do except wait for the jury to come back with a verdict. At that time – the period of *Brideshead*, the film of *A Voyage Round My Father* and the publication of *Clinging to the Wreckage*, an account of the first part of my life – the sentences were unexpectedly light.

After these nerve-racking occasions we went off for the first time to a new found land, the place of Leo McKern's birth, where air hostesses are known as trolley dollies and in Parliament the Prime Minister debates with the Opposition by flapping his lower lip with his finger and producing a derisory, bubbling sound. We went as a couple of Pommies prepared to whinge, who stayed to enjoy themselves ('What goes on whining after the BA plane's engines have stopped?' goes an Australian proverb. 'The Poms inside complaining about Australia'). We expected to find men with corks round their hats bolting down tinnies and yawning in technicolor over sturdy Sheilas. In fact Australia is distinguished by magnificent wines, excellent restaurants, and writers and artists who don't only bitch each other, but whose wives rush into print to bitch the wives of other writers for being a little standoffish and unhelpful on the holiday in Bali.

The inhabitants of this beautiful, wild and underpopulated country are ruthlessly eccentric and determined to be nothing but themselves. In an Italian restaurant called Senso Unico in the Sydney Surrey Hills, we sat having lunch with an unlikely character called Fabian Lo Schiavo. He is the Mother Inferior of the Sisters of Perpetual Indulgence and his friends, a gentle band with such names as Sister Mary Quite Contrary, Sister Matic and Sister Daisy Chain, who work as teachers, tenors or truck drivers, join him in such ceremonies as exorcizing the spirits of warships equipped with nuclear weapons from the harbour. When the Pope came to Sydney they stood on a street corner cheering and he smiled from the Popemobile until he noticed that many nuns in that particular group were wearing beards. Fabian said his father was an Italian Catholic dentist. 'He thinks the Madonna's great but hasn't much time for God. As for me,' the Mother Inferior told us, 'I converted to Anglicanism and, after a stint as a barman in King's Cross, I got a job in the public archives.' His mother once said that she would have liked him to be a priest. 'Mother' – Fabian comforted her with admirable Australian common sense – 'millions of mothers have sons who're priests. You're one of the few mothers in the world whose son's a nun.'

So we swam at Bondi, ate fish and Brought Our Own wine to Doyles on the Beach and flew up the Hawkesbury River in a tiny sea-plane which dipped and swerved as an ancient and superannuated pilot twisted round in his seat to talk to us. He got his seat-belt hooked on a door handle which was coloured red and marked Emergency Exit. I sat, white-knuckled in the back, and he said, 'Want to know something, John? It's a good thing you decided to set up as a writer and not a fighter-pilot. The trouble with this country,' he went on, as we flew further along the broad green river and high up above the shade under the gum trees, 'is that we've never had much sadness.' We went to Brisbane and I talked at a dinner of Labour lawyers. It was a highly dangerous evening when the 'chuck' was somehow delayed in the kitchen for two hours, by which time the Labour lawyers were in no fit state to deal with Chicken à la King or to listen to speeches, so the proceedings broke up in magnificent disarray. We travelled up to the deep north where the flowers get brighter and the foliage more lush and the politicians more like folksy southern American Democrats, or at least they were in those distant days of Joh Bjelke-Petersen. At last we got into a boat and went to Bedarra, a small island over the Great Barrier Reef, with a map which might have come out of *Treasure Island* and names like Lookout Post and Hidden Valley and Hernandia Beach.

The rain forest, filled with hibiscus and gum trees, swamp mahogany, bottle-brush orchids and, appropriately enough, the impenetrable lawyer vine (*calamus australis*), grew down to the sand and coral beaches. Sea-hawks soared over the trees, turtles dived deep into the water and jungle turkeys built huge nests in which the rotting vegetation slowly hatched out their buried eggs. There were about a dozen other guests housed in bungalows round the main hotel building and all the men seemed to be called Arthur. We never saw the Barrier Reef; it rained every day and the only sunshine was on the television news. There was a heatwave in London and the pictures were of sunbaked tourists leaping into the Trafalgar Square fountains. The wind came from the south, straight from the Arctic Circle, and the waitress, with bare arms and a cotton dress to preserve the illusion that we were in the tropics, went blue and shivered. I began to think of a new story and worked each day. In the evenings you could empty the drinks cupboard for no extra charge. We went through the Jacob's Creek claret, the Coonawarra Hermitage and the Hunters Valley red. We played Scrabble and one of the Arthurs usually sang the 'Marseillaise'.

Just after the First World War the island of Bedarra was sold for £20. In the thirties a modern castaway bought one end of it for £45 and set up with nothing but a natural spring and such things as might have been washed ashore from a shipwreck. He made a hut with driftwood, he caught fish, lived on a rare selection of tropical fruits and vegetables and built his own loo and shower. But he found his ambition to paint vanish in the demanding business of housekeeping on a desert island. One of the Arthurs, a horse-racing man from Sydney, invited us to his bungalow where he served us platefuls of lobster and Russian caviare and bottles of French champagne. 'Always bring this stuff with me,' said this Arthur, who had cruised round Honolulu, gone to Jermyn Street to have his shirts made and visited Moscow for the May Day parade, 'in fact I never travel without it.' He had also invited the castaway, now a lean, bearded man in his seventies, dressed in immaculate white. 'You can't get hold of a desert island now,' said Noël the castaway. 'I've had some girls there to share my life, but they were artists and writers and no good with the plumbing.' 'I never got married,' Arthur said, passing round the caviare. 'But I've had one or two photo-finishes.'

Noël told us of the Aboriginals who used to live on the next island. They performed ritual killings of those guilty of breaking family taboos and then ate a little of the victim's kidney fat to prove that the execution was legal. Exactly how eating kidney fat proved such a thing, he didn't explain.

The castaway didn't seem to live an entirely hermit-like existence, having visited Paris and once spent three years in Hollywood. 'When I got back,' he said, 'things were terrible. Morning Glory had smothered the kitchen and a huge poinsettia had grown up in the middle of the sitting-room. If the fridge hadn't still been working, I don't really think I'd've stayed.'

One afternoon the rain stopped and the cook lent us a hammer and gave us careful instructions about gathering rock oysters. We stood in the sea, under a grey and misty sky, vast as only an Australian sky can be. Penny became extremely deft at knocking oysters off the rocks. I washed them in the waves and disposed of them with a gulp of Castlemaine XXXX from a tinnie. We were far from home, on the other side of the world from the Law Courts and the television studios and all forms of anxiety. We were in a make-believe place which pretended to be a desert island with a pretence hermit. But the sea was real, Penny tapping at the rocks was real and the oysters tasted of all kinds of things like love and childhood holidays on windy beaches, and secrets which have never been published to the world. The happiness was real also. I had found a new land, and wouldn't find another until years later, when I went to South Africa in search of traces of my mother and father.

13

I'm settling into the back of a London taxi when the driver calls over his shoulder, 'You still doing those cases down the Old Bailey, are you?'

'I'm afraid not.' Was he a potential customer? 'I haven't done one of them for about ten years.'

'I did wonder. I was on the jury in that case you were doing when the bomb went off.'

I remember it well. A young man had filled his car with petrol and driven off without paying. A policeman who tried to stop him got lodged on the bonnet. The officer was unhurt but the young man was charged with attempted murder. The judge was quite unusually pompous. Just as he finished summing-up I saw a note being passed to him by the usher. He unfolded it slowly and spoke with great deliberation, 'Members of the jury, I have just received a note which tells me' — and then the words came tumbling out in a panic — 'there's a bomb outside the court!' Whereat, his Lordship shot out of the door like a greyhound from a trap. The bomb duly went off, breaking a good deal of glass. No one was injured except my client's unhappy mother, whose leg was cut, and a very stout, eccentric barrister named James Crespi, who was taken to hospital saying, 'I have a great deal of affection for the Old Bailey, so when the bomb was about to go off I interposed my body between it and the building.'

Later we stood in the street and the judge consulted his books to see if you could take a jury's verdict in Ludgate Circus. The books said no, so we *eventually returned to court. The judge repeated his summing-up and the young petrol-stealer was acquitted.*

'You were a very kind-hearted jury,' I tell the taxi driver, 'you let my client off.'

'Oh, that's all right,' he assures me. 'You see, you always said good morning to us when you came into court and the prosecuting gentleman, he never said good morning to us.'

Strangely enough this incident doesn't cause me to lose faith in the jury system or the virtues of politeness.

Both my father and I were guilty of infidelity to the law; my mistress was writing, his was the garden. He would break off conferences to get an early train, change his clothes and do a tour of the plants he couldn't see but could only smell before the light faded and my mother would no longer be able to describe the budding of the camellias or the blowsy attraction of the dahlias. The house and garden acted like a drug on him; the place was a Circe's island from which he found it harder and harder to escape. In time I also found myself less and less willing to leave it, to cover my head with itchy horsehair and put on a stiff, winged collar, to bow to someone for whom I felt no particular respect and say 'if your Lordship pleases', and to fight, over and over again, the same battles to save some client from being treated according to his just deserts. But then, as Hamlet said, 'Use every man after his desert, and who should scape whipping?'

Not, of course, that every fight was the same. The reasons for getting into trouble are the subject of infinite variation, from mere bad luck to the existence of evil. The Old Bailey was a mixture of the theatre of comedy, of tragedy, of the absurd and the macabre, and most often a drama in which these styles were alarmingly intermingled; as they were in the case of the murderous butler, a killer who, I was told, hoped to make the *Guinness Book of Records* on account of the number of persons he had done to death. In my childhood I remember my parents engaged a manservant, a tall fellow with crinkly hair who wore a grubby white mess-jacket which revealed the ends of his braces, called Tredgold. He used to ask me to go out on the common and bowl cricket balls at him, an invitation which filled me with fear. The butler in my Old Bailey case was pale, courteous and dignified. He had read a little law and discovered that in Scotland they had something which appealed to him greatly, a verdict of not proven. So he would drive his victims to Scotland, bury them on some barren heath and, if they were discovered, he hoped to take advantage of this ambiguous Scottish finding. He had been the butler of a very elderly ex-Labour MP who was no longer perfectly in his right mind. Having killed his employer's wife, the butler offered to drive the old man, who was quite unaware of the tragedy which had occurred, to the Odeon cinema in Leicester Square to see 'a nice travel film'. His victim saw no film but instead was driven to Scotland and there, beside a Highland stream, he was murdered.

Working for a county lady, the butler was recognized by her footman as someone he'd met during a spell in prison; for this the footman was killed and buried in the rose garden. Later, the lady in question wrote to the court to assure the judge that the butler was an absolute paragon who never failed to take the Labrador out each night for a run in the rose garden. I didn't act for this tail-coated assassin but for another footman who had been his accomplice. My client, I remember, complained that the butler was treated as a star in prison, enjoying the sort of deference which screws and fellow inmates accorded to such famous figures as the Kray twins, whereas he was treated with contempt and often had scalding cocoa poured over his head. At the end of the trial the judge sentenced the butler to life imprisonment from which 'you will never be released unless you are in the terminal stages of a fatal illness'. At this the perfect servant smiled faintly, bowed and left the dock as though he had been told that he might serve dinner now.

The most terrible crimes often take place in mundane surroundings and the evidence is commonplace. The story of one of the first murders I was concerned with started with a cleaning lady, employed by a very upper-class agency, let us say Dusters Ltd of Kensington. She was sent off to clean the Belgravia apartment of a family she had never met and was given the keys to let herself in. Accordingly she went to this select address, walked into the kitchen, took off her coat and hat and hung them neatly in a cupboard. She put on her overall, found the Hoover and emerged in a long passage, at the end of which she saw a young man, who was to be my client, in the act of murdering his mother with a weapon which was referred to during the trial as a 'salad knife'. Without a moment's hesitation, the cleaning lady returned to the kitchen, closed the door firmly, put away the Hoover, took off her overall, put on her hat and coat and returned to the offices of Dusters Ltd. When asked why she had come back so soon, she shook her head and said, 'No, that's not really the type of family I'd care to work for.' She told no one about the killing, which was not, in fact, discovered until a considerable time later. When the son was arrested, however, the statement he made to the police came out as a kind of lurid poetry, for he said, 'I have either buggered a prostitute or killed a peacock in paradise.' This may have been a lightning flash of lunacy or a well-contrived invention to get him to where he was destined to go, to Broadmoor.

Sometimes the plots of the dramas in which we took part might have been written, on a day when his fancy was running riot, by Joe Orton. Two young male prostitutes were standing under neighbouring lampposts in Bayswater and they struck up an acquaintance. Their names were Bob and Anthony. Bob was inclined to rob anyone who went home with him and Anthony was in the process of changing his sex. These two fell head over heels in love. Bob took his new friend, by now known as Antoinette, to live with his parents. Bob's father was a prison warder, a job which provided him with a house, and Bob's mother, overjoyed that her son had found a nice girlfriend at last, hoped for an early marriage. For a while all went well, but then Antoinette began to stray and took to visiting the Flying Saucer club in Leicester Square. One night Bob, overcome with jealousy, followed her to this resort where he found Antoinette removing her trousers whilst dancing with a young man. Enraged, Bob began to beat his friend about the head with a pink plastic piggy bank in which the club collected money for an annual children's outing. As a result of this attack Antoinette was fatally injured and the police were sent for. During the course of his questioning, Bob said to the Inspector in charge of the case, 'Have you got any idea what it's like to fall in love with a bloke who changes his sex, and you take him to live with your mum and dad, and then find him undressing on the dance floor of the Flying Saucer and making you so mad you hit him with a piggy bank?' To which the Inspector politely replied, 'No, sir. I can't say as I have ever had such an experience.' At the trial the judge said he was going to treat the case as a perfectly ordinary, run-of-the-mill matrimonial dispute. Bob was found guilty of manslaughter by reason of provocation and leniently treated – the reactions of judges at the Old Bailey were a source of continual surprise.

There was also a trial in which I got a startling insight into the home life of one particular his Lordship. I had a run of cases which arose from quarrels between married couples in bathrooms. Indeed, the shared bath is fraught with dangers for parties with cooling marriages; the situation in which they find themselves often gives rise to comments of a wounding and personal nature. One such dispute had led to an attempted drowning for which the husband was arrested and I was hard put to it to formulate a defence. Before the trial the judge asked us to his room for coffee and biscuits and a discussion of its probable length. He looked at me as though I was personally in the habit of drowning women in baths and said that it was a most terrible and serious case. 'Indeed it is, my Lord,' I told him. 'My client was seated at the tap end of the bath. He foolishly lost his temper when his wife adversely compared his physical prowess to that of her lover.'

'*What* did you say?' The judge looked at me aghast.

'I said she had made a comment of a personal nature which led to a violent quarrel,' I repeated, and added, 'I'm afraid the fight started when he was sitting at the tap end of the bath and –'

'The tap end!' By now the judge was seriously perturbed. 'Does the prosecution accept this evidence?'

'Yes, my Lord.' Counsel for the Crown admitted it cheerfully, not being altogether sure of what was going on.

'How long had he been in the habit of sitting at the tap end of the bath?' the judge asked in some distress.

'Throughout the marriage. His wife required him to sit in that position so he could rinse her hair after she'd shampooed it.'

'And how long had they been married?'

'About twenty years,' I had to tell him.

'For twenty years this woman required her husband to sit at the tap end!' the judge repeated and bit quite savagely into a digestive biscuit. And so it went on, and we were bound over to keep the peace, or pleaded guilty to common assault, before a judge whose wife had always sat, apparently without complaint, with her naked shoulders pressed against the taps. Eventually I did include this incident in a story, and no one thought it other than an extravagant invention. Rewriting what went on at the Old Bailey as fiction is a constant process of calming down the truth, so that it may achieve some degree of credibility.

Of course it wasn't always crime. The civil courts, in the huge, sham Gothic château in the Strand, with its mosaic floor where the secretaries used to play badminton in the gloom after all the judges, litigants and lawyers had gone home, was a far less jolly place than the Old Bailey. Wrangles over money in commercial courts go on in an atmosphere of unalleviated gloom; criminal trials, which concern life, liberty and the pursuit of happiness, proceed far more cheerfully. In the Law Courts I argued about wills and, unhappily, about the future of children. Contested custody cases are almost always battlefields in which embittered parents are fighting each other, using Christmas holidays and the choice of schools, days out and weekend visits, as weapons with which to wound each other. These are disputes in which advocacy has little place; lawyers ought to forget their clients for once and think about the children.

Now, it seems, almost every fought custody case contains allegations of child abuse. When I did them, divorced couples would scrape the barrel of unhappiness and bring up every conceivably hurtful accusation against each other, not leaving out dirty underclothes or demands for sex at inconvenient times and in bizarre outfits and positions. In almost twenty years I can only remember two or three allegations of child abuse. I can't believe that wives in these circumstances would have kept quiet about it, especially if it might win a custody case. Can these terrible activities have suddenly taken a hold on the British public, or have a few cases caused more to be invented? I have no idea of the answer; but life in the family division today must be far more grim than life in the Old Bailey.

With tousled grey hair, peering over half-glasses, Richard Ingrams looks like a popular but unpredictable schoolmaster, perhaps from St Cake's, his version of Beachcomber's Narkover. He is dressed in a succession of precisely similar tweed jackets, corduroy trousers and rust-coloured sweaters. He also wears a flannel shirt with a tie. His voice is unexpectedly precise, slightly out of tune with his rugged appearance, and he always seems in danger of bursting into laughter. No country but England could have produced him and, like many Englishmen, he is accused of hypocrisy. *Private Eye* ruined many reputations, mocked many serious people and spread malicious gossip, they say, and Richard went off with a smile and played the organ in his village church. My view of *Private Eye* has always been that it's kept a flame of irreverent common sense burning through many dark days, that serious people deserve mockery and that gossip is the stuff of history.

The magazine would also target various celebrities and, if they complained or threatened legal action, redouble the attack with delighted abandon. One such target was Desmond Wilcox, a television personality and producer, married to Esther Rantzen, also a cause of hilarity to *Private Eye* because of her habit of suckling her young in public. Desmond Wilcox was accused of plagiarism in that he had turned various scripts about explorers into a book which he published without sufficiently crediting, or rewarding, the script writers. *Private Eye*, with its tendency not to leave ill alone, also suggested that Desmond Wilcox had done the series in order to pinch the scripts and had, what's more, purloined a series about the history of the Jews from another producer at the BBC. Mr Wilcox at last sued *Private Eye* for libel.

'I appear for Mr Desmond Wilcox, my Lord,' said Anthony Hoolahan, his small, neat and invariably courteous QC, 'the plaintiff, and he needs no introduction from me.'

'Well, he does to me,' the judge said, 'because I have absolutely no idea who he is.'

So the proceedings started on a cheerful note for *Private Eye*, but when we came to the Jews, however, the ground began to give way beneath our feet. It seemed that the judge was a tremendous authority and had read every conceivable work on the history of the Jews, and at the drop of a question would lecture us on the diaspora. As the discussion of these matters became more and more detailed, Richard Ingrams passed a number of notes to my opponent, who was on his feet and cross-examining one of our witnesses, suggesting that Mr Hoolahan tell the judge about the 'diaspora of the Hoolahans, who fled from some Irish bog to scatter and breed all over the world, producing a race of Hoolahans who would bore us all to death in Queen's Bench Court Seven'. Far from being angered or disconcerted by these messages from the enemy whilst he was in full flow, Tony Hoolahan folded them up neatly, put them in his wallet and took them home to show to his children. I have never seen a client so calm and insouciant during litigation that might have cost him and his paper a very large sum of money. The fact that I lost his case caused no break in our friendship, nor was I targeted by *Private Eye*, although Richard did say that to lose it obviously called for a high degree of forensic skill.

Looking back on those days of murder, violence and sudden death, I wonder what that close association with killers did to us. I don't think it made us callous, lessened our hatred of violence, or diminished our belief of the sanctity of life on earth. I suppose we got a little nearer to understanding the nature of the crime. Very few of the murders I was engaged in were planned, or premeditated in any real sense. They were the result of moments which slid out of control: quarrels in pubs, quarrels between friends and lovers, husbands and wives. Those guilty of them had no time to think of the consequences and would certainly not have been deterred by the death penalty. Taking those pale, calm, curiously remote people out and hanging them would merely add further unnecessary killings to a sufficiently blood-stained society. The death penalty, as an American judge said recently, has nothing to do with deterrence and everything to do with revenge, which, as the man who didn't write the plays of Shakespeare told us, 'is a kind of wild justice, which the more man's nature runs to, the more ought law to weed it out'. And yet most of us, at the height of a quarrel, however passionate, don't kill. Why should anyone do so? Is it chemistry or morality, free will or the will of God? These are questions which no trial, however careful or prolonged, can hope to answer and so doesn't care to ask.

14

When Laurence Olivier played the cantankerous old painter in *The Ebony Tower* we took him down to see the artist in Fawley Bottom. As magical in its way as Le Nid du Duc, the Pipers' house is built, like all old Chiltern farmhouses, with brick and flints. It has a long, high barn where John Piper designed his stained glass windows. His other studio was a converted cowshed attached to the kitchen. There is an enlarged cottage garden – not the sort of gentrified garden which regards colour as vulgarity and all the flowers have to be white, or off-white or greenish (a horticultural and social snob once said, 'If you want colour in your garden, get your cook to go and buy the seeds!'). The Pipers' garden glows with huge poppies, peonies, golden rod and deep yellow anemones and petunias, stocks and irises; just as the walls of his studio glow with the great flower pieces he did in his last years and with his paintings of French châteaux, Welsh castles and parish churches under dark and dramatic skies. It was there that the painter showed the actor the movements he might go through while depicting the dark interior of a forest.

The rest of the house is similarly inviting, with stone floors, log-fires, an army of white candlesticks, flowers in big pots, two pianos (on which John and his son Edward, and sometimes Richard Ingrams, played jazz), tapestries, and one of those lowering portraits of Windsor Castle painted against the typical Piper sky, which caused George VI to tell John he was frightfully sorry about the weather. The kitchen has a great Welsh dresser full of bright mugs; posters for Britten operas, for which Myfanwy Piper wrote the words; and smells of unobtrusive cookery. Myfanwy, now over eighty, dives fearlessly into the pool when she comes to stay in Italy, and she's still writing – a libretto for an opera based on *Easter,* one of Strindberg's relatively cheerful plays – and cooking dinner for an infinite number of friends and her extended family. John Betjeman wrote a poem to Myfanwy whose 'fortunate bicycle' he mentioned and went on:

> Golden the lights on the locks of Myfanwy,
> Golden the light on the book on her knee,
> Finger-marked pages of Rackham's Hans Andersen,
> Time for the children to come down to tea.

And I remember him saying that he had amorous thoughts of Myfanwy, wearing a white overall with F for Fuller's embroidered on the bosom, serving him walnut cake in a tea shop. During the war, when petrol was short, Myfanwy drove a pony and trap round the narrow lanes. In her more advanced years, John Piper would ask her to put on exotic underwear and lace-up boots and make drawings of her.

John is in the house as though he were still alive, his paint table clean, his paints set out neatly, his collection of tapes and records in order. He was thin, grey-haired and aquiline, with a face like a cardinal and a taste for drinking a good deal of red wine with everything. He and Myfanwy met at a holiday cottage rented by another painter, Ivon Hitchens, and fell instantly in love. As they talked and argued, the old days came swimming back – the time when John was an abstract painter and not yet one of England's great topographical artists. Memories of Kenneth Clark and Sandy Calder, Ben Britten, Osbert Lankester and Betjeman, would come back to them and they would bicker gently about what exactly had happened and when, telling each other that they were completely impossible to live with in a way which showed clearly that their love had never died. All the same, John was a domineering character to whom Myfanwy devoted her life, and deprived herself of much time when she could have been writing. However, she says that without John Piper, she probably wouldn't have written at all.

John and I decided we would have a joint birthday party at Fawley Bottom on a summer evening. There were long tables covered with white cloths and flowers, and ivy climbing up the pillars of the tent. There were many children and grandchildren; small girls in white dresses ran between the tables and out over the grass as the light faded. A number of people met for the first time that evening and fell in love. John had always had a passion for fireworks, which exploded in great profusion at all Piper celebrations. He designed them, chose their colours and falling patterns for royal and state occasions, and a friend of his was a wizard with gunpowder. When the sky was blacker than even he painted it, it was filled with shooting stars and lazily descending coloured cannon-balls, which exploded and divided and reproduced, sending down showers of light and colour. And then, in letters of fire over the Chiltern hill, came the message HAPPY BIRTHDAY JOHN AND JOHN. That night John Piper was eighty, I was sixty – old by anyone's standards, but I had, I thought, very little excuse for not being entirely happy.

'I'm growing old,' the blonde girl approaching thirty said in a voice of doom. 'I know it. I'm getting lines. My face is growing old.'

We were at dinner with Niven in a Chelsea restaurant. He was bronzed by the sun and serene as ever, wearing no tie and a coat and trousers selected at random from different suits. He looked amused as he said, 'I can't feel too sorry for you. Even if I take every pill and hormone, and do whatever diet's going, there's no way I'm going to be alive in ten years' time.'

A few nights later he was interviewed on television. The stories were as funny as ever and even more brightly polished, but his speech was slurred. His doctor, who had watched the programme, left him a note at the Connaught saying that he might have had a slight stroke.

I don't remember how much later it was, a year, perhaps two, that I was driving across Switzerland. We had been staying at Verbier and I was on my way to Niven's other home in Château d'Oex. I knew what had happened. It wasn't a stroke but the cowardly and treacherous motor neurone disease, which either takes its time or kills you in a rush. Willing to wound and yet afraid to strike, it paralyses the nervous system so you can't eat or swallow. I knew that Niven had gone to the Mayo Clinic in America and travelled the world in search of a cure, but motor neurone disease, like God, moves in a mysterious way and no one has yet forced it to reveal its secret.

When I got to the house, a big, wooden chalet on a hillside glittering with snow, Hjordis was telephoning and seemed cheerful. She went out with a friend and then Niven came downstairs, gently, almost soundlessly, like a ghost, and when he spoke only the faintest sounds came out of him. 'Fundador!' he greeted me. 'What about a jar?' So we sat and drank white wine and he told me about all the cures he had tried. 'Someone advised me to sit in a bath of ice and water,' he whispered. 'So I sat there in misery and watched my lifetime's friend and companion shrink to the size of a gherkin! Now, tell me again about the dwarf you once defended.' We really didn't want to hear new stories; we wanted to enjoy old ones, told again. We sat together for a long time, until the sun had vanished and the snow was freezing hard, and I could hardly hear him when he said, 'I think it's having talked far too much during my life that's taken my voice away.'

So I drove back to Verbier, to the apartment full of ski boots and anoraks and exhausted children. We slithered down the street to a bar where chalet girls and middle-managers were laughing and shouting and throwing bread, and I never saw Niven again. A paparazzo got a picture of him sitting in his garden in the South of France, a photograph he must have hated, in which he looked even more ghostlike, almost transparent. He died soon afterwards and a great deal of joy and laughter slipped quietly out of the world.

I'm not sure what Niven felt as he faded slowly. Did he want to hurry on the process? I don't believe so. Euthanasia, or 'easing the passing' as Dr Bodkin Adams, who did away with many of his elderly patients in Eastbourne in the name of mercy, called it, has become a fashionable subject, and keeping old people alive has come to be seen as politically incorrect as fox-hunting or telling women that they look beautiful. I have doubts on this subject. I remember all the will cases I have done and the ruthlessness of relatives harkening after grandma's savings, or even her sticks of furniture. How easy it would be to persuade the old girl that she really owed it to her family to drift into painless oblivion so that the spoils might be divided. My doubts were greatly strengthened by a case I did, appropriately towards the end of my life as a barrister. I appeared for an elderly man who worked for an organization which exists to persuade the nation that passing should be eased whenever necessary.

The angel of death was called Mr Lyons. He wore a bobble hat and carried a white stick on account of impaired vision. His teeth were unreliable so he seemed to subsist mainly on tea and biscuits, which he called 'bicks'. He was the only man, I think ever, to have mixed up fish and chips and boiled sweets in a food processor and eaten the result. He was no great believer in free will but referred frequently to his puppet master, some unseen spirit who was in charge of his destiny. His terrestrial boss was a well-educated, youngish man who had come to a theoretical and philosophical belief in the virtues of euthanasia. People would ring Exit complaining of terrible pain and, the prosecution claimed, he would dispatch

Mr Lyons to put them out of their misery. This was done by encouraging them to wash down a special brand of sleeping pill with a good deal of whisky. A black plastic bag was then put over their heads and fastened with an elastic band. When they dozed off, the air in the bag would be reduced, they would suffocate and Mr Lyons was able to move on to another customer. If they took a long time dying, Mr Lyons was alleged once to have said something like, 'Hurry up, please. I've got others to go to this afternoon.' Before he left, he was thoughtful enough to feed any cats that might have been left unattended.

It's fair to say that all his clients embraced death voluntarily. Some cases, however, were clearer than others. A talented portrait painter with a brain tumour, knowing he would never work again, painted his last picture and decided to die, surrounded by his family, with the help of the strange man in the bobble hat. Other charges were more difficult. A suicidal young man with a drink problem rang Exit and it was alleged that Mr Lyons arrived to help him. He was also accused of having agreed to help a very sick woman out of this world without either of them telling her husband who came home from work to find his wife suffocated.

Unhappily, Mr Lyons kept a careful diary of his activities. The entries were short and gave little more than names and addresses, the times when the operation was complete and whether he got tea and 'bicks'. He also added a note of the money he had laid out on elastic bands and 'placcy' bags. Ever eager to provide evidence against himself, he started to tell the story of the passings he had eased to a pretty model he found himself next to on the top of a bus. She invited him into her house, gave him tea and 'delicious bicks' and, being a sensible young woman, and the daughter of the radio and television presenter David Jacobs, reported the matter to the police.

In England suicide was once a felony, and those who committed it would be buried at the crossroads with a stake through their hearts, and their property was forfeited to the Crown. Some unhappy people were imprisoned for unsuccessful attempts at suicide. When the crime of suicide was abolished, an offence of aiding and abetting the act was retained, and this was the charge faced by Mr Lyons and his director in Exit. It's remarkable that suicide has never been a crime in Scotland, so north of the Border Mr Lyons could have helped invalids on with their plastic bags in perfect innocence.

Mr Lyons was a verbose, not to say rambling, old man. His behaviour, and his attitude to life, did not make him the most sympathetic of defendants. When I first saw him, he was furious about his treatment in Brixton Prison, where he was remanded awaiting the trial. 'They pinched my copy of the Gilbert and Sullivan operas,' he told me. 'And the tea, well, you could hardly call it tea!' If the tea was weak, I thought it was hardly a secure foundation for an application for bail, so I told him that if he wanted to he could tell the judge about it. No sooner had the judge sat down and chosen a pencil but Mr Lyons started to harangue him from the dock and went on for a very long time indeed. When, at last, the stream of words ran dry, the judge, to my amazement, turned to me and said, 'You know, Mr Mortimer, I am extremely concerned about your client's copy of the Gilbert and Sullivan operas,' and he granted him bail. The next morning I arrived very early in court and found the judge, alone on his bench, working on his notes. He beckoned to me and, as I approached, leant down from his elevated seat and said confidentially, 'I say, John, I had a call from Brixton Prison.'

'You mean they want him back?'

'Oh, no.' He shook his head. 'They said, "Bloody glad to get rid of him!"'

The trial was long and depressing as it dealt with eight or nine cases of hopeless illness and the termination of life. Mr Lyons did not go into the witness-box, where he might have fallen victim to the plastic bag of cross-examination, but made a statement from the dock. He had been going for what seemed a lifetime – it was, in fact, several hours – when he started to talk about his puppet master who was giving him instructions through a small hole in the top of his head. At this, even the judge, who had been very kind to Mr Lyons, became exasperated and issued a peremptory order from the bench, 'Mr Lyons, will you please get your puppet master out of my court! I have no wish to hear his evidence.'

In the end, Mr Lyons was acquitted on the murder charges and found guilty of some offences under the Suicide Act. The young man who had taken the telephone calls and given my client his orders got a fairly severe prison sentence. The judge treated Mr Lyons with leniency, and when passing sentence had a singular conversation with the convicted man which, to the best of my recollection, went something like this:

JUDGE: Mr Lyons, you need someone to look after you. Some people seem to take a liking to you. Now, that young Miss Jacobs you met on top of the bus was an extremely attractive young lady . . .

MR LYONS: No thank you, sir. I prefer the older woman.

JUDGE: There, if I may say so, Mr Lyons, I think you're making a mistake. But, at any rate, there seem to be some very nice older ladies in the offices of your organization who might be pleased to keep an eye on you.

The case had an alarming sequel. Geoff Robertson, who had acted for the young organizer at Exit, fell ill with an attack of pneumonia. This fact must have been given some publicity, because Geoff heard a ring at his front door, went down and opened it to Mr Lyons, who was wearing his bobble hat. 'Oh, Mr Robertson, I heard as you weren't feeling very well lately?' said the old man whom Geoff thought might be eager for tea and bicks.

As I say, I have my doubts about euthanasia. Death may approach in many forms but none, I think, more alarming than Mr Lyons.

15

I'm sitting talking to an American author in his fifties. He has worked on both Esquire *and* Playboy *and served in intelligence during the war. He wrote a number of books with titles like* LSD: The Conscious Expanding Drug *and* The Marijuana Papers. *He lived in Cambridge with two pretty daughters who attracted the love and admiration of young students of chemistry. Whether the author became the guru of the group, or was merely anxious to prove his youthful credentials by showing himself part of the drug culture, I'm not sure. He became involved with some of them who took a Welsh farmhouse and there manufactured LSD on such a scale that the police officers, who finally entered the premises, became high on the air they breathed. I am talking to the middle-aged author in a cell.*

The police attack on the LSD factory was called Operation Julie, after a dark-haired member of the Thames Valley Force. At an early stage it became clear that one of the chemical constituents of the drug was being imported from Europe and Interpol was alerted. In fact it came from Switzerland and a car was stopped at the border by police who had seen The French Connection, *a film in which a car hiding drugs is systematically taken to pieces. The gendarmerie spent two days dismantling every bit of the car, and blowing down every tube and pipe, which they laid out on a garage floor. After a minute and lengthy examination, the verdict was* pas de stupéfiants, *and the young chemists were allowed to go on their way with a briefcase full of the forbidden chemical on the passenger seat. In the course of time, however, the police became more observant and the whole group was arrested.*

'The fuzz treated me very badly.' The author is complaining to me, as many clients do.

'What did they do, exactly?'

'They searched my apartment. They took away all my papers. They even analysed my mother.'

'They did what?'

'Oh, sure. You see, I kept my mother's ashes in a pot on the mantelpiece. They took it away, I guess, to analyse it.'

He has guessed right. Later I find that his mother has been tested at the forensic science laboratory in Reading to see whether she might be a hallucinogenic drug.

Barristers of a certain age get distinctly edgy. They are tired. All that standing up and sweating, that thinking on your feet and putting down questions like a gambler drops counters on the roulette table, has become as exhausting as spending days with an electric drill repairing roads. Most of them want to become judges, to spend the day sitting down, to stop caring who's going to win, and to have a title to take home to their wives. For these benefits, they will endure a life where they spend half their time on circuit, imprisoned in a large house with a butler and three or four other judges, having little to do in the evenings but discuss their cases and go to bed early. If no one makes them judges, old advocates soldier on, getting more forgetful and increasingly tetchy, sliding back to indecent assault and petty theft when they're no longer thought to be up to sensational murders. As the mug on my desk says OLD LAWYERS NEVER DIE, THEY SIMPLY LOSE THEIR APPEALS.

I knew I didn't want to be a judge. It was the Lord Chancellor's habit to send QCs round the country to do a little part-time judging to see if they had any aptitude for the work. It was after one such session that I told my mother I had spent a week being a judge and she laughed heartily. In fact Penny and I had been in Chester. A congress of florists was meeting in the town and we were hard put to it to find a room in the local motel. I only heard family law cases, so I was never, thank God, compelled to send anyone to prison. It is, as I found, a relief to be sitting down and it is also very strange to be in a courtroom and not have a client. A judge's chief duty is to keep his mouth shut for as long as possible, and this comes very hard to anyone who's spent his life as an advocate. It's the boredom induced by having to sit in silence for days on end which drives judges to say silly things, showing off or playing to the public gallery in a way which gets them into trouble and their names into the papers. I learnt all these painful lessons about judicial behaviour and I hoped I would never have to live by them. I also discovered the work to be fairly restful, and there is no excuse whatever for that lowering fury which so often exploded from the bench in my youth. The proceedings go at the pace you choose if you're a judge, and if you can't understand the law you can always get someone to explain it.

In the early seventies we still did nullity cases, granting decrees to unhappy couples who had failed to consummate their marriages. Either the wife or the husband would have to give evidence about the wedding night and, as they got to the heart of the matter, the court would be cleared and the public asked to leave. Penny, who had, with a slightly ironic smile, stood up and bowed to me as I came into court, left with the public when the preliminaries were over. She went for a walk in the park and when she got back the usher greeted her with 'The judge said you needn't have gone, but I'm glad you did. A nice girl like you's far better off in the fresh air than listening to all that filth!' I don't know if they still have nullity cases, which were insensitive and unnecessary proceedings.

The last case I was asked to judge concerned the future of two little boys; should they live with their mother, who was an opera singer in Norway, or stay with their father, who kept a garage in

Bournemouth? Their entire futures depended on this decision. I begged the parents to put their heads together and come up with an agreed answer. They said that their heads had been together for a considerable period without result and I was being paid to decide the case. If you write a book, you're not called upon to determine the whole course of some child's life. I saw escape from the law as a bright light at the end of a tunnel; even if it were the sort of beautiful and reassuring light that you see at the moment of death.

I wasn't sure that I was going to my final trial when I flew back to Singapore one Boxing Day and arrived jet-lagged, hungover and with no very clear idea what the case was all about. As I had started to read through a mass of papers on the aeroplane, the Singaporean hostess told me that the sleeve of a Rolling Stones record had been banned because it had a picture of a naked woman on it 'with a tiny black triangle between the legs'. She said, 'You run across the causeway to Malaysia if you want a good time, but the finest place in the world is Honolulu, if you want my opinion.'

Ben Jeyaretnam, my friend, the Secretary-General of the Workers Party, certainly hadn't been having a good time in Singapore. He enjoyed a triumph which made him the target of a relentless bombardment of legal proceedings, before which any average mortal would have retreated or run up the white flag of surrender. With irrepressible optimism, he soldiered on.

After we had lost his libel action against the prime minister, Ben had somehow contrived to pay his £35,000 of damages and costs. He was delighted when he won the Anson constituency for his party by some six hundred votes. At last he had a seat in parliament, but it was a moment of joy mixed with sadness because his English wife had died. The next morning he served at Holy Communion in St Andrew's Cathedral. Ben's seat in parliament could have done no possible harm to the government; indeed his

146

presence there as a single opposition MP would have enhanced its democratic credentials, but the heaviest legal artillery was trundled out to annihilate him.

First Mr Lee announced that 'Opposition is all theatre and doesn't make for good government.' Ben was ignored and isolated in parliament, told that he couldn't act as an adviser to the residents' committee in his constituency, and arrested for handing out leaflets with his party newspaper in the street. What had caused me to leave home on Boxing Day, and hover uneasily over the Indian Ocean, was a criminal charge against Ben and his party chairman, alleging their misuse of his party funds. The chairman, Mr Wong, ran the gift shop in the Singapore Hilton and at first I thought that the party funds were lodged in a drawer, with a packet of aspirins, a few condoms and some views of the harbour, and no doubt had got in a bit of a muddle. When I arrived at the hotel, I discovered that the case was far more complex. Very briefly, the trouble started with a debt owed by the party workers for the costs of an unsuccessful libel action lost many years before.

It was never suggested that Ben Jeyaretnam used money given to the party to line his own pockets. What was alleged was that they kept it out of the general fund because that had an order against it for old costs. It was also said that he and Mr Wong had made a false statutory declaration in relation to their accounts. I began to understand the danger for Ben. If he lost badly he could not only go to prison for a long time, he would forfeit his proudest possession, his hard-won seat in parliament. He would also be stripped of his solicitor's practice and his only way of earning a living.

So, after a sleepless and jet-lagged night's work on the case, I stumbled into the robing room of the subordinate court in Singapore. It looked very much like all the robing rooms I had known, from the Old Bailey to Manchester, from Reading to Ibadan. It was a shabby, unswept environment, the floor littered with old law reports and bits of newspaper, the armchairs full of barristers trying to sleep off their hangovers, with other barristers ringing up their wives in a vain attempt to explain where they were the night before. The place was presided over by an elderly Chinese lady who was brewing up Nescafé and pouring out Chinese cough mixture for barristers with sore throats. She took one look at me and called out, 'There you are, Lumpore of the Bairey!' In a dreadful moment I saw myself spending my declining years slogging round the Far East being called Lumpore. This alarming prospect may have had much to do with my final decision.

We went into court and Ben stood in the dock, looking up at the bench where he had once sat as a judge. Beside him was Mr Wong, whose perpetual smile I felt expressed neither happiness nor hope. The prosecutor seemed highly strung. During one of our differences of opinion he was so appalled by my criticism of his case that he asked for a short adjournment; this request the Chinese judge treated with disdain. If my second trial in Singapore was more pleasant, and seemed more likely to end happily, than the first it was because of Judge Michael Khoo. He was much younger and more talkative than the enigmatic figure who had presided over the libel action. I heard that he and his brother performed to the guitar and were known as the Singing Khoos. He behaved with great fairness and patience, so my last case was as well tried as any I had done at the Old Bailey.

In this trial, my junior was a plump, cheerful, fatalistic Indian lawyer who didn't mind appearing in cases which might annoy the government. After a hard day he asked if I would like to visit his club. 'The learned leader will find it most relaxing,' he told me. I thought the place would be a relic of the British Raj with peeling leather armchairs, ancient copies of *Punch* and afternoon tea. Instead he took me to the luxurious basement of a high-rise building, divided into small and discreet rooms, where Singaporean girls in thirties Hollywood-style evening-gowns knelt before the guests to serve them gin and tonics. 'You are English?' one of them asked me. 'Do you often bump into the Princess of Wales in London? She seems to us a very cheerful sort of person.' Her name was Tracy and during the daytime, she told me, she 'slept like a pig. I have no boyfriend, you see. I live only for my work.' Living only for my own work, I left her and spent another evening alone in my hotel bedroom with the accounts of the Workers Party.

One cheque had apparently been intended to pay the costs of an election petitioner, and we could argue that it didn't have to go through the party's account. There were other explanations of other cheques. One of the charges was that of making a false statutory declaration but there was a technical defence to that. There was no doubt that the financial affairs of the Workers Party were in confusion, but Ben had been unaware of the details and certainly had no intention of misappropriating the money. So we chased accounts and examined party supporters, and his Honour Judge Khoo, a Confucius come to judgment, found the prosecutor, who asked for a number of amendments, irritating. Halfway through the trial he dismissed one of the charges, but three remained. I escaped and had lunch with *The Times* correspondent in Singapore. I was tired, not looking forward to another afternoon in the steamy courtroom, and said I had a good mind to finish with the law when the case was over. The next day there was a story in *The Times* which announced that I was leaving the bar. I read it and felt that if it was in *The Times* it was probably true. Years before, when we drowned earwigs and I told my father I wanted to be a writer, he had asked me to consider my unfortunate wife, who would have me about the house all day 'wearing a dressing-gown, brewing tea and stumped for words'. He told me to pick a job which would get me out of the house and suggested I start by divorcing a few people. So my father decided that I was to become a barrister, and a newspaper told me when to stop.

The choices we make are few and the freedom of our will

149

exaggerated. If I hadn't been born the son of a divorce lawyer and raised, educated and clothed almost entirely on the proceeds of cruelty, adultery and wilful neglect to provide reasonable maintenance, I would never have gone near a law court and would have chosen almost any other day job. I might have been a waiter or an unsuccessful actor; I should have hated to have been a schoolmaster. I think it is important for a writer to have done other work and have come to know a world which has nothing to do with writing. He's greatly privileged if it is work where he meets people at crises in their lives, as doctors and priests and defending barristers do. It is also a relief, in the loneliness of a writer's life, to be part of an enterprise in which a number of people are working together to a single end: the production of a film or a play or the defence of a client in a long trial. If I hadn't been a barrister I should never have written *Rumpole*, and that would have been a subject of regret, at least to me. I am glad I went into the law, and very glad I came out of it. Perhaps, as is its great and often fatal weakness, it delayed me for too long.

Judge Khoo reserved his judgment in what was also to turn out to be a case which had a lasting effect on his legal career, and the Workers Party gave me a dinner in a downtown hotel. The Workers, who were not young, ate through numerous courses and were entertained by three singers: two girls who wore spangled tights, leg-warmers and crownless hats, and a Cliff Richard lookalike. They sang 'My Way' very loudly in Chinese and the Workers seemed full of hope and happiness, looking forward to a golden age to equal Britain in the sixties.

So I left the bar and went on my way, first of all on a flight to Los Angeles. Crossing innumerable frontiers of time I arrived at the Beverly Hills Hotel. Ancient men sat round the pool with their girlfriends, starlets, secretaries or manicurists and, it was said, writers and actors would ask their agents to ring them. The tannoy by the pool then called out their names and gave the impression that they were greatly in demand. Herb Schmerz, who as vice-president of Mobil Oil was a patron of British television (through *Masterpiece Theatre* and *Mystery*), used to bribe the telephone operator to announce calls for dead people. At the amplified announcement 'There's a call for Mr Clark Gable' or, 'Miss Carole Lombard to the telephone, please', the old men would look deeply worried and mutter, 'Carole Lombard? Isn't she dead or something?' Mr Schmerz had played this trick and was there to greet me by the Beverly Hills pool as I arrived, by way of Tokyo, at the end of my long flight from the law. He offered me a drink whereupon I collapsed, overcome with exhaustion, apprehension and relief, like a prisoner who has escaped. And, like an old lag, I had become institutionalized. I had stayed until I was a little arthritic and had to be helped over the wall by a *Times* journalist and a Chinese lady brewing up coffee in a Far-Eastern robing room.

My double life was over. Was I going to miss the variety: breakfast with a fraudster, down the cells to see a murderer, lunch with the judges and off to rehearsals at the end of the day? What wouldn't I miss? The fancy dress, the hours spent listening to other people's speeches (it's difficult to be completely bored by your own), and above all I wasn't going to miss the increasing responsibility for so many other people's lives.

When Judge Khoo delivered his judgment he acquitted Ben of all but one charge involving £100 and he fined him the equivalent of some £300. He didn't lose his liberty, or his livelihood, or his seat in parliament. The government of Singapore started a legal juggernaut rolling. Judge Khoo was removed from the bench. The prosecution appealed and a superior judge, who hadn't seen the witnesses, convicted Ben on two charges and ordered a retrial of the serious charge which Judge Khoo had thrown out at half time. At the retrial he was given a prison sentence that would still have allowed him to stay on as an MP. Ben appealed and his prison sentence was reduced to a month, but the fine was increased to a sum which meant he lost his parliamentary seat. Publications which showed themselves sympathetic to Ben in reporting these events – *Time* magazine and the *Asian Wall Street Journal* – were penalized. Later the Singapore court made an order striking Ben off the roll of solicitors. Happily this was an order that could be taken up to the Privy Council sitting in London. Ben could not take his criminal convictions to the Privy Council. His appeal was heard by a committee of five judges presided over by Lord Bridge, whose judgment contains the following passage:

> Their Lordships have to record their deep disquiet that by a series of misjudgments the appellant and his co-accused Wong have suffered a grievous injustice. They have been fined, imprisoned and publicly disgraced for offences of which they were not guilty. The appellant, in addition, has been deprived of his seat in parliament and disqualified for a year from practising his profession. Their Lordships' order restores him to the roll of advocates and solicitors of the Supreme Court of Singapore, but because of the course taken by the criminal proceedings, their Lordships have no power to right the other wrongs which the appellant and Wong have suffered. Their only prospect of redress, their Lordships understand, will be by way of petition for pardon to the President of the Republic of Singapore.

The Singapore government's response to this blast from London was to abolish appeals to the Privy Council in professional disciplinary proceedings. Ben's petition to the President to restore him to his seat in parliament was refused on the ground that he had 'failed to show contrition'. However, after about a year, he was restored to his practice. I last met him in a hotel in London where he sat, smiling as always, stroking his side whiskers and trying to face the fact that he now owes almost a million Singapore dollars as the result of another libel action by Mr Lee.

Not long ago, I was talking to some law students from Singapore. They were a group of girls, small, pretty, birdlike with wide eyes and gentle voices, who asked if I could recommend the practice of criminal law in their country. I thought of them in a world of brutal punishment and inscrutable judges and wished them luck. We have every reason to be proud of the fact that our judicial system has been adopted in so many distant parts of the world. At the heart of it is fairness to everyone who holds views with which the government doesn't agree, and judicial independence. Without these ingredients, the wearing of wigs, the humble submissions and the quoting of House of Lords authorities become a meaningless parade of archaic customs and costumes.

16

My youngest daughter Rosie and I are in the bath together; she is six *years old but I should presumably keep quiet about this fact or we're both in grave danger of being taken into custody by social workers. We are telling each other jokes, such as 'Who wrote* Where's My Sock?' *'Sonia Foot!' Or, 'Who wrote* Cutting It Fine?' *None other, of course, than Moses Lawn. We both find these titles wonderfully amusing. Then she says, 'I don't love you, Dad.'*

'Don't you, Rosie? That's very sad.'

'Yes, it's sad. But it is interesting.'

I look at her in dismay, having the uneasy feeling that we have given birth to a novelist.

When I fled from the law, and collapsed among the elderly brown bodies and sunbeds, heard the sound of wind in the palm trees and smelled coconut oil mixed with Givenchy perfume, I didn't think of myself as a novelist. It's true that I'd published my first novel when I was twenty-four, and gone on to write four more over the next decade. I had started early in the tall, silent house in Swiss Cottage and written my five pages before the children got up for school and I dressed as a dependable lawyer and went off to the divorce court; but for the past thirty years I had written nothing but drama, films and plays for the theatre and for television. Apart from the first, *Charade*, which seems to me to be original and caused very little trouble, these early novels are haunted by other voices: an echo of Graham Greene, a whisper of Waugh, a shot at Raymond Chandler. It wasn't until I wrote my first play, and heard actors say lines I had written, that I thought I had found a voice which, for better or worse, was entirely my own. The business of writing novels is long, lonely, and you get extremely cold. Plays have far fewer words and, as my father said of the divorce courts, they get you out of the house. I thought I would probably never write another novel.

I came back from Los Angeles, where we had been showing a new Rumpole series to the press, with no very clear idea of what to do with my life. I thought I might dramatize another novel like *Brideshead*, then decided I didn't want to do that with anyone else's novel and I would write my own. Brian Cowgill was running Thames Television and we met when I took part in the pleasant job of handing out slices of Thames's money to aspiring dramatists. On one of these occasions, he asked me when I was going to write a series about England since the war. At first I resisted the idea entirely, and then, thinking back over the years I had known, from the roaring forties to the awful eighties, I decided it was what I most wanted to do. This was the long novel I would write and then dramatize. I also had the insane idea that I would perform both tasks at the same time.

In thirty years I had forgotten the great gulf that lies between writing drama and prose fiction. In drama everything happens in action and dialogue scenes: people disclosing or, more interestingly, failing to disclose, their thoughts and feelings in direct speech. But most of the important things in life don't happen when we're talking to each other. They go on in silence and in solitude, while we're in the bath or on a bus, or waiting in the doctor's surgery. These are the memories, decisions and indecisions, unspoken love and unspeakable guilt, to which the novelist has the best access.

Both in the writing and in its effect a novel is far slower work than a drama. A theatre play has to hold the audience in a vice-like grip from the first line to the final curtain. A moment's lack of tension and the customers return to their usual occupations of unwrapping sweets or dying of bronchitis. A television play has to keep the audience from chattering, reading the paper, straying from the room, making love or making tea. In either case it's an event which fills a required time and must capture and hold captive its customers.

A novel is quite different. It can be tasted a few drops at a time or swallowed in a sitting. It can afford to relax, to take detours, to describe Exmoor or the Battle of Waterloo. It can change pace as often as life itself, and it's the reader's companion for as long as it takes him or her to finish it. Auden, comparing this painstaking work to that of the poets who can 'dash forward like huzzars', says that the novelist

> Must struggle out of his boyish gift and learn
> How to be plain and awkward, how to be
> One after whom none think it worth to turn.
>
> For, to achieve his lightest wish, he must
> Become the whole of boredom, subject to
> Vulgar complaints like love, among the Just
>
> Be just, among the Filthy filthy too,
> And in his own weak person, if he can,
> Dully put up with all the wrongs of Man.

There is another difference between the novel and drama: the reader has far more to do, and has a greater contribution to make, than the spectator. A great deal of the novel takes place in the reader's mind; if the writer describes a beautiful girl on the page of a book, it's for the reader to imagine her and supply his or her idea of beauty. If he is watching a performance, the spectator has an actress supplied and may not find her beautiful at all. The novel is an act of collaboration between the author and the single reader, whom he has to think of, during the act of writing, as himself.

Forgetting all these things, when I started to write the novel *Paradise Postponed*, it looked just like a television script with far too much dialogue and far too little thought. I had to think back to those early mornings in Swiss Cottage, before I had written a single line for actors, and come to my senses.

A politician, perhaps Denis Healey, said it was easy to keep Tories happy as they only believe in money and power, things which can be readily achieved. The left's belief in social justice is a paradise which almost certainly cannot be reached. The Labour Party, therefore, has to be kept going on a bright vision of the future which is unavoidably postponed. So I thought of a title, *Paradise Postponed*, and kept to it, as I did to the Elgar Cello Concerto as the music of a vanishing England, despite all anxious questions from the television company.

In 1945, the year when the war ended, paradise might have seemed just around the corner. There was going to be a welfare state, no great gulf between rich and poor, a free health service and a better education for all. Bliss was it, in those halcyon days, to be alive when the Labour Attorney-General, Sir Hartley Shawcross (eventually to become known as Sir Shortly Floorcross) said, 'We are the masters now.' Later, Churchill and Macmillan didn't forget what the voters had told them when the war ended. They had, as sensitive and intelligent Conservatives, been shocked by the poverty and social injustice of the thirties. They also remembered the soldiers who had fought and died in two wars, and had a paternalistic care for the workers. The idea of paradise was kept going by common consent; it would, of course, be postponed but, in the good times, no one seemed to doubt that it was worth hoping for.

Then the Tories in opposition went into a think tank and, inspired by Sir Keith Joseph, came to the conclusion that paradise was not only postponed, it did not, and could never, exist. In fact, even to hope for it was some sort of sick fantasy which led to political ill-health, dangerous anarchy and final madness. The business of politics had nothing to do with justice and much to do with permitting the rich to become richer in the hope that some small part of their wealth might dribble down and comfort the poor. Mrs Thatcher, the child of a corner shop in Grantham, swimming happily along behind Sir Keith, found this an enchanting idea; so the new Conservatism was born.

It was Mrs Thatcher's great achievement to take her party away from the paternalistic and easygoing knights of the shires and give it to − well, give it to whom exactly? In *Paradise Postponed* I invented Leslie Titmuss, who rises from being the most objectionable small boy in the village and, like his father, a clerk in the local brewery, to Cabinet rank. Mrs Thatcher and Leslie Titmuss achieved power by understanding the innate conservatism of the British blue- and white-collar workers. Leslie Titmuss thought that the real Conservatives were not like the old English gent and landowner, the chairman of the local party, whose daughter he was delighted to marry for the sake of advancing his career. When he's seeking adoption as a parliamentary candidate he says:

I grew up to understand the value of money because it took my father five years to save up for our first second-hand Ford Prefect. Every night he finishes his tea and says to my mother, 'Very tasty, dear. That was very tasty.' He always says the same thing. He falls asleep in front of the fire at exactly half past nine and at ten-thirty he wakes up with a start and says, 'I'll lock up, dear. Time for Bedfordshire!' Always the same. Every night . . . You can forget the county families and the city gents and the riverside commuters. They'll vote for you anyway. What you need to win is my people. The people who know the value of money because they've never had it. The people who say the same thing every night because it makes them feel safe. The people who've worked hard and don't want to see scroungers rewarded or laziness paying off. Put it this way, ladies and gentlemen. You need the voters I can bring you!

I thought I had given Leslie Titmuss a good case and I heard it was shown to some members of the Labour Shadow Cabinet at the time of an election, as a warning of the argument that had to be countered. The lesson wasn't learnt and Mrs Thatcher, and Leslie, resumed power. In spite of his ruthless and evil ways I acquired a certain affection for Titmuss; he was his own man, you knew where you were with him, and, although no good ever came of him, he was never guilty of grovelling to the electors in the way of politicians today. I have to say that my admiration for Titmuss was due, in great part, to the fact that he worked in the book and was a success on the page. I also have an irrational tendency to like people. I remember having a conversation with Norman Tebbit and, as he cracked his gallows jokes in that slow and deeply contemptuous voice of his, I felt a terrible affection for him stealing over me. This was cured, I am glad to say, when I heard his public pronouncements.

If I was going to be rude about the political right I had to be equally insulting to the left. The story centred on the will of the Reverend Simeon Simcox, a rector rather like that Canon Collins who was always seen with Michael Foot on CND marches to Aldermaston, the 'Red Dean' of Canterbury, or any other well-meaning and fairly well-off Christian Socialist. His wife was an elitist and rather grand lady with left-wing views of the sort you might have heard in Bloomsbury drawing-rooms in the days of Kingsley Martin (who edited the *New Statesman*) and Bertrand Russell. I wrote of her brand of mandarin Socialism that 'she wanted the working classes to rule the world, but she didn't want to have any of them to tea'. A similar sort of left-wing grandeur was displayed by Lord Mountbatten's family when a Conservative canvasser called on them. 'Why don't you try the servants' en-

159

trance?' he was told. 'Someone there might support your party. None of *us* is interested in that sort of thing!'

In the fifties and the sixties, when I started writing for the theatre, everything of interest seemed to happen in the North of England. Only there was life gritty, realistic and filled with ironic humour; where there was room at the top, the long-distance runner pursued his loneliness and the revels of Saturday night were followed by the remorse of Sunday morning. Girls from Roedean flattened their vowels and desperately sought a classless manner of speech, and I kept as quiet as I could about having been to Harrow. Now, I thought, the South should have its turn and I wanted to plot England's changes where I live, in a strangely isolated pocket of resistance to the implacable urbanization of our countryside. The hills and the valleys at the edge of the Chiltern escarpment, before the flat Oxfordshire plain, have not changed noticeably, although the few remaining beech woods are fighting a losing battle against the fir tree invasion. But the cottages that contained farmworkers, tree-fellers and chair-leg turners when I was a child have been converted, extended, equipped with car-ports and granny flats and are inhabited by weekending merchant bankers or couples in advertising. There are still secret woods, however, and strangely deserted valleys. I thought the country I knew best was the place to set my story.

While I was struggling with *Paradise Postponed*, a far more important act of creation was taking place. Rosie's birth seemed casual. The anaesthetist arrived late and left her ancient fur-coat and handbag on a chair in the corner. The gynaecologist was in shirt-sleeves, the waistcoat and trousers of a dark-blue suit, and gum boots. We were joined by another, hitherto unknown character, introduced as the doctor held her up high and said she was a beautiful little girl. I think we opened champagne in the room. Later I fetched Emily, who was thirteen, to see her mother and new sister. When we left the hospital and shared a Chinese dinner she wondered, a little nervously, how things would turn out when she was no longer the only child of a second marriage. I made a resolution to postpone dying indefinitely.

When Rosie was five months old the bad times started, and she became ill. We went to a variety of doctors who offered a variety of explanations. In Italy a doctor recommended a course of germs. We had tests and waited, sick with terror, for the results. At one time I was in a nursing home after an operation and Penny was in a hospital down the road where Rosie was on a drip. Months went by and there was no improvement and then, for no apparent reason, she began to recover. Now, as I'm writing, a nine-year-old girl with large eyes, long fair hair, a hatred of wearing dresses and an indomitable will is grooming a pony, getting ready to go out hunting with her mother.

The trouble I'd had during Rosie's illness was negligible by comparison. Careless Thetis held her child Achilles by the heel when she dipped him into the Styx for the purpose of making every part of his body invulnerable; this accounts for the peculiar weakness of the Achilles tendon. Keen squash and tennis players often hear a report like a pistol shot when this cord snaps; mine gave out quietly, discreetly, and over a long period of time. The operation to repair it caused a deep vein thrombosis in my other leg, which swelled up as though it had to support an ancient piano. For this condition I was put on a course of rat poison, which thins the blood. It's said to be advisable to avoid alcohol during this process, a warning which I have to say I disregarded entirely. I also spent a good deal of time in a wheelchair.

What I then discovered were some of the humiliations of childhood, because the chair reduces you to a child's height. At parties everyone talks over your head and forgets to include you in the conversation. The most ridiculous event occurred when I was asked to a charity dinner in the ballroom of a Piccadilly hotel. Because I was going to make a speech, I was ceremoniously piped in by a platoon of Gurkhas and propelled between their ranks by a hostess from British Caledonian Airlines, provided by the charity organizers of the evening. The air hostess pushed, the Gurkhas blew, the ballroom was alight with 1930s splendour – and then the wheel fell off my chair. I have been in many absurd situations during a long life, but none so ridiculous as when I found myself legless in a crowded ballroom, seated in a crashed wheelchair with a Gurkha band of honour resolutely blowing its bagpipes.

We also gave Rosie the name of Lucy, who had been almost the same age as Emily, lived next to us and was like a sister to her. When Emily and Lucy were quite young and we were filming *A Voyage Round My Father* they climbed into Laurence Olivier's caravan, experimented with his make-up and tried on his wig. Lucy was the daughter of Suzannah and the Pipers' grandchild. When she was nine, she ran out of the gate to catch the school bus and a car killed her instantly. I don't think any of us have recovered from this; in spite of his religious faith John Piper could never explain or get over it. It's a small paragraph in the indictment against God.

17

Taking over other people's houses is like taking over their lives. For many years I rented the homes of strangers to take my family to for summer holidays. The first was in Positano and I used to carry Jeremy, a small child in a white hat, up a thousand steps from the beach, while his sister Sally insisted that we were in Scotland. Later we took houses in Ravello, Greece and the South of France. I remember a strange house in Orbitello, where the gardener kept dead birds and rabbits hanging in the well. On one such holiday our landlord refused to move out but lurked about the house at night, accompanied by a silent parrot. He left threatening notes about the state of the bathroom for us to find in the mornings. When we told him we needed all the bedrooms, he and the bird spent the night in his car at the end of the drive. His case was an exception; for the most part we never met the people in whose pools we swam, on whose ping-pong tables we played and in whose beds we slept. We had answered an advertisement and had few clues about our hosts, other than some faded photographs of the house and a route which usually sounded dauntingly complex: 'Turn right by the large ilex tree shortly after the ten-kilometre stone on the left, past the Agip service station. Then double back down the dirt-track where a dog is chained by a shed with a pink door. Do not miss this turning or you will be returned immediately to the Roma–Bologna motorway.'

*

After the endless journey down the autostrada, with children who have finished their comics at Calais lying in the back, feeling sick, asking you exactly how long it will take to get to a place you've never been to before and making false allegations of longing for the lavatory in the next Motta bar, we would arrive at our home for the next three weeks. The description of fields of melons and strawberries surrounding the property may have meant only a burnt-out patch of withered sunflowers, the olive grove may have consisted of two stunted trees, but the bougainvillaea was in flower, there were bright geraniums in pots on the terrace and the swimming-pool was not yet afflicted by the drought. The thunder of a distant Lambretta would undoubtedly bring the formidable maid to unlock the front door, giving us that smile of daunting welcome perfected by air hostesses and hospital matrons. She was there to guard the rights of the absentee landlords and her chief duty over the ensuing weeks would be to watch hawk-eyed for signs of broken glasses, straw hats borrowed from the hall stand and dropped in the pool, or knives taken out on picnics and lost for ever.

As the children argued about the bedrooms, and after removing piles of comics, half-eaten sandwiches and half-empty packets of raspberry crush from the back of the car, I would start on my great holiday interest – detection. Playing the role of Poirot or Sherlock Holmes, I'd try to discover, from such clues as the empty house might offer, something about the characters we were dispossessing.

There are certain things which those who let their houses for the summer have in common. They are extraordinarily knowledgeable about the electrical and plumbing systems of their dwellings, and capable of giving instructions for their use in minute detail. These orders, accompanied by dire warnings of the disastrous consequences of disobedience, cover several sheets of duplicated typescript and are sent out like battle commands with the route and the photographs: *None of the following devices should, on any account, be switched on at the same time: the heater in the master bedroom, the*

swimming-pool filter or the dish-washing machine. If a hair-drier is in use,
it's wise to disconnect the refrigerator. More detailed instructions will be
found taped to the appliances concerned. Above all, avoid flushing the
lavatory next to the small sitting-room more than once in any half hour or
serious consequences may follow. Given the tone of these words of
command (*The chain requires one sharp downward pull! Do not, on any*
account, be tentative or give repeated tugs, which may be counter-productive),
every loo becomes an object of dread and you can't switch on the
record-player without fearing the sudden demise of the oven.

Some houses furnish clues in the shape of manuscript volumes
bound in marble paper and bought in Florence or Siena. These
may have been intended for tenants to write usually unrevealing
comments: 'Two weeks of bliss, the Thompsons will come again' or
'Tracy and Tim Maynard broke the Rioja-drinking record poolside
on Sunday morning and finally got Maria-Teresa to smile. *Hasta la*
vista!' In one house we thought we had struck gold: the owners
kept a bulky volume describing all the dinner parties they had ever
given. First came the menus, then the list of guests which included
such heavily dropped names as Tennessee Williams, Visconti, and
even Maria Callas on one occasion. Then came the comments. Did
these record the table talk of the great and famous? Did they
throw a flood of light on the lives and loves of hosts and guests?
They did not. The notes were strictly confined to such profound
observations as 'cannelloni a little too *al dente*' or 'saltimbocca on
the tough side but soufflé a rare success'. This too was, I suppose,
revealing in its way.

On very rare occasions the owners hand out straight information.
In one house in France they were clearly not getting on. The wife,
obviously a methodical lady, made a list of the attributes on which
she would have to rely were she to set out on a new, unmarried
existence. The document, left face upwards beside the telephone,
was headed MY ASSETS and began: 1. Extreme physical beauty 2.
A certain ability to type. She had also made a list WHAT IS
IMPORTANT IN MY LIFE in which the house itself came first,

someone called Gaston second and the rest of the family also ran. What was surprising about these lists was not that they should have been made (we all have to sort out our priorities) but that they should have been left so obviously to add interest and excitement to our stay.

It's often necessary, as the holiday sinks into its accident-prone middle period, to call the landlord about some disaster. In the dry Tuscan hills the water will run out, whether as an act of God or as the result of some dubious human conspiracy it is difficult to say. We have had to buy water by the lorry load from Siena which, on one nightmare night when we were reduced to boiling the spaghetti in San Pellegrino, was delivered into the swimming-pool by mistake. Into the same swimming-pool, on another memorable occasion, a horse fell during the hours of darkness and, unable to emerge, was found at dawn, blinking in the shallow end. Once the slenderest member of the party was lowered down the well in search of an obstruction. In another rented house, a rat regularly visited the kitchen. 'A rat?' said the landlord when we telephoned him. 'That's most unusual. But you'd better ask the maid to buy some glue.' Glue? He was no doubt sitting comfortably in his London office, a place where the water gushes out of taps and no one has to be lowered down the well; he was enjoying the luxury of not being on holiday. On that occasion we ignored his instructions. Far better to have a rat scuttling across the kitchen floor than one glued to it in squeaking immobility.

Holidays can be brutal occasions. Husbands and wives, usually protected by jobs, office routines, secretaries and bosses, are forced into each other's company for twenty-four hours a day. Teenage daughters are deprived of their friends, parties, nights at the Mud Club, the Café de Paris or assorted discos, and find little to do but change their clothes or collapse on their beds in terminal boredom. Aged grandparents sit in the backs of cars and try to keep up everyone's spirits; their efforts are not always successful. And yet in unaccustomed sunshine, paying unaccustomed visits to churches

Castle Howard visited: with Laurence Olivier, Charles Sturridge (director) and Derek Granger (producer)

With John Gielgud: chain-smoking, bubbling with reminiscences and eighty-five years old on the set of *Summer's Lease*

Penny with Rosie

Rosie and I, both under the weather

In the grounds of the Novodevichy Convent with
Henrietta Dobryakova and Emily

John Piper, with a face like a cardinal and a taste for drinking
a good deal of red wine with everything

Myfanwy Piper: John Betjeman wrote a poem about her fortunate bicycle

With Neil Kinnock and Barbara Castle: she's eloquent, scornful and unfashionably optimistic

In Tbilisi with the ghost of Stalin and a glass of Georgian red

Rosie, nine years old with large eyes and an indomitable will

Emily has learnt to speak beautiful lines in a language I can't understand

Sally: if the world's divided into patients and nurses,
she's one of the great nurses

Jeremy, gentler and calmer than his sisters

My Aunt Gertie known to the Zulu community as Umuthimkulu,
The Great Tree or The One Who Offers Shade

The children act us (*left to right*): Emma Hodge as Anna Ford,
Tom Ward as Katie Boxer, Emily as Rosie, Claire Boxer as me,
Katie Boxer as Tom Ward, Rosie as Penny

and cathedrals, pausing, however briefly, in front of great works of art, the visiting family may not only discover unusual and interesting things about their landlords but about each other. For these reasons I think it worth the considerable risk of renting a house and going on holiday.

I wrote much of *Summer's Lease* in an Italian house about fifteen miles to the east of Siena and, as the directions would say, you turn right past the castle and go on down a rough, dusty road, across a hillside that smells of wild fennel and wild thyme, until the road stops at the house and you can go, and would wish to go, no further. It's an old, converted *casa colonnica*, a farm manager's house; its big, cool rooms can accommodate many friends and a large assortment of children. The wine comes from the castle at the end of the road, and can be drunk in large quantities with no ill effects whatsoever. This castle, and a larger one built on the strangely Gothic lines of Balmoral, belongs to the Ricasoli family. I think it was early in the last century that, at a ball in Rome, the then Baron Ricasoli's wife danced twice with a handsome young officer. Her furious husband dragged her out into the winter's night in her thin ball-gown, threw her into his carriage and drove her to his castle in Tuscany. There he kept her prisoner and passed the long, tedious years while he stood guard over her, discovering the proper mixture of red and white grapes which became the classic wine of Chianti.

I suppose, if I didn't consider myself stuck for life in my father's house, that corner of Italy is where I would choose to live. There is nowhere else where you can travel so easily to see paintings, where you can sit in such beautiful squares in so many small towns, where trees are as green as they are in England and the sun is never too hot; where the food is fresh and, unlike food in France, or nowadays in England, tastes of exactly what it's made of, and where, on a warm night among the towers of San Gimignano, you can watch *Rigoletto* as the moon travels slowly across the sky. Is is also the place, again unlike England, where children are welcome.

The English have always been drawn to Tuscany, so that in the last century the common Italian word for foreigners, no matter from what country they came, was *inglesi*. One hotel porter in Siena was apparently heard to say, 'We've got six English in tonight: three of them are French, two German and one Russian.' The fountain of all knowledge about the Brits in Chiantishire was Harold Acton. Was he the original Anthony Blanche, the prickly aesthete in *Brideshead Revisited*? Admittedly he used to recite *The Waste Land* through a megaphone while at Oxford. When I visited him he lived in a villa, built by a Medici banker, on the outskirts of Florence. If it always seemed late afternoon indoors, the garden was full of sunshine. It boasted huge statues and a theatre made of lawns and hedges in which the Diaghilev Ballet, marooned in Florence during the 1914 war, once danced for the boy Acton. He was an old man, looked after by servants who may once have been handsome but now seemed grumpy in their old age. We sat together between two giant statues and his mind went back so far, to so many famous and notorious English visitors, that I asked him, in a moment of complete confusion, if he'd ever met Browning.

'Not *Robert* Browning, of course, but I knew his son Pen. Pen Browning had one great interest in life and that was (here he separated the syllables as delicately as though he were peeling a peach with a sharp silver knife) forn–ic–ation. In fact Pen was so fond of forn–ic–ation that his offspring were to be found in all the villages round Florence.' I thought of the cafés in Fiesole where the barmen and the customers are, perhaps, descendants of the Barretts of Wimpole Street. As the tall, bald man wearing a dark city suit in the Italian sunshine went on talking with immaculate courtesy in his precise accent ('My mother's family,' he said, 'comes from Chee – car – go'), great ghosts of the past seemed to steal out from behind the clipped hedges and wander among the white marble gods and heroes. There went a Miss Paget, who knew Browning well, and there Max Beerbohm ('A bit of an actor with a wife who was humourless although she had been on the stage'). And then D.H. Lawrence ('A genius as a writer but a disagreeable man with a ferocious German wife'). Also present was Reggie Turner, who was with Oscar Wilde when he died. Then came Ouida, the Victorian Barbara Cartland ('She died in poverty because she spent all her money on her dog'), and Ronald Firbank, 'the ornate and nervous novelist' who wrote *Valmouth*. ('Firbank admired Oscar Wilde so much that he bought armfuls of lilies and threw them at Reggie Turner, who was a very ugly little man with a face which looked as though it had been carved out of India rubber.') So why did these extraordinary English make their way to Chiantishire? 'Because,' said Sir Harold, 'the English and the Tuscans are very similar characters. We're both practical, unde-monstrative people with a love of proverbs. We both like the same sort of food, nursery cooking.'

Harold Acton said in *Who's Who* that his recreations were jettatura (which I take to mean putting the evil eye on persons) and 'hunting the Philistine'. When I asked him about this he said, 'It really comes from the time I was at Oxford. I used to go at them with my umbrella. They usually ran away. All Philistines are cowards at heart.'

Much of *Summer's Lease* goes on in the mind of the central character, a bothered housewife whose life takes on a new dimension during an Italian holiday. This made it a hard book to dramatize but thanks to the director and cameraman and an extraordinary cast I think the television version worked well. The book contains a lecherous old journalist, author of an appalling column called Jottings, which he fills with random and frequently pretentious thoughts. Haverford Downs insists on joining the family holiday and does his best to shock his grandchildren. Grandchildren are now, of course, quite unshockable, so he has to be content with shocking his boring solicitor son-in-law, which is rather too easy, and his daughter Molly, who is not quite so vulnerable. To my surprise and total delight, John Gielgud agreed to play Haverford, a consummation I had never hoped for when, a myopic eleven-year-old boy, I had sat in the stalls and heard the handsome and troubled student prince say, 'Nymph, in thy orizons be all my sins remembered', the line that always brought tears to my father's eyes.

I had got to know John Gielgud a little since we had met at Tony Richardson's London house. Emily was a baby then and we had brought her with us in her carrycot and left her in a spare bedroom. We were lugging this pink plastic box out of the front door when Gielgud saw us and said, 'Why on earth didn't you leave your baby at home? Were you afraid of burglars?'

The great tragedian became a great comic actor; this is understandable because of the number of jokes in *Hamlet* and *King Lear* (Macbeth's ambition ruled out a sense of humour). The wartime *The Importance of Being Earnest* has gone down in history because of the way Edith Evans said the word 'handbag'; it was equally notable for Gielgud's wonderfully serious-comical performance as John Worthing. His understated comedy and immaculate timing became apparent to cinema audiences with Tony Richardson's *The Charge of the Light Brigade*, in which he acted Lord Raglan. He had some, although not much, previous experience of war scenes and horses. He played King Louis of France in the film of *Becket* and played it on horseback. The director told him he would say the line and then the horse would move one pace forward. At the first take he said the line, of course impeccably, but the horse remained immobile. By the seventh take the horse had still not moved on cue, or at all. Then a puzzled Gielgud asked the director, 'Do you think the animal *knows*?'

The young Gielgud had the talent of all the Terrys ('poor lachrymal glands, you know') of crying at will. His movements were less certain; his first drama teacher said he walked like a 'cat with rickets', and a hostile critic said, I'm sure without justification, 'Mr Gielgud means absolutely nothing from the waist down.' But although he was never an athletic actor like Olivier, he arrived on the set of *Summer's Lease* at the age of eighty-five with a straight back, blue eyes bright with curiosity, chain-smoking and bubbling with reminiscences: 'You know Marlene Dietrich played me records of her concerts which consisted solely of applause?'; 'Elisabeth Bergner in *As You Like It* made Olivier film his scenes with Rosalind entirely by himself so she could work out how to upstage him'; 'Tynan said I only had two gestures: the left hand up, the right hand up. What did he want me to do, bring out my prick?'; 'Another critic, James Agate, came round to see me during the interval when I was playing Macbeth and said, "I've come to congratulate you now; by the end of the performance I'll probably have changed my mind!"'

During the filming Gielgud was taken ill and had to be flown to England for a small but necessary operation. He was soon back, as straight-backed and elegant, smoking and talking as energetically, as before. He had a scene with Chaliapin's son, who was also over eighty and played an aged Italian count with whom Haverford Downs gets into bed by mistake. 'Do you think,' Gielgud asked with genuine concern, 'the old boy will be able to remember his lines?'

We had a party scene to shoot that would require working all night in the garden of the huge rose-pink and floodlit Villa la Vignamaggio near Greve in Chianti. The Italian assistant shouted, *'Silenzio, giriamo!'* and the English assistant called, in more apologetic tones, 'Settle down now, we *are* shooting.' Word went out on the walkie-talkies and, on dark and distant roads, the shrill cries of Fiats and the falsetto solos of buses were silenced. Only films provide a writer with a chance of stopping the traffic. When we broke for supper, and the extras made a concerted rush for the catering van, I sat on the terrace with John, who had just been reading a book about Lord Lucan. 'Could you really get someone to do a murder for £3,000?' he asked with genuine curiosity. 'I suppose Donald Wolfit might almost have paid that to get rid of me. He did *hate* me so much.'

And then he remembered, as Harold Acton had, relics of the heyday of Oscar Wilde and the friends and enemies who survived him. 'Lord Alfred Douglas was a beautiful young man who ended up sour and ugly. Can you believe this? He was at the first night of *The Importance of Being Earnest*, so I asked him how it was played. Was it done as satire or as a comedy of manners, and how broad was the comedy? Do you know, Douglas just couldn't tell me! He was Wilde's closest friend and he couldn't remember anything about the production at all.'

John Gielgud went to bed early, long before we finished work on the other scenes. It was five o'clock in the morning, the nightingales in the villa garden had fallen silent and there was an increased sense of urgency. The night scene had to be finished quickly before it was flooded with the cruel light of day and would become completely unreal.

18

Poor times are good times for the countryside. Bankrupt developers are unable to pollute what they like to call 'greenfield sites'. The eighties brought a curse which some people called prosperity. It was the age when self-respect went with two cars and owning your own house; if you had less than these minimum requirements you might well be living in a cardboard box. House prices in our valley spiralled to dizzy heights; a cottage with a leaking roof and a handkerchief of a garden could cost as much as a sizeable London house. Motorways were built and seemed in instant need of repair, so travellers who might have been speeding along in trains crawled, at the speed of a slow nervous breakdown, among the cones. Market towns, which had boasted wide streets, Georgian town halls and ancient churches were developed, operated on and degutted. Dreary and lifeless pedestrian precincts and shopping centres were inserted like useless pacemakers into their hearts. In such centres the wind blew empty Coca-Cola tins among concrete pots in which shrubs died, and the shops sold nothing anyone might want – such as fish, meat or ironmongery – but specialized in 'gifts', padded coathangers and embroidered knicker-bags, and greetings cards. These shops rapidly went bankrupt and the pedestrian precincts became places where the outcasts of the monetarist society might urinate and sleep, or where pupils from the local polytechnic, now called a university, could deal in more or less harmless drugs.

Henley, a small riverside town, suffered from the current malaise. It has a handsome bridge, decorated with sculptured masks of Thames and Isis; a fourteenth-century chantry house; the Red Lion, where Coleridge was billeted when a dragoon; and a small Regency theatre where, it's said, Sarah Siddons once acted. Cavaliers and Roundheads fought a battle in Duke Street. William Lenthall, the Speaker of the parliament that defeated Charles, was born there and Prince Rupert hanged a spy on a tree outside the smaller post office. In the eighties, rapacious landlords made its tradesmen's lives impossible, useful shops vanished and an ever-changing assortment of boutiques and pine furniture stores took their place. The small shops not only had to struggle with their landlords but with the local supermarket, part of a prosperous chain, which planned to grow enormously in size and pull down the cinema.

Some people said we had a greatly exaggerated affection for the Henley cinema. It was a 1930s building, but perhaps not to be mentioned in the same breath as the Hoover building or the Odeon, Leicester Square. However, it had one of the finest cinema organs in the land, which rose up miraculously from the bowels of the earth in a beam of changing purple, green, orange and scarlet light. At the end of the recital ('Deep Purple', 'Smoke Gets in Your Eyes' and 'The Isle of Capri'), a disembodied voice would tell us that 'All the music played at this performance is available from Messrs Woolworths.' I first saw Fred Astaire and Ginger Rogers there, and Bob Hope, Dorothy Lamour and Bing Crosby, and Greta Garbo in *Queen Christina*. I saw, and shall never forget, a film called *The Mummy* in which some long-entombed Egyptian prince left his hieroglyph-covered case and slowly crossed the room, trailing his bandages behind him. On the way home I pretended to be asleep in the back of the Morris Oxford in order that I might be carried up to bed, where I lay for hours with my eyes open, terrified of seeing a trail of mouldering linen curling round the door.

The fight for the Henley cinema was protracted. We gave star-studded concerts in the theatre, law-suits were financed and, at one mass rally, the marketplace looked, for a glorious moment, something like Wenceslas Square at the collapse of Communism. Waitrose Ltd and the South Oxfordshire District Council proved, however, harder nuts to crack than the red peril and were quite unwilling to surrender to any velvet revolution.

Fighting for the countryside broke out on all fronts. Bands of developers, buying options on land from greedy farmers, were constantly seeking to build new towns. One such scheme was suggested near Thame, which would have swallowed up a number of villages and village churches and caused even more traffic confusion. Any person wishing to provide housing, which is no doubt needed, could have built a new town on the outskirts of Cowley. Of course greenfield sites were cheaper and the developers applied for permission for Stone Bassett – soulless urban sites are always given charmingly rustic names such as Broadwater Farm and Blackbird Leys, a god-forsaken housing estate where stolen cars are raced and then burnt.

The fight against Stone Bassett cost the local villagers, who had never invited it, huge sums of money. Michael Heseltine, the member for Henley-on-Thames, gave evidence in support of the view that Stone Bassett would do great harm to the district. After the case was won, I congratulated him on behaving extremely well. He thanked me but begged me not to repeat my kind words in public. Any praise from me, he was convinced, would ruin his chances in the Conservative Party. He seems to be one of the few remaining politicians with anything like a personality, so I assured him I wouldn't breathe a word in his praise. I went further. I promised that if he went on behaving admirably, I would write a scathing attack on him. He seemed grateful for that.

It took over a year to make *Paradise Postponed*, which filled eleven hours of television. In time, if nothing else, it was like writing the three parts of *Henry VI* or a couple of pretty hefty Wagner operas. Michael Hordern, who had made *The Dock Brief* a success, played the comfortably off left-wing vicar. There were memorable performances from Jill Bennett, Zoë Wannamaker, Peter Egan, Annette Crosbie, Paul Shelley and many more. The production was not entirely happy. The director was Alvin Rakoff, who had done *A Voyage Round My Father* very well. I was delighted when he said he'd do the series. Then things began to go wrong. He quarrelled with Jacquie Davis, the gentlest of producers, who, as always, was desperately anxious that every detail and every performance should be exactly right. The enormous schedule took its toll and the days often ended in tears. However, the shooting ended without any serious casualties. The greatest embarrassment was caused to the business man who rented part of his converted vicarage as Michael Hordern's home. During the Easter break he invited a Conservative politician to dinner without telling him that he had hired out some of his house for filming. On his way back from the loo the politician stumbled into a room we had dressed as the vicar's study. He was astounded to see a bust of Karl Marx, numerous CND posters and Left Book Club hardbacks next to bound copies of *Tribune*. He came to the conclusion that our landlord was a closet lefty of the most dangerous variety.

The discovery was David Threlfall and the credit for it must go to Alvin. I had only seen Threlfall as Smike, the ill-used, put upon and pathetically grateful victim of Dr Wackford Squeers in *Nicholas Nickleby*. I had no idea he could play that political rottweiler the Rt Hon. Leslie Titmuss, MP, and his performance only emerged slowly. At the read-through the older actors sat on one side of a long narrow table, referred to by Michael Hordern as the 'generation gap', and the younger actors sat on the other. The gap was immediately apparent when the reading began. Older actors perform, are audible, rush to meet their characters with open arms; the young ones give a muttered rendering that is little help to the author and take care not to give away what they plan to do.

Nothing emerged from David in the first days, but the performance, when it came, was extraordinary. The cold, classless, carefully ironic voice, the pale intensity, the unremitting tension and moments of sarcastic delight – David Threlfall became Titmuss in the way Leo McKern became Rumpole. When he acted, it was impossible to think of the part being played by anyone else.

I thought it might be interesting to follow the fortunes of Leslie Titmuss past the Falklands War, when *Paradise Postponed* ended, into the late Thatcher years. I thought we might see Titmuss in love. And then Nicholas Ridley, a cabinet minister who always expressed himself as being passionate for freedom from government restrictions, was found to have been just as passionately in favour of the planning laws when there was a building development threatened near to his Georgian country house. I thought of facing Titmuss with a similar dilemma. All we had gone through trying to save the cinema and stop the new town should provide ample scope for comedy.

To make the television version of *Titmuss Regained* and our subsequent productions, Jacquie and I started a production company and became, if not complete converts to the Titmuss view of life, at least entrepreneurs, mini-capitalists running a small business. The risks we took were not enormous. Thames Television provided the money, but we had the responsibility of spending it; we could engage the performers and technicians and we had to keep within our budget. On the first day of filming we looked at the great army we had recruited – the Winnebagos for stars' dressing-rooms, the make-up and wardrobe vans, the catering lorry, the honey wagon, where the army could pee, and the huge bus where they could sit and eat breakfast, elevenses, lunch and tea (unlike schools, television companies still have to provide free dinners) – and I, at any rate, felt a certain terror. I have absolutely no head for figures and, when a barrister, always avoided fraud cases for that reason.

One small piece of money was well spent. I'd seen Kristin Scott

Thomas in a film of *A Handful of Dust* and I thought she was just the right wife for Titmuss. She could be beautiful and vague, determined to avoid, if possible, any uncomfortable reality such as his character. And he would be utterly confused by the delicacy of her feelings. Finally, he would even reject forgiveness because such behaviour was not in his nature. We found Kristin living in Paris with a French gynaecologist husband and two children. She'd had a strange career. She was doing a stage management course at a London drama school and she said she wanted to be an actress. Apparently she was greeted with some such caustic phrase as '*You, an actress!*', at which she not only gave up her course but gave up England, went to Paris and studied acting there. After the Waugh story, she had been in many French and German films. Jacquie, the director Martyn Friend and I took her out to lunch in a restaurant near the Sorbonne and she was clearly the character I'd written. She acted it perfectly, looked beautiful and would be a great star if only we had a film industry.

The organizations which seek to protect the countryside are sometimes fatal to it. No doubt when the South of England is mostly under concrete, with motorways joining new towns, car parks leading to more car parks, with a maze of pedestrian precincts weaving between them, there will be some green areas. Those will be left for the ramblers' associations, where the senior citizens' 'nature walk opportunities' will be clearly marked and children may be allowed to pick wild flowers on the first Thursday of every month. This is the urban attitude to country living: the longing to tidy up the country and make it less alarming. It leads to hunt saboteurs and the RSPCA endangering animal farming in Southern England by endless prosecutions. The country flourishes on neglect and has to do with dark woods, where fallen trees are left to rot and crawl with life, where animals hunt and are hunted, where life and death, birth and decomposition are not interfered with or inspected too much.

What would the world be, once bereft
Of wet and wildness? Let them be left,
O let them be left, wildness and wet;
Long live the weeds and the wilderness yet

wrote Gerard Manley Hopkins, who had never even seen a multi-storey car park or a pedestrian precinct.

Titmuss Regained begins with a scene in which a couple are making love in an uncultivated meadow, beneath a stretch of woodland. They are interrupted by a furious and bearded warden, who says they might be crushing a stone curlew's egg and shouts, 'Can't you lot read? . . . This place is reserved for nature!' The couple who performed this on a cold October day did it well enough, but such scenes, now mandatory in all television plays, are often better left to the reader's imagination. I discovered that these performances are sometimes taken extremely seriously. An actress, whom I'll call June, told me that she was asked to do a 'struggling-about-in-bed' scene with a male star. The star said to her, 'We don't go in for this type of work, do we, June?', and she agreed. So male and female stand-ins (or lie-ins) were engaged to do the rough work in their place. The male stand-in, not realizing that June wasn't to be his partner, came up to her in the canteen and said, 'How'd you like me to play our scene, dear? Full erect, half erect or limp?' I suppose it's a talent of a sort to have such range.

For one moment during the filming, truth intruded on fiction. We staged a protest march in the valley, where the road leads down to the double gables of Fingest church. We had a large number of extras carrying placards saying SAVE OUR VALLEY and SAY NO TO FALLOWFIELD COUNTRY TOWN. Commuters, on their way to work in London that early morning when we were filming, stopped their cars, got out and asked if they could sign the petition.

19

Emily is *twenty-one. I am sitting in a rehearsal room in the Moscow Arts Theatre watching her acting lesson. The room is large and apparently airtight. Like all rehearsal rooms, it's dusty, unswept and provided only with a few clapped out pieces of furniture. The director is tall with floppy hair and, unlike English directors who sit motionless, making notes, he acts all the time, giving a larger than life demonstration of all the performances. The scene takes place in the bedroom of a suspicious husband who has just brought his wife home from a ball. Everyone is smoking tirelessly while they act or direct. Emily has a long speech and is making beautiful sounds which I cannot understand. The play is by Lermontov, the director is an actor at the Moscow Arts Theatre, the others are students. All Russians act hugely, with thrilling voices and flamboyant gestures. During a break I ask the director how he gets his actors to act so energetically, when it's quite hard to persuade English actors to move their mouths. Large and expansive gestures come naturally to Russians, he says, and tells the following story: 'A man is lost in a strange city. He sees a local inhabitant coming down the street towards him, carrying a huge watermelon, so he asks him the way to the Nijinsky Prospekt, or whatever the street he wants is called. "Just hold my watermelon a moment," the local inhabitant says, and when relieved of his burden he opens his arms in a great gesture of comic despair. "How the hell should I know?" he says, and then he asks for his watermelon back.'*

It was in the sixties, during Russia's bad times, that I first saw Moscow. I remember being sent out, armed only with a phrase book which contained no apposite entry, and a hazy memory of the Greek alphabet, into Red Square on a Sunday morning to buy sanitary towels. Russia is always unpredictable but, surprisingly enough, my mission was successful. In this it was unlike our attempts to get permission to film a version of Anthony Burgess's novel *Honey for the Bears* in what was then the Soviet Union. At endless meetings in a variety of ministries our requests to make this story, which concerned the illegal importation of a suitcase full of nylon underwear, were greeted with encouraging smiles until the final, unvarying *niet* from the top.

I remember the long car rides through birch trees, the children in their red pioneer uniforms dancing for us in restored palaces, and then applauding us with well-drilled charm. I remember a night in a Leningrad hotel, watching a Chinese general in full military uniform waltzing with an elderly gentleman who looked like a senior civil servant in a black jacket and striped trousers. I remember the breakfast that took three hours to come, which I used to order a careful two and a half hours before my then wife woke up, so that she and the cold hard-boiled egg and bottles of beer might, if we were lucky, arrive in the dining-room at the same time. I remember the first sight of gold, onion domes and spires across the water, and men stripped to the waist standing to sunbathe against south-facing walls. Through all the smiling, meaningless conversations in the offices of the film bureaucracy I never forgot Chekhov.

I had first read the plays during the school holidays, and I thought his characters very like us, members of a doomed middle class, living an uneventful life in the country, carrying on a daily battle against boredom. I read them sitting in the garden on long summer evenings, tormented by midges, lonely because my father didn't encourage visitors who might be embarrassingly sympathetic about his blindness. The empty time, aching to be filled, was something I could recognize, as were the unexpected moments of high drama, which came, like all great tragedy, mixed with farce. Later, and with growing excitement, I read Dostoevsky. I revelled in the bizarre comedy and the courage of characters pushed beyond the limits of endurance. I could admire him from the rational calm of an English home where religious passion, self-abasement, wild extravagance and epileptic fits would all be greeted with a nervous smile and a retreat into the shrubbery. In those days Russia meant the story of a seagull shot beside the lake; lovers kissing in the snow of the Nevsky Prospekt; the huge, comical, grotesque, weeping figure of the father of the Karamazovs; and the tap of a hammer on the wheels of Anna Karenina's train. Russia was all in books, and Moscow still seems to me, even after its conquest by McDonald's, the most literary city in the world, the place where people still read seriously on the metro.

During the war the Russians were our heroic allies, standing firm at Stalingrad, luring Hitler to defeat, afflicted neither by Chekhov's poetic uncertainty nor Dostoevsky's penetrating hysteria. After the war Winston and Uncle Joe, smiling broadly, carved Europe up and we discovered the full horror of Stalinist dictatorship. We settled down into that comfortable ice age, the Cold War, where everyone thought they knew who the enemy was and the world was kept comparatively quiet by an imaginary balance of terror. I didn't go back to Russia until the start of the thaw. It was 1988, Gorbachev was in power and he had just stopped a particularly senseless war in Afghanistan. The future seemed warm and bright and no one imagined that the melting ice would end in a torrent of uncheckable racial hatred. I went to Moscow with our National Theatre which was performing Shakespeare's three last plays, autumnal stories of forgiveness. The Company was led by Tim Piggott-Smith, an actor who had shown great power in the television version of *The Jewel in the Crown*, Eileen Atkins and Geraldine James. I was there to chronicle their progress through a land an American president had called 'barbaric'. It was also a place of beautiful buildings, hilarious evenings and people of great generosity and warmth.

Actors on tour, and film units on location, bring their own world with them, like snails in shells or armies on the march. They bring their jealousies, love affairs, rivalries, disappointments and the expectation of five-star treatment once they are sent abroad. Such luxury was not readily available in the Peking Hotel in Mayakovsky Square, a gloomy building, decorated inside like an old touring set for *Chu Chin Chow*. When, after prolonged formalities, I was shown into my vast bedroom it became apparent, in the gloaming, that two men in blue suits were lying on my bed, eating cucumbers from a plastic bag. Having no Russian I didn't know how to invite them to leave, so I unpacked, hung up my clothes in cavernous cupboards and, when my visitors started to refresh themselves from a carton of milk, I went off to find the lady at the end of the passage. These custodians of the keys used to be large and unsmiling; with the advent of glasnost I found a youngish blonde wrapped in an eiderdown and she, after some argument, persuaded my visitors to leave. One of the actors was less fortunate. Coming back late at night, he found a man in his bed watching television. When he protested, the girl at the end of his passage nodded understandingly and fetched a camp bed which she erected so that he, and his newfound friend, could watch television together.

Peter Hall, who directed the last plays of reconciliation with great simplicity and understanding, did not care for Russia. I had known him so long, off and on through his various marriages, and we had sat together so often in the National Theatre boardroom, where he displayed those extraordinary political skills which are even more impressive than his understanding of Shakespeare's verse. His life had been a marvellously organized flight from the small town where his father was stationmaster, the single bar of an electric fire to study by, and the relations who called birth a 'happy event' and death a 'merciful release'. Moscow seemed, to him, to be everything he had escaped. Breakfast at the Peking Hotel, consisting as it did of pork and roast potatoes, rice pudding, buttermilk and cold soft-boiled eggs, appealed to him not at all. The ponderous Russian critics, trained in Marxist dialectic, said they failed to find a 'social message' in his productions. Glasnost, Peter judged, had changed nothing and Moscow, hot as Antibes and smelling of lilac and petrol fumes, was irredeemably working class. Some of the actors were invited to Sunday lunch in the country. Unfortunately their journey took them through a prohibited military zone and they came back with tales of having been chased by the police, hiding in ditches and lying flat on the floor of their host's bedroom when the authorities came to look for them. Peter, it seemed, had taken a wiser course: a taxi to the airport and a plane back to London. He left the Russians a marvellous production of *Cymbeline*, which had no message except its story of past injustices and old brutalities forgiven. As the king at the end of the play says, 'Pardon's the word to all.'

'In the West I know you can go into a shop at the end of the street and find twenty-five different sorts of yoghurt. Here you are lucky if you find one sort. I tell you, life for us is so hard. We have so little and have to queue for it so long. What can we do but live a rich inner life? So we read books and poetry and, when we can, we go to the theatre.' I was talking to Olga, a university graduate and a poet who had translated for me at the Theatre Workers' Union. She said she had not been feeling well recently; it seemed to her that she was about to die. The reason, of course, was that her mother was casting spells on her. 'Why on earth should she do that?' I asked, not questioning the spells. 'Mainly, I think, because she wants to get me out of the apartment where my husband and I and our child are living with her and my stepfather and his child by a previous marriage. I am sure that my mother is burning a candle in church from the wrong end, which I know is the way to kill someone. When I was a small girl my mother loved me, but now I have grown to be a beautiful woman she is very jealous. Of course, I have to pray very hard to recover from the illness my mother has brought upon me.' The conflict of families and incantations in one small apartment was terrible to contemplate. Not only Orthodox religion and the love of icons but a reliance on witchcraft seemed to have survived Lenin, Stalin, Brezhnev and the age of reason.

'I am translating this short story,' Olga told me as we were walking down what was then still Gorky Street, 'and I came to the following sentence, "He called in to the motel for a meal and a good bonk." How should I translate, please, "a good bonk"? Is it a beer, perhaps, or a cup of coffee?'

'It takes a bit of explaining,' I told her. 'Shall we go and have a drink at the National Hotel?'

'Oh, you mean,' she smiled charmingly, 'have a good bonk?'

We sat at lunch with our new friend, Henrietta Dobryakova, a short, plump, middle-aged woman with the eyes of a schoolgirl. She worked at the Stanislavsky Museum, sitting among the master's furniture and luggage, his books, photographs and the costumes he had designed for him by Gordon Craig, longing for a cigarette. Her husband, surprisingly young-looking and slender, made children's films. Henrietta spoke English caressingly, in a voice which seemed to be making a gently amorous approach to the language. We were entertaining the Professor, small, grey-haired and opinionated, an elderly man whose son had been imprisoned for his beliefs in the Brezhnev era. Now he spent his time caring for his sick wife and studying the life and works of H.G. Wells. Geraldine James was with us, the actress with a mass of red hair, Imogen who became the boy Fidele, at whose supposed death the lines 'Golden lads and girls all must, As chimney-sweepers, come to dust' are sung. Geraldine was a good friend to take to the holy city of Zagorsk or share champanski and red caviare with in the National Hotel.

Henrietta was talking about a previous short-lived thaw, the momentary appearance of glasnost when Khrushchev was in power. 'He promised us freedom,' she told us, 'but all we got were the Olympic Games.'

'My mother was English, my father was a Russian working in China,' the Professor told us. 'They chose Russia as the best country in the world. So see what a life they gave me! A good deal of war. A lot of Stalin. A moment of hope with Khrushchev and then years of Brezhnev, who was too stupid to open his mouth without a bit of paper in his hand. And now freedom when I'm too old to enjoy it.'

'Are the workers really interested in freedom to write books and plays? Don't they want more food to buy?' I asked. A huge shop window in Gorky Street contained no more than three yellowing cabbages, each mounted on an ornate stand.

'I have no idea what the workers want.' The Professor gave me a lofty smile. 'I am of the intelligentsia. I know little of the workers.' I thought Peter Hall had been mistaken in thinking Russia a working-class society. 'I do not know what will happen, quite honestly,' he went on. 'We would like Gorbachev to win but Russia has eighteen million bureaucrats who have their jobs to look after. They don't want too much change.'

'In Stalin's time,' Olga said in a wistful fashion, 'the bureaucrats could have been killed off, but that's not the way we do things now.'

'What will you take?' The Professor was studying the menu, prepared to eat for the intelligentsia. 'The red caviare, I think. And then will you take piglet? I see that they have it.'

'I don't think I'm very keen on piglet,' Geraldine confessed.

'Why not?' The Professor fixed her with a gimlet eye. He was at his most challenging. 'Why shouldn't you like it? Haven't you an actor in your company, Tim Piglet-Smith?'

'Do you ever feel tempted to leave Russia?' I asked, remembering his account of the political history of his lifetime and trying to drag the conversation back to world events.

'Leave? Why should I leave?'

'You're a Jew. Your son was in prison. Didn't you ever think of leaving?'

'Of course not. This is my country. Anywhere else I should be a stranger.'

Henrietta took me to visit the Director of the Moscow Arts Theatre – Mr Yefremov, thin, fine-boned, as elegantly dressed as one of the light comedy performers of the Rex Harrison period. Acting as an interpreter, Henrietta was unusually nervous and in considerable awe of Mr Yefremov. I also knew that she was afraid to smoke in his presence and was longing for the moment when she would be free to dash to the room in the Arts Theatre dedicated to smoking and, feeling her way through grey clouds as thick as those that hang over the stage during a Royal Shakespeare battle scene, light up a Cosmos. To add to her torment, Mr Yefremov himself applied a gold and tortoiseshell lighter to a Chesterfield. 'When all books and newspapers were censored,' he said, 'the theatre had to speak out and take the lead with new ideas. Now the newspapers are free to discuss everything and the theatre can return to its proper work.'

'Which is?'

'Plays about people. Their individual souls. The new kind of plays will be the old kind of plays.'

The night before, during an interval in *The Winter's Tale*, I was having a glass of sweet champagne with a writer. 'What kept the soul of Russia free in the bad years?' he said. 'I will tell you. The theatre. During the 1960s and 1970s, do you know what was the most popular play? Chekhov's *Ivanov*.'

'Because it's against authority?'

'No. Because it's against everything.'

The complex, even Byzantine, diplomatic strategy of the tour was organized by Thelma Holt, small, dynamic, loquacious, and a great figure in the theatre. She ran the Open Space with Charles Marowitz and the Round House in Chalk Farm before it surrendered to the drug culture and she went into world drama. With a high sense of Catholic morality and utter fearlessness, she thrives on disaster and difficulties which amuse her, entertain her and provide her, if serious enough, with a challenge worthy of her great talents for organization. She had to plan the movement of the three last Shakespeare plays from Moscow to Tbilisi in Georgia. This operation proved one historical fact to my entire satisfaction: in spite of all the horror stories during the Cold War period, the West never had anything to fear from a Russian invasion. On the night they were to load the scenery from the Moscow Arts Theatre, the three British truck drivers were told they couldn't have permits to make the journey to the Caucasus. What was offered by the state touring organization, the perpetually accident-prone Goskonzert, was a number of open army lorries with Russian drivers forbidden to go more than some two hundred miles a day. The whole trek, it was calculated, would take five or six days, so the scenery wouldn't arrive in time. Could we get a Jumbo jet, or should we decline to go? For most of the night, ministers, ambassadors, hugely important people, were bombarded with phone calls. At last, the British drivers, who had brought the productions from England, were given permits. After many hours' delay they set off to cover unknown, potholed and mountainous roads with two interpreters, one of whom hardly spoke English, and the single available map, which they had to promise to return.

Our hotel in Tbilisi was said, in a 1982 guidebook, to have a swimming-pool on the roof and 'terrible plumbing'. We found the swimming-pool locked up, in a temperature soaring to the nineties, and the plumbing, one actor said, 'makes your bathroom sound like Fingal's Cave'. In any event, the tower block hotel did little justice to the town, set in a steep valley by a fast-flowing, dark brown river. The streets of archways, trees and fretted balconies make Tbilisi look like a dusty Nice without the cafés or a more beautiful New Orleans.

With its moustachioed men, sloe-eyed women, flower markets, perpetual singing and Cossack dancers, Tbilisi feels less like a communist city than a set for a musical comedy by the late Ivor Novello. Yet Stalin was a Georgian; a local taxi driver had a picture of the dictator on his dashboard, and children still went up on the funicular to the Stalin Park of Recreation overlooking the city.

So we waited in Tbilisi, as touring thespians used to hang around Crewe Junction, for the sets and costumes. We were entertained by the directors of the Rustaveli Theatre. We sat under trees, beside a railway line, drinking red wine as soft and smooth as any Chianti and eating course after course of savoury meat pasties, cheese pies, spring onions, corn bread, strawberries and fat sausages held in square pancakes. During the first course, the toasts began, and they continued, almost without interruption, through the prolonged feast. A Georgian director would stand and fill his glass. The interpreter then said, 'This gentleman would like to pronounce a toast to the ladies.' The gentleman would place one hand on his heart and, in basso profundo tones, say something like, 'What is life without spring, without flowers, without heart? And flowers, heart and spring are united in one wonderful blessing. That is woman!' We would all clap loudly, stand, clink glasses and see off another bottle of Georgian red. In this way art, peace, the theatre, our 'better halves' as the Georgian interpreter called them, and absent friends, such as William Shakespeare, were celebrated. When the toasting began it seemed an unstoppable process; if you feel a toast coming on, it's impossible to keep it down. After a certain amount of wine I rose to my feet and, as a train thundered by, heard myself proposing a toast to peace between all nations and good luck to Sir Peter Hall and the British truck drivers.

My toast was sadly ineffective. Somewhere, after days of travel, our drivers had to fill up with diesel. The concrete tanks in which the fuel was stored had cracked and were half filled with water; this caused the engines to stall somewhere in the Caucasus, and telephone calls to Tbilisi were at best unreliable and at worst impossible. So *The Winter's Tale* and *The Tempest* and *Cymbeline* were played on a bare stage by a cast wearing sun hats and their own skirts and jeans. Needless to say, the plays appeared even more exciting in these conditions. The best performance is always at the last run-through, before anyone dresses up or worries about the set. Nothing then gets in the way of the acting or the words.

The opera house in Tbilisi is an imposing building where the inhabitants of the city can bring their children to fill in their colouring books and chatter among the gilt and plush. There were some visiting English critics who went to see the director and he told them he wanted to do more Weber. 'You mean *Der Freischütz?*', Michael Billington, who was of the party, asked him. 'Or perhaps *Oberon?*' 'Oh, no,' the director shook his head impatiently, 'I mean Andrew Lloyd Weber.'

When Geraldine James and I went to see *Salome* they locked us into our box, which we found sinister. The leading role was taken by a mountainous singer who was clearly not going to undertake the Dance of the Seven Veils. When the time came for this number, she removed a satin house-coat and stood, completely covered by a thick, black, nylon nightdress, waving a scarf amid a number of children dressed as Walt Disney animals. I saw a man in the circle eagerly viewing these proceedings through a telescope. We had arrived in Tbilisi without the headless corpse needed for *Cymbeline*. We wondered, in the opera house, if we could pluck up the courage to ask for the loan of John the Baptist's head.

We had all been warned, before we went to Russia, not to have sex with strange partners. An actor who ignored this warning in the Peking Hotel was robbed of his money and his Raybans. 'Take care of Georgian men,' a lady from the Moscow Arts Theatre warned the English actresses. 'They will put you on the back of a horse, or shut you in the boot of their car, and drive you away into the hills.'

The mixture of sunshine, flowers and English actresses was clearly irresistible to the locals. One Shakespeare star was walking along the street when a young Georgian came up to her and asked her age. Somewhat taken aback she said, 'Thirty.' 'That will do,' he said. 'I am twenty-three and you have very nice breasts. I know a quiet courtyard near to here.' Another actress was making a telephone call when an eager Georgian entered the kiosk and solicited her urgently; whereupon she punched him sharply in the stomach. He looked at her with huge, sad eyes and said in a plaintive voice and perfect English, 'You shouldn't have done that. You see, I'm a very decent chap at heart.' Geraldine James was offered an aphrodisiac in the lift. It's fair to say that in all these cases the suitors retired defeated, no doubt to spend years of their young lives denouncing the coldness of English women, until they were liberated from the Russian yoke and could devote themselves to the more macho business of killing each other.

Only one more encounter sticks in my mind. I was sitting on the terrace of the Tbilisi Hotel, wondering how I could persuade a waiter to take my order, when I saw a huge, laughing Georgian drinking a bottle of champagne with one great hand on a make-up girl's knee. I thought that if I went to sit with them I might be offered a glass, and indeed I was and much else besides. As I drank gratefully I felt a weight like a Sunday joint on my leg and discovered that my kind host had transferred his hand from the make-up girl's knee to mine; then came a curiously moist sensation in my left ear and I discovered in terror that I was being kissed. The foreplay was broken off, however, when he offered to buy my spectacles for forty roubles. When I told him that I couldn't be left to stagger short-sightedly round the Soviet Union, he withdrew his favours, saying, 'You English have a great deal of charm and absolutely no business sense.'

*

When we left from Tbilisi airport we saw our trucks full of scenery arrive and gave them a cheer for a brave attempt. I suppose I fell in love with Russia in Moscow, and out of love in Georgia. Moscow, the town the Three Sisters pined for, is full of unexpected beauty: the churches in the Kremlin, the view across the river, the streets full of peeling stucco and once-elegant houses, the cemetery of the Novodevichy Convent, where Chekhov, who called for a glass of champagne and refused all further medication as he was dying, lies under a little stone hut next to his wife the actress. In the same cemetery a general, monumental in stone, is for ever answering a telephone – to what eternal commander-in-chief no one knows. The people look forbidding, solemn, marked by that impossible ideal, Communism, which, like Christianity, seemed to demand too much of humanity and, falling into the wrong hands, led too easily to horrible brutality. And yet those who scowl at you on the metro will welcome you into their tiny, overcrowded flats and lay out every morsel of food, every ruinous slice of ham and herring, every hoarded scrap of red caviare, with more vodka and wine than you can cope with, blowing three months' salary on a single evening with friends. They have been slaughtered, tyrannized, spied on and betrayed. They remain stoic, funny, smoking and drinking far too much, with their heads full of poetry and music. I wasn't to come back to Moscow for five years, when my schoolgirl daughter Emily was a grown-up student and the high hopes of glasnost had somehow got lost between the free market economy and the Mafia.

20

*O*nce *upon a time, much more than twenty years ago, a girl's voice on the telephone was telling me she wanted to see me urgently, about something very important. She arrived and was extremely beautiful, with heavy eyelids and long, blonde hair. She was dressed in white. Without much preliminary chat she told me that she had discovered that she was an angel of God. She decided to share this secret with various religious leaders so she called on a Catholic cardinal, who said perhaps he could find her work with young people. An Anglican bishop asked if she had a family history of mental instability. A leading Methodist said he could recommend a reliable psychiatrist. She had come to me as the statutory atheist for a fourth opinion, and I told her that I had no doubt at all that she was, in fact, a genuine angel. This seemed to reassure her, because we then went to lunch at Alvaro's in the King's Road, and saw each other from time to time until she took up with a colony of Sufis and emigrated to France. A short while ago, almost in the present, I went to lunch in the country, near to where I live, and there was the angel again: a smiling, short-haired, middle-aged woman wearing woollen stockings and sensible shoes, surrounded by her cousins. Time devours most things, including angels.*

My family were completely unmusical; when my father's fingers strayed, as they often did when we weren't being sufficiently entertaining, to feel for the wireless, it was never to find a concert, always to follow the adventures of Paul Temple and Steve, or to stop the mighty roar of London's traffic to meet some of the interesting people who were *In Town Tonight*. Words were his music and he had no need of an orchestra. He would repeat lines from Shakespeare's sonnets: 'Not mine own fears, nor the prophetic soul / Of the wide world dreaming on things to come', 'When in the chronicle of wasted time', 'From you I have been absent in the spring, / When proud-pied April, dress'd in all his trim' and 'Farewell! thou art too dear for my possessing', proving the immortality of these poems of love and despair. If he had no classical music in himself he wasn't therefore fit for treasons, stratagems or spoils, but for Shakespeare.

My musical tastes came from my unbounded admiration for Gershwin, Cole Porter, Irving Berlin and Jerome Kern. Performing for my long-suffering parents I would sing and tap dance in a top hat, trying to manage a silver-knobbed cane, but as my dancing was rudimentary and I have never been able to sing in tune these performances must have been even more embarrassing than my one-boy Elizabethan tragedies. I had a banjolele, a small drum set and a kazoo; and I could just about get through 'Isn't This a Lovely Day to Get Caught in the Rain'. My favourite of all the films was *Top Hat*.

> I'm steppin' out, my dear,
> To breathe an atmosphere
> That simply reeks with class
> And I trust that you'll excuse my dust
> When I step on the gas.
> Puttin' on my top hat . . .

The effect, as I sang this clumping down the stairs, must have been truly awful.

The next step in my musical education came at Oxford, where I was introduced to Mozart and Brahms and W.C. Handy. My closest friend, Henry Winter, sharpening his thorn needles and polishing his records with a velvet pad, played me *The Magic Flute*, the Brahms Fourth Symphony and 'St James Infirmary Blues'. His soul was full of music but, as I have said, he went on to become a country doctor and, in an extraordinarily Wagnerian end to his life, murdered his mistress and, swallowing the contents of his medical bag in a parked car, committed suicide.

I came to opera, as I came to murder, late in life. I was asked to write an article on a month in the life of Covent Garden and I saw all the operas then in the repertoire, culminating in a new production of *Luisa Miller* with Pavarotti and Ricciarelli. Gautier was commissioned to write a guide book on Greece and, with the money he made from it, was able to visit Greece for the first time; in the same way I came to the opera house because of a job.

I also came to opera with all my prejudices intact. I had been led to believe that the plots were improbable and that no rational audience could take to a drama in which lawyers, soldiers, cigarette-makers and courtesans not only fall instantly in love on first clapping eyes on each other, but are able to burst into elaborate song about it without exciting the instant mirth of their friends and relatives. The words of these songs, I suspected, would not be tolerated if translated into ordinary dialogue. In short, I agreed with Beaumarchais that if a thing is not worth saying then people sing it. But two of the greatest operas ever written derive from works by Beaumarchais and no one would dream of complaining that the singing in *The Marriage of Figaro* spoils the play.

In that first season of opera my enlightenment began. I discovered many of the plots are about real people in recognizable situations. The stories of Carmen, Violetta and Rigoletto are true and moving, and Da Ponte's libretti for Mozart are among the best plays ever written. I also began to understand the dramatic role of the music; for what is sung is what we all feel beneath the flat and polite surface of our lives. The aria is the subtext of our trivial conversations; only in the opera house does it come out into the open. A man and a woman may meet and say no more than 'What was the traffic like in the Marylebone Road?' but somewhere inside one of them may be singing 'How strange this is', *'Sia per me sventura un serio amore? | Che risolve, o turbata anima mia?'* ('Would a real love be a misfortune for me? | What do you say, my troubled spirit?'). Opera is all subtext; we are spared the chat about the weather and the traffic information. The tenor or soprano within us all, and struggling to get out, is released.

So our deepest feelings, but not our spoken comments, easily translate into operatic numbers. Who would not recognize the crying aria from *La Festa Dei Bambini* (*The Children's Party*), the terrible, vengeful lament *'O la mia alimonia'* from *Il Divorzio*, the seductive duet 'Are you | Am I coming up for a drink?' from *L'Appuntamento* (*The Date*), the fearful 'Is He after My Job?' quartet from *La Conferenzia Dei Venditori* (*The Sales Conference*)? These and many other old favourites are the perpetual accompaniment of our inner lives.

I had learnt these important lessons about the operatic theatre and came to play Mozart, Rossini, Verdi and Puccini in the car, in the bath, when I was working or getting dressed. I had no idea that I would ever be fortunate enough to take part in a production at Covent Garden. I was extremely surprised when John Tooley rang and suggested I might translate *Die Fledermaus*, an opera which Covent Garden used to perform in a strange assortment of languages, each character apparently speaking his or her favourite tongue, around Christmas time.

My experience of translating was limited to Feydeau farces, which had achieved some success at the National Theatre (mainly due to the genius of the French author) and a German play called *The Captain of Kopenick*, the end of which I changed, much to the author's surprise. Translation seems to me a matter of finding an English equivalent to the play's period, keeping as closely as possible to the spirit of the original. The ideal is that the audience should think they are watching a play in a foreign language which they happen to understand perfectly. Although full of pitfalls, this is a far easier task than writing a play of your own. Accordingly I accepted John Tooley's suggestion with enthusiasm. I would have, he told me, about four years before the first night. Accustomed to write for papers coming out tomorrow or television shows due to go into rehearsal next month, I said that would probably be enough time.

I had, I realized, been over-confident. I should have read Auden's essay on the extraordinarily difficult business of translating opera libretti. He starts with a quotation from an old translation of *Ernani*, which illustrates the depths of banality into which the translator may fall in pursuit of rhyme and words which have to be forced to fit the music:

SILVA: The cup's prepared, and so rejoice;
          And more, I'll let thee have thy choice.
          [He proudly presents him a dagger and a cup of poison.]

After this dire warning Auden goes on to define the task:

In comparison with the ordinary translator, the translator of a libretto is much more strictly bound in some respects and much freer in others. Since the music is infinitely more important than the text, the translator must demand no change of musical intervals or rhythms to fit it. He, therefore, has to produce a version which is rhythmically identical, not with the verse prosody of the original as it would be spoken, but with the musical prosody as it is sung. The difficulty in achieving this lies in the fact that verse prosody is both quantitative like Greek and Latin verse and accentual like English and German.

This means that your translation must not only have exactly the right number of syllables to fit the musical phrase, but the long and short syllables must be properly positioned and the accents, or emphases, must fit the appropriate musical notes. No doubt the author of the original libretto had a far easier task. He could ask the composer to write for his words. The modern translator is entirely bound by the long-established and much-loved music, and there was no possibility of my asking Johann Strauss if he could see his way to giving me a couple of extra notes or moving an accent a couple of centimetres to the left.

So I began my task, ignorant of Auden's warning, but I was soon faced with the difficulties he describes. I sat on an Italian beach with my literal translation and my Walkman and started to fit English words to the German libretto. I would think of what I hoped was a joke, but when it was reduced to the exact number of syllables as there were in the German, when I tried to follow the German rhymes and get the stresses on the same syllables as the German, the joke began to look a little contorted, not to say strangled. So I started again, this time in Switzerland on a balcony in the snow. My family grew used to seeing me on our holidays sitting with an extremely worried expression and an opera in my ears. I found the big solo arias the easiest. The trios were like solving a difficult crossword puzzle in a foreign tongue.

At last I had what I thought was right and fitted, and then I spent happy days with a charming lady *répétitrice* and a piano in the catacombs below Covent Garden. She was exceedingly generous, and if my words didn't quite fit she would pop in an extra note or two that Johann Strauss never thought necessary. Later I was handed over to Covent Garden's learned and brilliant head of music, who was far stricter with me. He took away my extra notes, all except one, which I challenge any musicologist to discover. Then, one happy day, I sat in a big rehearsal room where the opera chorus, taking various parts, sang the whole of my translation to me. By this time, miracle of miracles, it seemed to fit, more or less, but the carpet could not yet be tacked down; the supreme test was yet to come.

Weeks before Christmas I was in another rehearsal room, at a read-through with the cast. Now read-throughs are part of my life. I'm used to the draughty rooms, the instant coffee, the set plan taped to the floor and actors who murmur, 'I don't think I'd say this.' But a cast who said, with great politeness, 'This has got too many consonants,' or 'If I say "divorce" on a high note it comes out as "div*a*rce",' or 'Please don't give me a "th",' added a new and alarming complexity to a writer's life. The confusing thing is that the rules don't seem to be universally applicable; while one singer abominates a 'th', another can put up with it and give it welcome.

There are general rules, however, which Auden has stated: 'An aria contains a number of high notes, long runs and phrases which repeat like an echo. Any English version, therefore, must provide open vowels for the high notes and runs and phrases which can sound like echoes.' So there is yet another burden the joke or moving phrase has to bear; it's no good its 'ee' sound coinciding with a high note. Once again the music is of supreme importance. It also seems to me that the singer's task is so indescribably difficult, that if the likes of Carol Vaness and Thomas Allen, who sang my *Fledermaus*, shy at a 'th', they must be accommodated by the translator. So far as I am concerned they were welcome to all the open vowels they needed.

Just to be in the great gilt and plush horseshoe of Covent Garden was a pleasure, and a lot of rehearsals seemed to take place on the stage, with the conductor in command and the director wandering about, quietly moving the singers as though they were pieces in a gigantic game of chess. I had strayed into a new world and, when I thought I shouldn't be there because I can't sing, I comforted myself by remembering that Johann Strauss the younger couldn't waltz.

Entertainments vary from the sublime to the deeply embarrassing, venues from the glories of Covent Garden to a huge gathering of fairly elderly comics at a dickie-bow and rubber chicken do in a London hotel. The invitation to speak at their dinner came as I queued up with an actor in a canteen during a rehearsal; like death it seemed sufficiently far away to be acceptable. As with death, the date inevitably came.

I looked round the vast room and saw that every one of what seemed hundreds of comics was male. The one I was sitting next to, who enjoyed, for the evening, the title of Commander, told me that this was so the jokes could be 'free and easy with no holds barred'. It was then I realized that I was in hell. 'I only played in a small family circus' – the Commander was as nervous as I was – 'and a function like this scares the wits out of me. What's more, I do not read with fluency.'

The melon balls were hardly on the table before a wispy old comedian got to his feet and yelled, 'I say, I say, I say, Commander,' at the top table. 'Yes, Sandy,' the Commander stammered back uncertainly. '*What* do you say?' 'I say, what's the difference between *soixante-neuf* and a terrorist?' 'I do not know, Sandy. What *is* the difference between *soixante-neuf* and a terrorist?' 'With a terrorist you can see the bugger coming!' The answer was drowned in a wave of laughter, but the Commander was deeply frustrated. 'I had a great act worked out with Sandy,' he was telling me. 'When he said, "I say, I say, I say, Commander", I was going to ask, "Who the fuck let *you* in here?" It would have been a great gag and, I tell you, we worked on it. But it slipped my mind at the vital moment, you see, and now the act's fucked up.'

From then on the 'I say, I say, I say's' volleyed and thundered from every distant corner of the vast room and the poor Commander, nervous as ever, stood up, flinching, to the cannonade. Then we had a trip down memory lane, golden oldies, the dirtiest jokes of long-dead comedians, disinterred. At last the Commander's dreaded moment came and he had to stand up to speak. His words were written in very large letters and a kindly fellow comic stood beside him, running a finger under each word, the task Hollywood producers are said to perform for themselves when they read scripts. His speech was frequently interrupted by shouts of ribaldry. 'How did I do?' he asked his helper when he sat down exhausted. 'You did fine, Commander,' the kindly comic did his best to be reassuring. 'All the laughs was at you and not with you. But you did fine.' My speech, which has been considered racy and once caused a blue-rinsed lady to walk out of a literary lunch in Chichester, sounded in that company like the address of a celibate vicar to the Women's Institute.

At the end of the evening a hitherto silent comic got up to propose a vote of thanks to me, the visiting speaker. He was a ventriloquist and he held a sort of Gladstone bag at arm's length, from which emerged a disembodied voice. From then on the evening sunk to even greater depths, for he opened the bag and removed from it a two-foot model of an erect penis, with which he held a lively conversation. 'Does this chap work much?' I asked the Commander. 'Not in public,' he assured me. 'It's mainly private functions.' At which the ventriloquist's doll began to compliment me on my speech. I sat there in full black-tie depression. This is my life, I told myself, surrounded by an all male audience and being thanked by a prick.

21

'*What is the 20th of June Group?*'
   The person who asked this question was the chairman of the fringe meeting at a Labour Party conference. We had eaten at a Blackpool restaurant and were now off to talk. In fact our collection of around twenty writers and journalists got its name because we first met, in a Campden Hill sitting-room, one 20th of June 1988.

'It's called that,' I said, hoping to raise some sort of laugh in the car as we drove past the Waxworks and the Tower to the conference centre, 'after the well-known Luxemburg revolution of the 20th of June 1849. A group of intellectuals, you will remember, took part in a failed coup d'état. There was a show trial and they were expelled to Paris, where they sat drinking champagne in La Coupole and remembering their glorious past.' I didn't get much of a reaction to this at the time, although Penny smiled tolerantly. However, when the chairman introduced me to the comrades and brothers, he said that I would talk about the 20th of June Group, which was named after the well-known Luxemburg revolution of 1849. At this, I heard some murmurings of assent from the audience and whispers of 'Of course, Luxemburg, 1849.' Our movement was, it seemed, easily misunderstood.

I had known Harold Pinter since the late fifties. Michael Codron had taken the old Lyric, Hammersmith, for a season when it was in its rightful place in the middle of a whirl of traffic and hadn't been moved, in all its beauty, into a grey building where it's stuck like a once-glamorous actress in an old people's home. He put on Harold's *The Birthday Party* and my first plays, *The Dock Brief* and *What Shall We Tell Caroline?*, and a production by Michael Elliott of Ibsen's *Little Eyolf*. Harold was some seven years younger than I and he had the unnerving habit of standing closer to you than you had bargained for. The fates, in handing out qualities, had given him the gift of aggression. He made some use of it, indeed, in life; but it was a boon beyond price in the theatre. It's his characters' aggression, expressed, suppressed, always unexpected and often terrifying, that gives his plays their supercharged energy. He also has, perhaps from his experience as an actor, an infallible a sense of theatre as some people have a perfect ear for music. Added to all this, he has a marvellous feeling for the rhythms of dialogue. With all these gifts it's idle to say that Harold's plays mean less than they hint at, when they hint so effectively at so much.

It's no secret that Harold's theatrical sense of aggression sometimes explodes into real life drama. It's less well known that he is kind and generous, loyal to the friends he helps in all sorts of unheard of ways, seeing them out of difficulties or getting their poems printed. On the morning after dramatic and seemingly serious quarrels he is a great one for sending flowers.

After the season of plays at the Lyric we did a revue (a vanished form of entertainment, greatly to be regretted) called *One to Another*, which was largely written by Harold, N.F. Simpson and me. Harold's sketches were unforgettable and greatly applauded, in contrast to *The Birthday Party* which, with the notable exception of Harold Hobson, had been quite misunderstood by the critics. As a trio we wrote an evening of three plays, which were also done by Michael Codron at the Arts Theatre and the Criterion. It was during rehearsals for this triple bill that the late Emlyn Williams said to me, as the oldest writer present, 'Well, you just got into the New Wave as the tube doors were closing!'

In all these years Harold seemed quite unpolitical, as far removed from the business of party politics as his hero and mentor Samuel Beckett. The only event which might be called political, and which moved him to anger, so far as I can remember, was the fact that his son was expected to take part in religious teaching at school. Later, I think much later, he became concerned with American imperialism in South America. He was also convinced that in Britain police horses are trained to shit on demonstrators. The aggression of dictatorships and power politics had been strongly confined in the claustrophobic world of his plays; later his feelings became more widely diffused and, perhaps, less focused.

It was the end of the eighties, the world had changed, and those headily optimistic days when we had done our plays together had receded as deeply into the shadows of history as the fighting forties or the tinkling twenties. Penny and I went out to dinner with Harold and Antonia Pinter and I happened to regret the apparent absence of left-wing journalists; even old lefties such as Woodrow Wyatt and Paul Johnson had fallen victim to the stentorian siren song and apparently erotic allure of Mrs Thatcher. The *New Statesman*, once powerful and respected, had sunk into a swamp of sociology and political correctness; the *Spectator* had captured the young who, dismissing all political ideals as airy-fairy claptrap, had become middle-aged long before their time. All we had believed in was dismissed as dangerous or absurd or both. After I had gone on in this vein for a while, Harold had me rattled by exclaiming, 'Do you realize what you've been saying! What're we going to do about it then?' It was some time since the Bishop of Durham had dismissed miracles as vulgar conjuring-tricks, so I didn't think we could convert conservative newspaper-owners or bring Bernard Levin out in favour of Neil Kinnock overnight. But it did seem we might get a few friends together to discuss the situation. Antonia, who, having been married to Hugh Fraser, a leading Conservative MP, was experienced in such gatherings, said the great thing was that someone should read a 'paper'. So invitations were sent out for the first meeting: the date the 20th of June 1988, the place Harold and Antonia's sitting-room. I think that what I, at any rate, wanted to do was to redress the balance of the political debate and remind everyone too young to remember that we had done pretty well with a Labour government.

As Antonia suggested, we had a 'paper' and Anthony Howard read it. He said that it was quite inconceivable that Labour could ever win another election, and we listened in growing gloom. In the subsequent discussion we did our best to raise our spirits with more optimistic forecasts. Germaine Greer came, and Salman Rushdie, Melvyn Bragg, Peter and Thelma Nichols, Margaret Jay, Michael Holroyd, Margaret Drabble and many others. In the subsequent meetings, when Denis Healey, Jonathan Porritt, John Smith and Barbara Castle came with 'papers', we began to educate ourselves. As David Hare said, the meetings were our evening-classes.

We did, however, have an immediate and hilarious effect on the world outside Campden Hill Square.

News of our meeting, ferreted out by Frank Johnson, who worked at the *Sunday Telegraph*, first appeared in his paper a few days after our inauguration. The reaction that followed showed how far the press had moved towards the Thatcherite ideal, which was, put briefly, that there is no such thing as society so we needn't worry about that; private citizens should devote their energies to getting on in the world, making money, buying shares and voting Conservative at appropriate intervals, and for writers and artists to worry their pretty little heads about politics is simply laughable. Even such a respected columnist as Peter Jenkins in the *Independent* thought that the idea of a Socialist intellectual had become absurd and, with a surprisingly vogueish view of political history, said that 'radical chic' had gone out of style and 'reactionary chic' was now the rage. So we awoke to find ourselves ridiculously newsworthy. In numerous London houses Tory groups were meeting and discussing politics unpilloried; indeed, Mrs Thatcher's ideas for government emerged from smoke- and claret-filled rooms. It was clear that no such luxuries were to be allowed to the left. We were meant to assemble in draughty church halls, drink strong tea and wear anoraks with bobble hats. A *Spectator* diarist went so far as to accuse Antonia of some kind of treachery because she allowed leftish bottoms to perch upon the sofas on which the Conservative Philosophy Group had once sat listening to 'papers'. The headline on the *Spectator*'s cover, LADY ANTONIA'S INFIDELITY, promised more revelations than the paper was able to deliver.

There is another assumption and that is that only the poor should be allowed to complain on behalf of the poor. If you earn a regular income, or have put by a few savings, you should forget the unemployed and avert your eyes from those sleeping in doorways. This is a convenient belief for those in power as it may silence eloquent voices of criticism; my only regret now is that our voices were not more eloquent, and that we didn't make better use of the free publicity awarded us. A final objection was that a belief in social justice imposes on those who hold it an obligation to adopt habits of particular austerity, Conservatives being free to lead the life of Riley. This seems absurd to me. A taste for champagne didn't stop Nye Bevan introducing the Health Service, any more than an occasional whisky deterred Mrs Thatcher from imposing on British politics the moral values of the Chamber of Commerce and the corner shop.

Looking back on that summer I think we should have thrown our meetings open to the public. Harold, it must be said, thought otherwise. Perhaps his way of writing gave him a taste for secrecy; at any rate he saw us as conspirators faced with deeper and more complex conspiracies, with moles burrowing into our midst and throwing up earthworks for the amusement of the public. Perhaps, and he may have been right, he thought that secrecy made us more interesting. In any event, our meetings were to be shrouded in silence. With Campden Hill Square staked out by journalists, we retired to Ruth Rogers's Italian restaurant on the river at Hammersmith, just opposite the building which will always be known as Harrods Suppository. There we were to hold a meeting at which Harold was to be the chairman. He was greatly concerned that our revolutionary plots should not be leaked to the press by the waitresses.

Of course our hiding-place was discovered; not a particularly hard task as one wall of the restaurant is mainly glass. I arrived with Penny and Ann Mallalieu in her van, out of which rolled two empty beer cans, none of my doing, when I got out. My arrival with the falling cans and *'two women'* was described as part of the lingering evil of the permissive society. But, as the restaurant was besieged by reporters, Harold became more and more determined that no journalist should be admitted.

One potential customer had been promised a table, in error, on that night when the River Café was filled with what the paper called 'literary lefties'. He was someone who worked on a news programme at the BBC and he had booked dinner for four. He entered the restaurant and, seeing such people as Germaine Greer and Melvyn Bragg, David Hare and Gavin Ewart dotted at various tables, he looked forward to a delightful evening in a well-patronized eatery. To his surprise, someone he later described as 'a man with a black pullover and heavy horn-rimmed glasses' approached him in a hostile manner and asked if he was a journalist. When he was compelled to admit that it was, indeed, his profession, he was unceremoniously turfed out. Then he sat on a wall and consulted his Filofax to make sure he'd got the right date. Nothing daunted he made another attempt to enter the restaurant, but *'the same man'* was ready for him and ejected him once more. In the end the River Café had to provide a free dinner for this innocent journalist and his friends on a safer date.

Behind the glass door we listened to an investigative journalist telling us about his inquiries into the ways of the army. 'When the police searched my place,' he said, 'I knew how women feel when they are raped.' 'When we get a Labour government,' a Socialist member of the House of Lords muttered indignantly, 'we'll have that chap behind bars in no time at all.'

Our meetings continued and grew in interest, at least to us. We discussed the programme regularly with Harold and Antonia and the four of us met one night over a pub in the Portobello Road. We had reached agreement on the next subject for discussion when Penny said, in all innocence, that she'd seen *Scandal*, a film about the Profumo affair. Harold, forever as unexpected as his plays, took the greatest exception to this and felt it was a terrible thing to make a film about Mr Profumo and discreditable to watch one.

'I don't see why,' Penny was brave enough to say. 'I thought in art no subject was taboo.'

'Art!' At this there was a Pinter explosion. 'Oh, "art", is it? Of course that makes it perfectly all right, doesn't it? I'm so glad it's "art"! It doesn't matter what sort of harm it does so long as it's "art"! How wonderful!'

We were already in the Theatre of Menace but Penny went on to say, 'Well, I was a child at the time of Profumo. I mean, to me he's a figure in history. Like Henry VIII.'

'Henry VIII!' If Harold had been at the end of his tether it now snapped. 'Did you say Henry VIII? That does it! Henry VIII absolutely puts the tin lid on it. I just can't sit here and be told that Profumo's just the same as Henry VIII!'

At which point, coming, somewhat late, to Penny's assistance, I was moved to say something controversial, such as, 'Piss off, Harold!' The Pinters left us and we sat thinking about life without the 20th of June Group and decided that we could probably endure it; but then, after a very short while, they were back, smiling in the most friendly fashion. I expressed my sincere admiration for Harold's writing and the awkward moment was soon forgotten, particularly as the Pinters explained that they felt sensitive about *Scandal* because they feared a film might be made about them one day. We have filled many empty moments since then in trying to cast such a movie.

In time Harold left the 20th of June Group, but we continued to meet without him. The occasions were less dramatic and no longer grabbed the headlines. Whether we helped the Opposition I don't know. At least we made it clear that a number of writers hadn't fallen for the mercenary charms of the new Conservatism. We owed the dissemination of this message largely to the newspapers which came to mock us.

Mrs Thatcher was toppled by the machinations of her own party, and Labour was deprived of its greatest electoral asset. In her book she has dismissed Neil Kinnock as a leader always to be relied on to play into her hands, and after the election they both departed into the political shadows. He left abruptly and with him went, so it seemed to me, a link with the heady old days of the Labour Party. He was the holder of the torch which had been passed on from Nye Bevan and then by the somewhat tremulous hand of Michael Foot to Neil, his protégé.

When I first met Neil he had only recently become leader of the opposition. If Mrs Thatcher had a poor opinion of him, he had little time for her. 'She retreats into stylized arguments,' he said. 'I don't rate her highly at all.' His wife Glenys had given him a Gothic ornamented board from a chapel into which hymn numbers could be slotted; he said he would use it to keep the score in his Question Time bouts with the Prime Minister. He had to fight against heavy odds: a huge Conservative majority which often shouted him down, a press which gave him more bad notices in a week than most writers get in a lifetime, and an apparently irresistible temptation to pack too many words into every bulging sentence. But fighting is something he understands. He has said he has a certain contempt for those who cower in the gents during pub fights (as I certainly should) and don't join in. As the election drew nearer, journalists followed Neil around in the hope of tempting him to blows, just as they followed his son Stephen round Cambridge hoping he'd drift into some newsworthy love affair. In neither of these doubtful activities were they successful.

This red-haired, pugnacious character is best seen at home with Glenys and their two glamorous children. On his own ground Neil's charm and enthusiasm seem irresistible and the wonder grows at the fact that the great British public found it so easy to resist them. It's hardly enough to say that the voting millions had never found their way to Acton and so never realized that England might have become a brighter and more enjoyable place if Neil had moved into Downing Street. It's not enough to know that the Kinnocks are the sort most people would like to have living next door, which could hardly be said for the members of the Cabinet they finally voted into power. Something, in those heady months that led up to April 1992, got lost. Perhaps it was the great British bottle.

Neil had considerable achievements. In a dramatic and eloquent speech he managed to defeat Derek Hatton and the militant left. Over the years he forced the Labour party, an organization much inclined to shy away nervously from power, to unite as a body capable of winning an election. 'Of course, I've no doubt we'll win.' At home in jeans and a sweater, a couple of years before the election, he blew an unexpectedly perfect smoke ring from his metallic-stemmed pipe, a scientifically improved version of Harold Wilson's showpiece. 'I should think by about twenty seats.' Glenys, similarly dressed, had, as I remember, as untroubled a faith. 'Of course,' she said, 'I've no doubt Neil's going to be prime minister. Just as, when I first met him, I had no doubt he was going to be an MP. He was one by the time he was twenty-seven.'

Glenys's grandfather was a deacon who sat in a big chair in the local chapel and sang hymns very loudly. Her father was a railway signalman and she said she had her first political experience at the age of one when she was pushed around with her pram full of leaflets during the 1945 election. Neil is the only son of a disabled miner and a nurse, a mother who was always ambitious for her son. Not only was he the first working-class boy to become a Labour leader since Ramsay MacDonald, he was the first member of his family to go to university. It was there, at Cardiff, that he met Glenys in the canteen when he was handing out Socialist leaflets. 'I must confess' – Neil Kinnock was honest – 'that what first drew me to her wasn't her political intelligence, although I found out about that later.'

There was a by-election at Monmouth, a very English constituency over the Welsh border. The Labour candidate was called Hugh Edwards and he appeared very nervous. Neil made a speech. Hugh Edwards made a speech, even I made a speech, and then, looking fragile and lost but always beautiful, Barbara Castle, who had been stuck on some draughty station platform, came wandering into the hall. Her eyes are blue, shining and almost blind, her hair still reddish, swept back appealingly. 'Keep your sex,' she once advised Emily. 'Use it for power but don't give it away.' Such, apparently, was her technique at the Ministry of Transport. When Penny expressed a moment's doubt about Neil winning the election, Barbara had called her a flibbertigibbet and said 'careless talk costs lives'. Now she was standing on the platform, holding a few notes she was unable to read, and when she spoke she was vibrating with energy. She scorned the government and stirred the audience in a way which reminded us, after so many years, why we should want to vote Labour. When the meeting was over we went back to the plastic hotel in a sprawling urban development and Neil sang, in a light baritone, a number of songs to the candidate, such as 'Hugh are My Sunshine', 'If Hugh were the Only Boy in the World' and 'Comes the Moment Divine When All the Things Hugh are are Mine'. It's scarcely necessary to add that Labour won the seat with a majority of ten thousand and lost it again at the general election.

*

211

It was Neil and Glenys's silver wedding party in the Inner Temple Hall, my manor. The singing and playing of Johnny Dankworth and Cleo Laine, the guitar of John Williams, woke the sleeping courtyards. I went to the gents in the special facilities reserved for Benchers of the Inn and I saw that my gown, hanging there unused, had stolen up a number of pegs as various judges and QCs had dropped off the twig. When I came back to the party, the Welsh relatives were singing and Neil and Glenys were dancing with the bewildering expertise they must have learnt in their student days. Even hardened journalists, who had followed his campaign for papers committed to the Tories, muttered that Neil would make the best prime minister but admitted that they couldn't possibly write that.

I don't know exactly when it was that Neil became sure that he was going to lose the election. There were certain warning signs, the Labour lead in the polls was perilously narrow. There was a somewhat overstated rally in Sheffield in which Neil and Glenys dropped from the sky as though he were a successful American presidential candidate with his lovely wife; this was unfortunate but I doubt whether it would have deterred anyone who seriously intended to vote Labour. So much had changed in the past decade. The unions had become the victims of a policy of overkill and pubs had died. Men and women no longer met in public bars, drank beer and small ports and argued about politics, life, love and the state of the nation. Pubs have become places for deafening music, space invaders, white wine and lasagne verde. Many people stay at home watching videos and have lost the habit of worrying about the state of the nation. The last decade has almost washed politics clean of ideals and pity. The voters went to the polls and decided to stick with the ghosts of the government they had once admired. They forgot what they had said to the pollsters, and forgot that, whatever your political beliefs, our constitution fails to work unless rulers change and there is an Opposition with some experience of government.

In David Hare's play *The Absence of War*, the defeated Labour leader, faced with apparently endless Conservative rule, says, 'Let's join the Tory party. And then let's all fuck it up.' Neil was still smiling, also full of jokes, only he looked smaller and thinner. It was understood that he would have a job as a European Commisioner, and Glenys was to stand as a Euro MP. He told us that when he had been walking up to the steps of the throne at the opening of the new Parliament he said to Mr Major, 'Well, here we are, in the same position as we were before.' Major said, 'I know just how you feel. It could have gone either way, and I'd be feeling just like you if I'd lost. Anyway, you did a great job for the Labour party.' 'As a matter of fact,' Neil conceded, 'he was being rather nice.'

Some months later I met Mr Major, in the unusual surroundings, for me, of a cricket match. Being stumped for words I told him what Neil had said about going up to the steps of the throne. 'That's very *nice* of you to tell me that,' Mr Major said, 'and how nice of Neil to pass that on to you. And how nice of you to remember it. That is very nice.' I felt I had to move away before my principles sank in a sea of niceness. Even this quality didn't allow Mr Major to give Neil his expected job at that time, and, in his early fifties, a tough and extremely competent politician was left to enjoy the sudden popularity the newspapers would allow him, and to perform on radio and television. For a while he was as unemployed as our political hopes and aspirations.

22

I am sitting in the boardroom of a television company where we award bursaries to playwrights. We interview writers who come with someone from the theatre which is prepared to sponsor them. The plays are mainly concerned with old people's homes, or Northern Ireland, and so make for gloomy reading; but surprisingly often we discover a new talent operating on a different subject and then giving away the money becomes a positive joy. What sort of questions can you ask a writer? When did you start? Whom do you admire? Have you thought of writing about your job as a pornographic phonecall answerer? Did you find you learnt a lot during the rehearsal period? If we give you this money, will you promise not to write for television? The young man answering the questions has small, gold glasses and designer stubble. His face goes blank when someone mentions Look Back in Anger. Beside him sits a plump, balding, middle-aged man in a black T-shirt and an earring. He smiles anxiously at every answer his protégé gives. Suddenly, in mid-sentence, they both vanish. I look at the committee members on the other side of the table. They are reassuringly visible. The sun, shining unusually brightly across the Euston Road, comes through the wide windows and picks them out in sharp focus. They show no surprise at the sudden nightfall on the candidate. I take off my glasses, breathe on them heavily and clean them with a red-and-white spotted handkerchief. No amount of breathing and polishing will alter the fact that half the room is in deep shadow and Peter the playwright is no more than a voice in the night saying, 'In my new work I thought of having a go at the environment.'

The retinas departed from the backs of both my father's eyes and he went to Switzerland in search of the best eye surgeon. In his day the operation was horrible. The eye was removed while you were conscious and operated on. For weeks afterwards you had to lie motionless, your head fixed, in some cases, between sandbags. If anything has improved since his time of blindness it's surgery. By the next morning I am dressed in a short nightgown and a sort of plastic mob-cap, looking like the unwilling participant in some surrealist ballet, and ready to be pushed up to the theatre in Moorfields to replace the retina which had slid off the back of my left eye. As with my father, the operation is less than successful. I can see a little with my left eye but nothing that I am looking at. This hasn't, so far, made a great difference to my life but, in spite of my love for my father, I never wanted to follow him in the matter of retinas. He was the man who told me to 'avoid the temptation to do anything heroic' and yet he went through his many operations with great stoicism. I don't know how I would behave if both my eyes went and I was left to feel my way across the room, my arms stretched out, my knees bumping into the furniture, calling helplessly into the darkness for a wife who might not answer.

None of this has occurred. I was well able to find my way to South Africa, to discover the extended family I had never met.

'Your Uncle Will married into the Jackson family and the Mortimers didn't approve of the Jacksons because they danced and committed suicide.'

The Mortimers were West Country Methodists. My grandfather John had been a Bristol brewer. In the early 1890s he came to the conclusion that drink was wicked, signed the Pledge and departed for South Africa with his wife and three children, Will, Gertie and Clifford, my father, who was then four years old. He set up as an estate agent, an occupation which he thought, strangely enough, more innocent than brewing. His youngest daughter, Irene, was born in Pietermaritzburg. The firm, known as Bale & Mortimer, did very well; the family grew and apparently prospered until, long after my grandfather's death, my cousin Jack Mortimer was

215

forced, much against his will, to go into the family business. He took his revenge by embezzling a great part of the funds and spent seven years in gaol. The firm never recovered and the Victorian building in Church Street, Maritzburg, which housed it has now become a bottle store.

My father always told me that, after he became a teetotaller, my grandfather drank nothing but a temperance beverage of his own preparing which produced all the outward and visible signs of drunkenness. I don't know if this was just one of my father's stories; like Niven's they improved with age and were honed and polished in the retelling. Before the great emigration my grandfather had visited Natal; he'd gone there because of the asthma he suffered from in the damp air of Clifton, and then his favourite tipple was undoubtedly cocoa. I have his records from the 1870s, written horizontally across a Letts diary and then cross-written vertically, presumably to save the expense of another diary. The resulting confusion can't be intended to mask any intimate and scandalous confessions; apart from work and chapel, he chronicles the most innocent treks by horse and wagon to the Orange Free State where he slept under the stars and ate horrendous meals washed down with cocoa.

'Sent on the Kaffir to bring back my horse and also to take up some beef, bread, vinegar, rice and cocoa to the wagon', he writes. Soon after they started, a yoke broke and then an axle. In this last accident the wagon overturned, depositing a bag of sugar on the hillside. 'We made the best of it and had a healthy laugh over our misfortune, which didn't interfere with our appetite and we set about getting some scoff cooked and prepared some cocoa. We made an attack on the potted salmon and then had a rusk with some sugar and cocoa (the rusks we soaked in a saucepan) . . . A delightful view by a little creek where I washed 2 handkerchiefs and myself. Mutton and cocoa for breakfast.' Later the party crossed a river, some of them on the backs of 'Kaffirs' and shot a wildebees and so had 'venison' with cocoa. The evenings were spent playing the concertina and, on Sundays, reading sermons. Late one night, after they had fried some bits of a buck (which a Dutchman had sold them off the back of his horse for half a crown), a Mr J started to talk about native education and suggested that the 'Kaffirs' should be treated as equal citizens. This was a conversation which seems to have been about a hundred and twenty years ahead of its time. It was to this strange land of cocoa and 'Kaffirs', chapels and concertinas that my grandfather decided to transport his family.

It was my father and not his elder brother Will who seemed, for some reason, to get the expensive education. Clifford was sent to Michaelhouse, Maritzburg's imitation of an English public school, and he was there during the Boer War. The school magazine records that various old boys and masters took part in 'the Historic Struggle', including a W.S. Bigsby of the Natal Carabineers who, says the magazine, returned from the Siege of Ladysmith 'a perfect wreck'. My father contributed a number of short stories to this publication; one was called the 'Autobiography of a Post Office Mauritius Stamp'. Another, 'The Green Diamond', began with a group of men discussing the relative merits of Lord Kitchener and Lord Roberts on the verandah of the Sea View Hotel, Durban. They are startled by a deep voice from behind them saying, 'If you would care to hear it, gentlemen, I should very much like to tell you the tale of the Curse of 'Mpala the witchdoctor, the son of Hesheth of the Bapadi, and of the effect it had on the lives of the men on whom it fell.' A formative influence on my father was Sir Henry Rider Haggard.

I don't know who reads Rider Haggard today. He wrote thirty-four adventure novels that made him famous; the best of them are set in Africa and deal with its hidden magic and mysterious history. Recently a reviewer, wishing to insult a contemporary novelist for telling anything as vulgar as a story, compared him to Rider Haggard, but the author of *King Solomon's Mines* was admired by Tolstoy, and Jung used *She* as a striking example of the anima concept. Horace Rumpole, who hasn't read much Tolstoy and practically no Jung, adopted Haggard's phrase 'She Who Must Be Obeyed' to describe his formidable wife. Queen Ayesha or 'Hiya', Rider Haggard's *She*, is extremely beautiful, has round, ivory-coloured arms, lived for thousands of years and was fluent in various languages, including Arabic, Latin and Greek, and was a 'terrible but most fascinating person'.

King Solomon's Mines was published in the year before my father went to Michaelhouse and *She* a year later. Rider Haggard had the same idealized picture of the noble Zulu warrior as British writers, such as T.E. Lawrence, had of warlike Arabs. There was Umslopogaas 'the splendid savage' with his razor-sharp axe Inkosi-Kaas and, clearly adored by the author, Umbopa, a servant, who turns out to be king of a remote country 'beyond the Lukanga river'. Umbopa is described as a magnificent man, six foot three and broad in proportion. 'I never saw a finer native,' Haggard writes, and he is clearly a gent to equal Sir Henry Curtis, the blond and bearded British landowner who sets out to find King Solomon's treasure. In the final, blood-stained battle scene, Sir Henry is dressed in Zulu war-gear – black ostrich feathers and a leopard skin – as he wields a great battle-axe: 'We are men, you and I,' Umbopa says to Sir Henry. This implanting of British public school virtues on an African king would be regarded as politically horrendous today; but no doubt my father, a short-sighted schoolboy in the year Mafeking was relieved, found these adventure stories irresistible.

Haggard used a curious biblical prose, even more archaic than the way Kipling wrote *The Jungle Book*, for the way natives talked: 'Down, my son, down my Baboon; down on to thy hands and knees. We enter the presence of *She*, and, if thou art not humble, of a surety she will blast thee where thou standest' and '"Ah stranger," She answered with a laugh that sounded like silver bells, "thou wast afraid because mine eyes were searching out thine heart, therefore wast thou afraid."' Writing in the Michaelhouse magazine, my father's version of this style was, 'Now this is the curse of 'Mpala and the vengeance that he swore upon the hand which humbled him, and that hath slain him.'

The implacable enemy of Rider Haggard's Umbopa is the witch Gagool, who creeps on all fours, is centuries old but shrunk to the size of a child and whose face might have been taken for 'a sun-dried corpse had it not been for a pair of large black eyes ... which gleamed ... like jewels in a charnel house'. Fears of witchcraft still bedevil South African politics. It's whispered among conservative whites that the ANC has infected the blood oranges with Aids. More devilish still is the ANC plot to infect the mice in Sun City (also known as Sin City), so they will bite the rich whites who go there to gamble and purchase love, causing their early death.

When he was at school, the headmaster was Canon Todd and my father would sing me, to the tune of 'Lives of Great Men Still Remind Us', the verse he had made up about this cleric.

> Todd's old slippers still remind us
> Not to case our feet in grime
> And by passing leave behind us
> Odours which are not sublime.

When he left Michaelhouse my father was sent to Cambridge to study law. His elder brother may have felt some jealousy about this, because Will afterwards refused to employ anyone who had been to a university. After he'd got his degree, Clifford came home for a few years and was admitted to the bar in Natal. He also entertained the children of the family by building dams and treasure islands in the stream at Hilton. He drew a map of one of these islands on which such places as the Dontchu Sea and the Tellme Strait are marked, leaving Rosie a blood legacy of appalling puns. One of his most vivid memories of this period was of seeing a black prisoner being taken to gaol with his wrist chained to the stirrup of a horse on which his gaoler cantered and the man had to run for his life. Soon he was back in England and joined chambers at Number One Dr Johnson's Buildings in the Temple, which specialized in wills and broken marriages.

He always wrote at Christmas to Rene, his favourite sister, but stayed away from that land of witchcraft. I also stayed away as an empty gesture, a protest I now see as pointless against apartheid, and only went recently to discover a great number of relatives, cousins, second cousins and cousins several times removed. It was my cousin Pam Edkins who told me over dinner in Johannesburg about the dancing and suicidal Jacksons.

It was my father's elder brother who married into the Jacksons. Will was a pillar of the chapel who washed in a tin bath on the roof of his house and would, if dinner guests outstayed their welcome, slowly and methodically unwind the bandages which supported the swollen veins in his legs. Mabel Jackson, however frivolous her upbringing, was apparently devoted to Will and would peel grapes for him as though he were Mae West. There were also lighter moments in the family life, however, and I have seen strange photographs, taken in the early 1900s, of a party where all the men, including my father, appear to be in drag. And then there was my father's elder sister, the exotic Auntie Gertie.

Gertrude Emma appears in photographs, less beautiful perhaps, but just as daunting as Queen Ayesha. She wears huge, brimmed hats and feather boas, her waist is hauled in, her skirts flow outwards. Without a hat, her hair, spread out in snakelike curls, looks as elaborate and ornate as the yucca in front of which she stands. She was known to the local Zulu community as Umuthimkulu, The Great Tree or The One Who Offers Shade, and she used to drive a pony and trap at a spanking pace down the Victorian streets of Pietermaritzburg. She specialized in Cockney imitations and sang 'Twilight' to the mandoline at local concerts where she was billed as Mrs Norman Pechey.

Norman Pechey was a considerably older man. Because of the rough way his nurse pulled his foot out of a grating, where it had got stuck when he was a child, he was lame, a total abstainer and couldn't keep up with his wife, Gertie the Go-er. She became the mistress of Sir Duncan MacKenzie, a savage old general who, after the Bambatha Rebellion, led a punitive expedition into Zululand, slaughtering and setting fire to huts and, presumably, returning to the welcoming bed of my Auntie Gertie, who liked a man with 'dash'.

Her home, for many years, was Dimity Cottage, a pretty Victorian bungalow in the middle of Maritzburg, dwarfed today by a large building which was once the police headquarters and now houses the ANC. As she grew older she would sit, wearing a black dressing-gown patterned with huge pink flowers, on the red, polished verandah with a green trellis. She would call out in what Graham Pechey, her grandson, has described as 'a harsh and rasping voice of such volume that she seemed to imagine the rest of the world was deaf', 'Hello, lassie, how are you today?' to young women, or, 'Are you two ger-fuffling?' to those she suspected might be lovers. Somewhere in the nether regions of her bungalow there lived an elderly gentleman but, Gertie explained to another of my relatives, 'We only sleep back to back.'

Gertie had a manservant called Mkhize, which was actually his name. To call your servant by his surname was considered extremely liberal in her day. Graham Pechey remembers that some less enlightened employers called their servants after the wages they received, such as Half-a-Crown or Sixpence. Mkhize would squat outside his quarters in the afternoons, still in his white apron and khaki uniform, selling muti – magical cures for all diseases. He would have to pack them away hurriedly when Gertie, awake after her siesta, screamed at him from the verandah.

I only saw Dimity Cottage almost forty years after Gertie died. It became a dentist's, and then a doctor's, surgery.

There were two big houses at Hilton, in the hills above the steaming heart of Maritzburg, one for my grandfather and his wife Selina, one for my Uncle Will and his wife Mabel, née Jackson. They are long, low, red-brick buildings with cool verandahs, marble floors, tiled fireplaces and roofs of that corrugated iron which seems to cover all Natal buildings from regimental headquarters to pigsties. The houses had a good deal of land and the Mortimers sold most of it for the building of St Anne's School. St Anne's always had English mistresses to teach the well-heeled South African girls who, bicycling in white dresses among the trees in faded photographs, look like Proust's *jeunes filles en fleur*. The St Anne's magazine for 1913, the year before Europe embarked on four years of dedicated self-slaughter, announced that Miss Robinson the art mistress had left 'rather suddenly' to be married and her place was taken by Miss K. Smith, my mother, who couldn't have been much more than twenty.

I was driving down to the Wild Coast on a hot Sunday morning when the Zulu driver took off his rhythm and blues and replaced it with a tape made by Will's daughter Mavis shortly before she died. On it she remembers old times. She spoke of my mother as 'a beautiful thin girl with huge dark eyes', who never seemed entirely happy at St Anne's. She had been born and brought up in Leamington Spa and bicycled each day to art school in Birmingham. She made friends with Leslie Brockhurst, who became an RA and a glossily competent portrait painter. She also met Dick Stubbington, who had a flaming red beard and used to visit my mother after she was married. I suspected, I'm sure wrongly, that they were having a torrid love affair and used to burst into the room unexpectedly when they were alone together. My mother's chief memory of St Anne's seemed to be of mealtimes, when a platoon of black servants came running at high speed into the dining-room carrying great plates of wobbling blancmange.

In 1916 the St Anne's News announced that 'the children have been admirably taught by Miss Smith, who left at Easter to go home'. Before she went the Mortimers, who still lived in the school grounds, suggested that when she got back to England she might care to 'look up Cliff', who was waiting to be sent to France, where the expectation of life for an infantry officer was about four weeks. I have a photograph of him wearing a khaki uniform and a gold pince-nez. He must have been one of the few people who ever thought of going into battle wearing pince-nez. When Miss Smith, just home from Natal, looked him up, he bought a picnic and took her on the river at Hammersmith. This was the start of their strange, life-long romance.

When my father told his commanding officer he was getting married, this unusual soldier said, 'No point in going out and getting killed then, not if you're just getting married. I think there's a job going in the Inland Waterways.' So began my mother's life of unfailing love and dedication and, tragically, the end of her life as an artist. They always shared the same bed and I can remember her saying, 'It can't be true. It can't!' as we tried to bandage up my father's jaw which had fallen at the moment of death. After his funeral she wrote, 'I am very lonely and nothing can quench my regrets.'

When I married my first wife, Penelope, she had four daughters. Our first child together was also a daughter, Sally. Much loved by my mother, affected, perhaps by my father's blindness, Sally started, when she was still at school, visiting and looking after handicapped children. Now she lives in Bristol with her artist husband and two sons, supervising the care of extremely handicapped and blind children over a large part of Avon. When my father, with great subtlety, was trying to put Penelope off the idea of marrying me, he warned her that I was useless at looking after the sick and said, 'If your temperature goes up a couple of degrees, he'll be off like a shot in the other direction!' Like all his wilder generalizations, this had a grain of truth in it; I'd've made a hopelessly squeamish and impatient doctor. Sally has more, much more, than made up for such defects. The painter Walter Sickert once said that the world can be divided into patients and nurses, and Sally is, like all the great nurses, an extraordinarily efficient organizer. She has helped take over and equip a building in Bristol where handicapped children can spend time and be encouraged, by a battery of toys and other ingenious devices, to look, listen and discover that even the slightest movement of which they are capable can produce astonishing results. One of these is a ray of light which, if you move a hand or an arm in it, will produce notes of music which rise or fall. Children, so handicapped that they have lost all incentive to move, suddenly discover that, by doing so, they can produce magical sounds in the air and are lured into unusual activity. This is Sally's work, her great talent and her consuming passion. She becomes, I sometimes think, more interested in me as my handicaps increase.

After five daughters, Penelope had, to our amazement, a son. Jeremy is the only male person among the eight children that have made up my life, and he always seemed gentler, calmer even, than his sisters and half-sisters. He met Polly Fisher when they were at school; they have been together almost ever since, married, and now have three small children. Polly's grandfather was the Archbishop who crowned the Queen and had a brother, it seems, of uncertain sanity, who had to be handed into a nearby mental hospital. When the authorities weren't looking, the brother escaped through a window and the attendants arrived and put their hands on Polly's grandfather. 'Let me go' – he spoke with the full authority of the head of the Church of England! – 'I'm the Archbishop of Canterbury.' 'We know all about that,' the men in white coats told him. 'We've got twenty-three of you in here already.' Polly's father, a most distinguished lawyer, is so sane that he gave up being a High Court judge out of boredom with the job.

Radio doesn't blast, like television, from the corner of a room; it speaks to people alone in cars, in bedrooms, workrooms and kitchens. It can command the services of great actors because it doesn't call for long rehearsals and they don't have to learn their lines. Jeremy has always worked in radio drama, where many writers got their first chance of hearing their lines spoken by actors.

I persuaded him to join me in search of our relatives in South Africa. I had got to know Graham Pechey, who had been exiled during the darkest days of apartheid and is now teaching at an English university. He sent word to Maritzburg and soon the telephones, like tom-toms, were summoning the Mortimer tribe to gather from areas as far apart as Durban and Pretoria. I had no idea what to expect. Would they be grim Calvinists, Methodist abstainers or last-ditch racists with steel shutters and a plentiful supply of small arms and Rottweilers in the garden? Would they be as eccentric as my father, as scandalous as my Auntie Gertie or stick to cocoa with their dinner like my grandfather? I had absolutely no way of telling.

I arrived, a little ahead of Jeremy, on Peace Day in Johannesburg. There were two minutes' silence and all the traffic stopped. In the dining-room of the hotel black and white waiters and waitresses, black and white cooks in tall hats, were standing with their heads bowed, praying for peace. As I got to know these people better, I learnt their names. One waitress was called Sweetness, another Birthwell, because, it seemed, she gave her mother an easy delivery. A waiter told me his mother called him Adolphus 'because she was always a great admirer of Hitler'.

Half a dozen close relatives whom I'd never met arrived for dinner. I was pleased, in a way, to see they were wearing blue ribbons in their buttonholes, the symbol chosen for the day of peace, but disappointed also. Could the Mortimer family not produce one outrageous apartheid apparatchik for me to describe and mock? It seemed not. The ghost of my grandfather, being carried across a stream on a 'Kaffir's' back, the raucous tones of Aunt Gertie – The Great Tree and adulteress, screaming from the shadows of her verandah – had, it seemed, been stilled for ever. It was the sort of amiable dinner party you might go to in Hampstead with a family who supported the Liberal Party. Pam Edkins, grey-haired and pretty, handed out photographs of my bearded grandfather, my father as a schoolboy at the famous drag party, my beautiful Aunt Rene, my father's favourite, and Gertie in her prime, her jutting sleeves and billowing skirts making her look like a tall ship sailing out to war. But these people were long dead. The later generations scorned cocoa, did complete justice to the Coastal Region Cabernet Sauvignon and accepted the fact that Nelson Mandela would be the next State President and that they had no alternative but to be nervously optimistic. It was a perfectly enjoyable evening. The Peace Day was held to be a great success as there were only three murders. A few days later twenty-five people were slaughtered as they waited for taxis to take them to work. It was, once again, as the whites comfort themselves by saying, 'black on black'.

Death is so near and yet seems, for most of the time, so safely far away. The road from the airport into Cape Town is said to be dangerous. Soldiers line it and helicopters guard the sky over a city of fragile shacks where almost half the adults are unemployed and one in five of the young men is going to die by a shot from a hand-gun. And yet so near, it seems almost next door, are the watered greens and manicured tees where white people are playing golf in the sunshine, apparently without a care in the world.

On the aeroplane we had been looked after by cheerful Afrikaner stewards and stewardesses, and wondered how it was that the Dutch, who have produced such a liberal and tolerant society at home, became violent racists south of the equator. Every brand of human being in this strangely isolated part of the world seems characterized by personal generosity and hospitality. No doubt many Boers cared well for their own servants, and their servants' children, and their servants' children's friends. An open house is easy to keep when you don't have to do the cooking and white South Africans who'd been to London were amazed that you had to give a fortnight's notice, and wait for a formal invitation, if you wanted to take your child to tea in the house of a schoolfriend. The situation, of course, changed when the servants became insolent and asked for things like votes. The Afrikaners are a South African tribe, like the Zulus and the Xhosas, and tribal warfare and private generosity seem compatible. The English, however long they stayed, never really became a tribe raised in the dark heart of Africa. The Boers called them 'salt pricks', men with one foot in Natal and the other still in England, with their genitals trailing in the salt water of the Atlantic Ocean.

The Cape is undeniably beautiful. From my bedroom window it seemed I could almost reach out and touch the side of Table Mountain, which changes perpetually, appearing and disappearing, standing out with daunting clarity or withdrawing into the clouds. When we drove up to Signal Hill, we were lost in a grey mist, barely able to see the bright blue flowers on the side of the road and the wild guineafowl that scuttled across it. We drove down to the beaches, brown strips between the mountains and the white-crested breakers, and to the fish market where oysters, mussels, crabs, lobster and huge kingklip were arranged in patterns on ice, like gigantic flowers.

At dinner we met a couple who ran a small independent publishing house. They had been arrested, and their daughter put in detention, during a long political struggle. From across the street police, with strong binoculars, had looked into their windows, seen the titles and immediately got a banning order. Against enormous odds these publishers managed to keep going and made a living. With the death of apartheid, books about the fight for human rights have gone out of style; now that change is inevitable everyone longs for entertainment. The couple in publishing are suffering badly and, in the theatres, Athol Fugard may have to give way to Noël Coward.

At Durban airport we were met by my second cousin Peggy, the beautiful Rene's daughter, and her husband Dennis, who wore long khaki shorts, long woollen socks and said very little, being an ex-army man, while his wife spoke quickly, full of memories and family news. 'We came to see you once in a house in Swiss Cottage,' she accused me, 'and you stood in the corner of your room and asked how many black people we'd had to dinner lately!' I thought how intolerable I must have been, a smug North London pinko far removed from the land of Umbopa and Gagool. We were taken to lunch in a grand house on the Berea, a pillared mansion, once used as an officers' mess, surrounded by jacaranda trees on the hills above the centre of the city. Peggy's son Michael is immensely tall, a huge Ian Botham look-alike, with gentle good manners and a crushing handshake; his wife Cass and two daughters are blonde and pretty. Michael is preparing a journey to Europe in an exhausting attempt to market an all-plastic supermarket trolley. All young South African Englishmen seem giants, their women change often and own a multiplicity of outfits. That evening we drove down the short Durban street given over to shacks and shanties, between two pieces of waste ground on which the black families don't dare to trespass. Their homes are made of plastic sheeting and cardboard boxes. One dark room, which might blow away on a stormy night, houses a family of ten. There's no water or electricity, no loos, no place to wash. Tsotsis, sometimes children from this and similar streets, have nothing to do except steal cars and rob people. If they mug you, the whites complain, you can't just give them the money and hope to be allowed home in peace. It's probable that they will take the money and shoot you.

There was an orange sunset behind the palm trees; we were on the hot, Riviera-like Durban seafront. We walked down a long slender pier out over the ocean. We had been drinking Margaritas and were a little unsteady on the planks. The gently undulating waves were covered with small black dots, which I took for sea birds. Closer examination proved them to be the heads of people, business men and hairdressers, Michael told us, relaxing after a heavy day, bobbing about and waiting for a wave to wash them into shore. For some people, life in South Africa is still idyllic in spite of a soaring divorce rate and a plummeting currency.

Pietermaritzburg has been called the last outpost of the Empire; the Union Jack still dangles in the heat above the entrance to the Victoria Club, which has relics of the days before the Union, when Natal was governed by the British as though it were a large Home County. In the shadowy recesses of the club, with its own small house, a patch of lawn and a large quantity of salad, there lives an elderly tortoise called Doranda. A brass plate secured to his shell announces that he was presented to the club in September 1914 by a captain in the South Staffordshires. That regiment was quartered in the barracks on a Maritzburg hill and, when they paraded during a famous thunderstorm, lightning struck their fixed bayonets causing some deaths and a good deal of madness. Whether this captain was affected I don't know, but he certainly gave the club a tortoise which has outlived two wars and most of the old outpost's inhabitants. We were in the Victoria Club with a local schoolmaster who told us that Doranda was the Latin name for tortoise. It's a weakness of the English public school system that many hours spent learning Latin leaves you with such a tenuous grasp on the subject, but Jeremy and I looked at each other in surprise, remembering the Roman military formation, with shields held over bent backs, which was called a 'testudo'. Careful research revealed the late Latin form 'tortuca', a derivative of 'tortus', meaning 'twisted'. The ancient reptile of the order Chelonia, with its trunk enclosed between a carapace and a plastron, chomped its salad and the schoolmaster, with a slight loss of nerve, suggested that Doranda might mean tortoise in Greek. The privileged and poshly educated citizens of Maritzburg go round with hazy memories of the Empire, and even hazier memories of the classics.

Another relative, a pale Scot in pallid clothes, took us on a lengthy tour of the Maritzburg cemeteries, introducing us to the gravestones of numerous Mortimers. I discovered that my grand-mother Selina, who had been brought from Bristol with her three children to this strange country, died when she was forty-eight; and my asthmatic cocoa-drinking grandfather lived to be sixty-five. They are all there: Will and Mabel, and Aunt Gertie, quiet at last, and the twelve-year-old daughter of Jack the embezzler, who died of hydrocephaly and could hardly move her gigantic head. The spirit of Maritzburg lingers on the tombstone of a certain Frederick George Mapstone (Sergt Natal Carabineers) who died fighting for his country at Ladysmith on the 4th of November 1899 aged 33 years: 'He has fought the good fight', the tombstone told us, 'and his Captain has called him to a high promotion.'

Bill Bizley, who lectures in English at the University of Natal in Maritzburg, had helped us to find relatives and plan our trip. There have been strikes and demonstrations at universities, particularly in Johannesburg, by students wishing to extend the principle of one man, one vote to one student, one degree. Some find it a racist outrage that any black student should ever fail. This is unfair treatment as the English universities never surrendered completely to apartheid, and they have to struggle with the hideous legacy of a system which provided no proper black education. Now Bill Bizley was lecturing his students on *Kim*. Kipling, the awkward, often bloody-minded imperialist genius, is being dragged towards the South Africa of President Mandela.

Maritzburg seemed too hot and its hotels too noisy, so we chose a place in the Natal midlands called, dauntingly, Granny Mouse's Country House. The drought had burnt the hills to the colour of coconut-matting and the streams and the waterfalls were dry. The feeling that you were driving through a scorched version of the Home Counties was strengthened by the place names: Caversham, Richmond and South Downs.

Our destination was a cluster of thatched cottages where a short lady, standing in the shadows beside the reception desk, introduced herself proudly as Granny Mouse. To call the hotel twee would be an understatement. Laura Ashley patterns, flounced pelmets, tartan scatter cushions and flower prints abounded. My room had a frenzied American feeling to it. There were any number of small cushions dressed up in the stars and stripes, the flounced curtains were red, white and blue, as was the patchwork quilt. There were a number of framed photographs of President Kennedy, and others of his assassination and his funeral. Seated on the lavatory in my bathroom there was a bewildered teddy bear. In the dining-room the black waitresses were huddled together and giggling, perhaps at the decor or more probably at the Mrs Tiggywinkle costumes they had on: big mob-caps, ribbons and aprons. These Beatrix Potter illustrations laughingly brought us liver and bacon. There was trouble near by; Zulus had attacked an area lived in by Indians and there were further massacres in the Natal heartland. It was the only moment in my South African journey that I felt fear. Who would wish to be hacked to death among a lot of Laura Ashley patterns?

Jeremy and I sat in Granny Mouse's English country garden, by a tiny swimming-pool filled with black and brackish water, with hadedahs, the glossy ibis, calling out above us as raucous as Aunt Gertie. The rainbird uttered its single tedious note. We talked as we hadn't found time to talk for years; not, perhaps, since Jeremy was at school and we made a list for our day out in London – lunch, a cinema, finally a theatre. Even further back he was a quiet boy among a crowd of older, bossier girls or, dressed as a Roman soldier, was standing beside my father's garden stool being asked, as I was asked at that puzzled age, 'Is execution done on Cawdor?' We went to a game reserve where black rhinos slowly crossed the road and giraffes and wildebeeste stood patiently, waiting to be photographed as though they too were tourists who'd come from another country.

Not too far away a dog was wandering in a township with a human arm in its mouth; an American girl, dropping her black student friends off at their homes near the airport, was butchered; white racists were stealing weapons in enormous quantities. Gagool was still scuttling about, full of malice, looking forward to the great dance when innocent men and women would be picked off at random for instant death: '"Good! Good! Good!" piped out that aged iniquity. "Are your senses awake? Can you smell blood? Can you purge the land of the wicked ones?"' Can the story ever have a happy ending? My numerous relatives, the salt pricks, are doing well to remain nervously optimistic.

23

For a long time the children have been preparing a play. We heard them whispering. They locked themselves away from the Italian sunshine. We found our clothes vanishing, hats and sunglasses went missing, make-up was depleted. After dinner, we go down to what is labelled on the bunch of keys Il Salone. It's the coolest and most comfortable room in the house. Through the high French windows, now shuttered, you walk down stone steps to the patch of grass, the roses and lavender, to the olive trees and the wood where there is a stream and snakes – perhaps an occasional wild boar snuffling. At one end of the room there is a platform, a grand piano, music-stands and piles of sheet music, a place where the true owners of the house play string quartets. We, the grown-ups, the old and the not so completely young, sit in darkness. After we have told each other how excited we are, we fall silent. And then the stage is bathed in light, performing as sunlight. Some people are having lunch, no doubt on the terrace, and then we see that the people are the children and the children are us.

Rosie is wearing her mother's shirt, her mother's earrings, her mother's skirt, and between her fingers rests one of her mother's fags, and she is gazing dreamily at a glass of wine. When Tom introduces her, in the manner of a gossip columnist, she pushes away her glass and says wearily, 'Piss off, Tom!' Claire Boxer, aged twelve, is wearing my hat, my glasses, my shirt, with a cushion acting as my stomach. Other children play other parents. They are us, in a new, fresh, well-lit and entertaining version, while we sit tongue-tied in the shadows, trying to put the best possible face on it.

'All women become their mothers,' Oscar Wilde said. 'That's their tragedy.' It may not be tragic, but it's inevitable, just as men turn into their fathers. We may wear different clothes and dance to different music, but we take over the same parts, the same loves, the same loyalties and the same old quarrels and unforgivable wrongs. Your mum and dad don't necessarily fuck you up, they just step into the darkness and invite you to take their place.

Humanity doesn't so much progress as constantly renew itself, carrying the same old baggage down the centuries, and in this luggage the grievances are greatly treasured. It's impossible to understand the bloodshed in Bosnia without some understanding of the Roman Empire and the Ottoman invasion; just as Ireland is still suffering from Oliver Cromwell. The British Civil War is now long over but the divisions are still clearly marked between the Roundheads and the Cavaliers. It's not just a split between left and right, for there are many Conservative Puritans and left-wing Cavaliers. It's not only the opposing claims of guilt and pleasure, the voice of duty or the hymn to Dionysus, the urge to gather roses on earth or lay up treasure in heaven. The division is stronger and more subtle. We live among Civil War battlegrounds, on a hill between two valleys where two families conscripted their servants to fight against each other.

Sometimes it wasn't even war between families but brother against brother. In Hambleden church there is the seventeenth-century tombstone of a husband and wife; half their kneeling children are dressed as Cavaliers, the others are in the uniform of Parliament. This may have been an astute political move to make sure the family would be seen right, no matter who won. I suppose anyone wanting an easy life would mix their Cavalier and Roundhead qualities like a sort of cocktail. The trouble with that is one of these heady draughts is bound to taste stronger and drown out the other.

Just past the rare orchids and the trees, on the other side of a

234

sunken road from us, is a great and seldom visited valley with a house, once disintegrating, in which lived the descendants of Colonel Scrope, a regicide who signed Charles I's death warrant. The last member of the family to live there had kept Oliver Cromwell's boots in his downstairs lavatory. The Cavaliers were on the other side of the hill. Mass has been said at Stonor Park, it seems, since the Norman Conquest and the Camoys family withstood persecution and huge fines, hid Father Campion, the Elizabethan martyr, in a priest's hole and maintained the observance to this day. It was only broken on one Sunday during the present Pope's visit to Britain, when the priests went off to catch a glimpse of His Holiness. When I was young the inhabitants of Stonor village were loyal to the old religion and the village school was Catholic.

Graham Greene and Evelyn Waugh used to visit Stonor and the 1930s chapel has its romantic echo in *Brideshead*. They came, I'm sure, out of affection for Sherman Stonor, the late Lord Camoys, who knew a great deal about wild flowers and came to the mistaken belief that he had been a parachutist during the war. After some long, and no doubt happy evening, he fell off a table and broke his leg. When he appeared in the House of Lords on crutches and was asked how he'd come by this injury, he is alleged to have said, 'When your parachute fails to open at twenty thousand feet, you are rather inclined to break a leg, aren't you?' He often set off for London, sometimes getting no further than the Angel pub by the bridge in Henley. If he achieved his goal he would spend his money unwisely on a large variety of objects, including unsaleable pictures, and visit his good friend Eartha Kitt. He was a man with a sweet nature and a fine turn of phrase. When asked why a relative had his term of training in a priests' seminary cut short he said, 'I believe he was jumping a little too low at the leapfrog.'

Our friend was Jeanne Camoys, Sherman's widow, the dowager, the avenger, the endlessly quarrelsome, whose abundance of malice made her excellent company. She was a small, pale, dark-haired woman who had been a great beauty in the thirties, with the exotic habit of painting her fingernails green. At some time a dose of Spanish blood had been pumped into her, making her liable to take instant offence and she was singularly unforgiving. Her features were small, but her jaw was strong and could set like an iron trap. Although from some upper-crust family, she had been hard up when she met Sherman and working in a hat shop. When we met she was living with her youngest son Bobby, at whom she would hurl demands from various parts of the house in a voice which was alarmingly powerful in so small a woman. She had been able to equal her husband in the matter of serious and devoted drinking.

I liked her because she carried the strange art of being herself to unbelievable lengths. When she first invited us to lunch and we suggested we should ask her back, she said, 'No need to swap cutlets.' She regularly visited the King of Nepal, whom her son had tutored, and on her return would immediately ask for and obtain an audience with Mrs Thatcher to discuss the affairs of that remote kingdom. When a rat appeared on her garden wall she rang up Michael Heseltine, then Minister for the Environment, and told him to do something about it at once. When he failed she vowed undying enmity to Heseltine and said she was voting Labour. Bobby prepared himself to fight the minister for his Henley constituency as a Gay SDP candidate. She was extremely well read and had worked in some capacity for Edith Sitwell. She hinted at a distant, passionate relationship with Graham Greene, but I noticed that he was nervous of visiting England when he heard she was in the country.

Jeanne was the only character I put directly into a work of fiction. One day she came to lunch, loud-mouthed, fragile and beautifully dressed. As I was sitting on the sofa beside her, she asked me to admire her shoes. I did so obediently and told her that she had very pretty legs, if I might say so. 'You already have said so, I think. *In your book*.' I apologized for the use of her, and she smiled tightly. 'Better to be lampooned than ignored,' she said, a motto for everyone who suffers from the attentions of *Private Eye*.

She sold the Dower House and bought a small, rather ugly building which she renamed Camoys Cottage. She would sit there at a long lunch, eating like a bird and discussing her rival beauty, the Duchess of Argyll. 'Having an affair with her nowadays must be like making love to a kipper,' she decided. Sometimes the room was full of treasures: Georgian bookcases, silver candlesticks, china and paintings of Stonor Park. Suddenly these rare things would vanish, as she had sold them when she and Bobby went off on a spree to London. Then, as she paid a surreptitious visit to the family mansion, coming away with a few pictures, a collection of antique cutlery or a set of Carolean lace-bordered napkins, some traces of splendour would return to Camoys Cottage. At the end, when she took to her bed, it seemed that the living-room was equipped with only a few pieces of garden furniture.

I remember one night, when we were drinking the proceeds of some small antique, she began to talk about her wedding and produced scrapbooks of yellowing press-cuttings. In the photographs she looked brilliantly young, probably dangerous, and desirable, with Sherman smiling modestly as he carried off the prize she agreed she was. And then, at the command 'Bobby, fetch the wedding dress!', her youngest son went upstairs and came down with a battered suitcase. 'Norman Hartnell,' Jeanne announced, 'did this for me. Open it, Bobby!' The suitcase was opened, releasing a cascade of white satin sewn over with seed pearls. Jeanne looked at it with wonder and longing for a past that may have seemed more alluring in retrospect, and then collapsed into its lengthy and voluminous train. Penny helped our hostess upstairs and then into bed. As I sat downstairs and Bobby poured another drink he said, as though it were the first article of his creed, 'A fellow should not be called on to undress his own ma.'

At the end she seemed to shrink and become a child again, and a small, thin-armed, deprived child at that. She was in bed and Bobby and I were sitting with her; the drinks were poured out and we were discussing old scandals when a jovial Irish priest arrived from the local Borstal. He also brought a small case, from which he took the materials for a Mass. As he lit the candles and kissed and put on the stole, I said I ought to be going. 'Stay,' Jeanne said, 'do stay. Father won't mind, will you, Father?' 'It won't worry me in the least.' So Bobby poured fresh drinks and we continued to chat while some unction was given. It was not extreme. She lived on for many subsequent drinks and Masses.

The soul of Jeanne Camoys eventually floated off, no doubt complaining vociferously, to await the forgiveness of her God. The chapel at Stonor was so crowded that the funeral service had to be broadcast to those who stood outside in the park where she was to be buried. The aged monsignor who conducted the ceremony said that she had always been a 'strong character'. It was, unlike most religious pronouncements, a considerable understatement.

Unconvinced of immortality, and not having the Stonors' privilege of burial on their own bit of land, my mother and father are commemorated on one extended stone, which lies flat on the ground, often overgrown and covered with dead leaves, in Turville churchyard. On one side of them the graves give way to the tall grass of a field; on the other the path winds to the church door. The name of the village has a Danish ring, and it might have been the site of an Anglo-Scandinavian settlement. It's certain that the King of Mercia's son gave the place, and the lands round it, to the monks of St Albans in the year 796. The squat tower and body of the church are built in flint – the only material available in the stony Chilterns – but because 'flint can't turn corners' the edges are stone. The nave is simple, with a Norman font. In one wall is a piece of stained glass, a hand holding a lily, which is the work of John Piper. A new aisle was built in 1733 by William Percy, who had become Lord of the Manor. He married Elizabeth Sidney of Penshurst in Kent, whose daughter was to be Shelley's grand-mother. The arms of the Percy family are displayed in the church and twenty-eight quarterings of families from whom Elizabeth Sidney claimed descent. This great show of ancestors is largely fictional. Sir Henry Sidney, two centuries before, had commissioned a pedigree from a researcher, who found it both simpler and more impressive to forge it. All the same, Elizabeth Sidney was proud of the display.

During some restoration work in 1900, a huge stone coffin was dug up in the south-east corner of the nave. It has a single cross on the top and was carved some time in the thirteenth century from a block of that Oxfordshire limestone which is composed of rounded granules, like the roe of a fish. At the time the coffin seems to have been made for a single man – he must have been both tall and rich – who lay there, unaccompanied, until the seventeenth century when he was joined by the body of a woman. A hole had been driven through her skull; so was this body the result of a successfully planned murder? Did some man unknown kill his wife or mistress and lift the great stone lid of the coffin to conceal her? 'Where does a wise man hide a pebble?' Father Brown asks, and the answer comes, 'On the beach.' 'Where does a wise man hide a leaf?' 'In the forest.' From this it follows that a wise man hides a body in a graveyard.

There are a number of miscellaneous bones in the coffin. Up till the mid eighteenth century the villagers didn't enjoy the luxury of a box, but were buried in the earth, wrapped in woollen shrouds. When the graveyard boasted more bones than soil, they were dug up and put in any old coffin that had room for them. So the tall and wealthy thirteenth-century landlord had his privacy further invaded.

Through the Middle Ages runaway serfs and outlaws lived in the surrounding woods. Now an MP who wants to retire becomes Steward of the Chiltern Hundreds, which was not always a sinecure; in the old days his task was to catch and hang all such

malefactors. Turville was also, for many years, the home of highway-
men who held up coaches on the road to Oxford.

By the 1930s things were more peaceful and the artist John
Nash, writing of that period, describes the chairmakers, sitting in
the sun, at work in front of their cottage doors.

Paul Nicolson has been the vicar of Turville for a decade or more.
He's a tall man with a balding head, glasses and a perpetual smile,
which is bravely worn through all adversity. He came to the
priesthood late in life, having worked for many years in his family
wine business, supplying Veuve Cliquot to West End nightclubs.
On fund-raising expeditions it appears that he was in the same
regiment or is, at least, a distant cousin of the establishment gents
in charge of charitable funds. He has the quality essential to all
friends, and indeed worthwhile human beings, of being entirely
unpredictable. He was violently opposed to the poll tax, holding it,
as most people did, to be a grossly unjust imposition on the poor.
However, he went further and refused to pay it, and would have
been imprisoned for this offence had not the church, to his extreme
disappointment, paid it for him. He is a high churchman who
blesses domestic animals at a special service on the village green, a
country clergyman whose life has not always been happy and who
spends much of his time caring for the poor and homeless in High
Wycombe, to the annoyance of Turville commuters who think the
church should keep its nose out of politics. He can be whimsical.
When his daughter, who won the title of Miss Henley, took to a
spiky pink hairdo he made no comment at all, but sat at breakfast
reading *The Times* and wearing a purple female wig. In church he
gives a feeling of excitement to the prayers as he commends both
the employers and the TUC to the particular attention of the
Almighty, to sharp intakes of breath from kneeling Conservatives.
He is a resolutely good man and we have to depend nowadays, for
sane and liberal opinion, on the judges and on the church.

*

My father knew about Turville because a friend of his, a stained-glass artist, lived there over a butcher's shop. At the end of the war my first wife lived in the same cottage and I used to walk across the fields to visit her. The pub was then kept by a fat, winking, moustached rogue who could obtain anything for anybody and, in the time of rationing, had petrol on draught behind the saloon bar. Rationing also caused the death of the couple who kept the sweetshop. They couldn't understand the points system, which regulated the sale of chocolate bars and gob-stoppers to children, and were reduced to such a state of despair by this that a suicide pact seemed the only way out. The husband shot his wife and then himself, and the shop never reopened.

Later the village school was also condemned to death. Edicts went out from a local council closing a number of schools, inflicting long, exhausting bus journeys on the children and robbing the villages of youth and vitality. One of the last cases I did as a barrister was a fight to keep our village school open. The judge was charming, the vicar an anxious supporter; good sense and justice were on our side but bureaucracy triumphed. For many years the school was an empty shell, and the voices of children were no longer heard on the green. This, it transpired, was exactly how many of the wealthier inhabitants, who had moved to the country after the school's death, wanted it to be.

The school building belongs to the church, and the local clergy-men thought it should be bought from the diocese and turned into a place where inner-city children might come for holidays, discover that bacon doesn't come from pink packages in Sainsbury's and something more of life and death in the countryside. What was suggested was that about a dozen primary school children should visit at a time with four adult minders. The bishop thought it an excellent idea, others of the clergy were enthusiastic; but this modest proposal, apparently so harmless and admirable, divided the village and the surrounding countryside more bitterly than anything since ship money and the Battle of Chalgrove Field.

Strangely it was the Cavaliers, some actors and certain barristers, together with older inhabitants who had pleasant memories of the school when it was alive, who favoured the plan. The Puritans from the city, perhaps anxious about the commercial value of their properties, were rigidly opposed to it and were deeply shocked when the vicar suggested that their views were not entirely consistent with Christian charity. Some of them had, after all, agreed to read the lessons in church.

We heard, by chance, of a character called Brother Jonathan who lived in the West Country and had run a similar holiday home for inner-city children. He had grown too old to continue running it and the money he had collected might, by the grace of God and the Charity Commissioners, be transferred to our school. Full of hope we found Brother Jonathan in his priory, which also served as the shop and post office in a West Country village. Part of the premises sold cornflakes, cheese, ham and postage stamps; the other represented the priory and had been consecrated. There the two monks of an Anglican order, Brother Jonathan and Brother John, who had periods of absence as a part-time schizophrene, conducted services, administered their charity and, judging by the smell which hung about the place, cooked a good deal of cabbage.

Brother Jonathan was one of six children of a London docker. He was a big man with strong hands and considerable charm. He'd had success with all sorts of people who needed help to get off drugs. The world also missed a talented tycoon when he took his vow of poverty, for he had managed to acquire a number of properties for his trust. He told us that holiday homes for children ran perfectly smoothly so far as the children were concerned, but you had to watch the adult minders carefully.

He seemed to be entirely in favour of transferring his funds to buy and run the Turville school for a similar purpose. So we were still optimistic when we left Brother Jonathan, but we had underestimated the Ironsides of the opposition. They fought a long and laborious campaign, voicing their objections to any charity which might have helped us; dropping, we suspected, a word or two in the ears of persons close to the Charity Commissioners. Brother Jonathan died unexpectedly and then Brother John died also. The West Country post office and village shop was bereft of monks. Our schemes were not approved and our troops were disconsolate. Paul had a number of inner-city children to stay in his vicarage; they required endless bowls of cereal and seemed most at home in the environment of the Wycombe supermarket, but they caused no disturbance at all.

I suppose there may still be some hope, but it seems likely that the diocese will sell the school and it will be turned into a desirable residence for a stockbroker or a person in public relations. There will be no sound of children to disturb the contemplation of the town dweller who, moving to the countryside, takes out summonses to stop cocks crowing, sheep baaing or guns being let off to scare birds off the crops. A heavy blanket of smothering silence will now fall upon our landscape, where the sounds of living have come to be seen as an intolerable nuisance.

24

In the grimmest days of tyranny, Jaraslova Moserova used to translate my books into Czech. She is small, bright-eyed, with a bell of grey hair and a face on which life and history have drawn lines which she shows as honourable scars. Apart from being a translator, she is a doctor who specialized in burns and an artist who drew illustrations for Rumpole.

During the bad old days she visited England for a medical conference. We drove round the village churches and pubs where I live and she was overcome by the sight of so much freedom. The regime she had to return to was unspeakably stupid, brutal and oppressive. She felt she was going back into a long tunnel with no particular sign of life at the end of it. At the end of our days together she was near to tears. Would we come to visit her in Prague? Would I telephone from time to time just to cheer her up? After a number of such calls I telephoned Jara to say that we were at last coming to Prague to visit her.

Czechoslovakia's bloodless, velvet revolution had taken place and Vaclav Havel had been transformed from prisoner to President. For Jara freedom was no longer a tourist attraction to be found in Henley-on-Thames. Yet her voice still sounded tragic as she said, 'That is so sad.'

'Jara, why is it sad?'

'I shall not be here. I shall be in Australia.'

'What are you going to be doing in Australia?'

She answered as though it were a minor inconvenience. 'As a matter of fact I have just been made our ambassador.'

'I thought for a long time before I accepted,' she said when we met for breakfast in a London airport hotel as she was about to step into the first-class cabin of the BA flight to Sydney. 'I had to be careful before the revolution because of my job at the hospital. When the change came I stood as a deputy in the countryside, and I won the election. Then I was in the council and Mr Havel asked me to go to Australia.'

Her husband, a lawyer who had been reduced to painting bridges by the Communists, smiled at her proudly as they dissected their kippers. In Canberra, as an ambassador's spouse, he would have to sit with the Middle-Eastern wives drinking coffee and talking about shopping while his wife discussed affairs of state with their husbands. I said goodbye to Jara and saw her small figure disappear through the revolving hotel doors. At least the victory of the West had one indisputably good result. Her Excellency Jaraslova Moserova was off to represent her country in the southern hemisphere.

In Prague Jara's sister Boska, a gynaecologist who gets about 15p an hour for doing hysterectomies and Caesarian sections on the night-shift, made us welcome. She drove us through the eighteenth-century squares which look like sets for *Don Giovanni*, immaculately kept. 'These houses are all lived in by ordinary families paying controlled rents,' she told us. 'Now they're going to be given back to people who are living abroad and owned them long ago, before the war. I really don't know what will happen. Some of them will be pulled down to build hotels, and we don't want that.' We were on the way to call on Dr Ota Motelj, the chief judge of the Supreme Court, who was, so Boska told us, a great man for the ladies. She also told us that her son, a film editor who had been kept busy on Czech films that won international prizes, was now unemployed as no one had any money to put into

245

films or plays. The National Theatre was empty and everyone stayed at home to watch American television. We passed an area of dark trees and bushes near the Central Station. 'We call that Sherwood Forest,' Boska said, 'because it's where the outlaws rob the men and rape the girls.'

The chief judge sat at the head of a long table where all the judges meet and confer. He was short, square-headed, with a deep, gentle voice, and he smoked with the energy and enthusiasm of someone who has to spend many hours in court, deprived of cigarettes. Outside was the place where the Communists carried out executions. Not far away is the street where a woman dissident was hanged; it now contains one of Prague's first sex shops. Dr Motelj talked of what seems to me a complete nightmare, the life of a lawyer under a long reign of terror.

'The worst time was just after the Communists took over,' he said, 'when they got rid of proper judges and the cases were decided by workers' committees. If you weren't one of the workers you had no hope at all, but if you were, you were bound to win. Things got a little better after a while, but now we have to get rid of a lot of old Communist judges. We are in desperate need of judges. Lawyers can earn about three times as much as judges now, so no one wants to take on the job.' I discovered that a Czech judge earns the equivalent of £250 a month, and I told Dr Motelj that an English High Court judge makes more than £6,000 a month. 'I'm glad my judges cannot read English,' he said. 'I would not like them to know that.'

After a morning in the law courts he drove us, at an alarming speed, to lunch. Menus are not enormously varied in Prague and conversations with waiters start with the simple question, 'Pork meat or beef meat?' The chief judge told us his recent trip to Canada had been the first time he had ever been outside Czechoslovakia. 'All the time the Communists were in power they said that, because I had defended in spy trials, I couldn't go abroad in case I betrayed the official secrets.' So the lawyer who risked his life in defending dissidents became a prisoner of the state. Then he thought of happier times in Ottawa. 'I told them that in Prague we only had one woman Supreme Court judge, and she's not even beautiful! The newspapers said that I was a sexist. I am very proud of that. Does it mean that they found me sexy?'

When we had got to the coffee and the plum brandy I asked the judge what sort of society he would like to emerge finally from the velvet revolution.

'I hope we keep a little Socialism. Just a little of it.'

'What would have been the real difference, if we were sitting having lunch in this restaurant in the days of Communism?'

He thought, ground out a final cigarette and said, 'Under the Communists, it would have been cheaper.' He was joking, of course.

I remember talking to an English general who admitted that when he'd heard Reagan say that the Berlin Wall should come down, he felt a few moments of pure fear. Now this unthinkable event has occurred and the West is deprived of the enormous comfort of feeling that we have an easily defined enemy.

Some people arrived from the frontiers,
And they said there are no longer any barbarians,
And now, what shall become of us without the barbarians?
Those people were a kind of solution.

C.P. Cavafy summed up the bewildering situation in which the West finds itself. The Russians, like the Czechs, must have been equally puzzled to be suddenly landed with a free market economy without a market; and such western-style benefits as crime on the streets, pornography, unemployment and a newly formed Mafia, swollen by out-of-work KGB men, with even more dangerous habits than those of the fraternity in Palermo or New York.

I went back to Russia to see Emily, who was spending her third undergraduate year there to improve her Russian and take an acting course at the Moscow Arts Theatre.

It was the Russia of Boris Yeltsin, hero of the failed coup and the CNN news, enemy of the speaker Khasbulatov and the endlessly obstructive members of parliament. Moscow was now a capital city where Gumm, the great glass shopping arcade just off Red Square, which once specialized in fur hats and voluminous knickers, houses Benetton and Christian Dior and the Galleries Lafayette. 'What sort of people,' I asked, 'queue outside these shops?' 'Mainly crooks, members of the Mafia and hard-currency prostitutes,' was the answer. In fact the sort of people who shop in such places all over the world.

Victory in the Cold War is so complete that the only currency worth anything on the streets of Moscow is the dollar. Pounds are derided, francs laughed to scorn, hold out a fistful of roubles and the gesture is ignored; but a few dollars will buy you huge pots of caviare, a fat goose to cook for a party of friends, any one of the eleven thousand prostitutes who now patrol the streets and bars, or many hours in the massage parlours which boast genteel names like The Welcome and The Prince of Wales. Forget the Peking Hotel where strangers in blue suits may be found on your bed eating pickled cucumbers out of a plastic bag. The Metropol, restored to its full art deco glory, is one of the most efficient hotels in Europe, with a first-floor restaurant so expensive that, having booked, I had to feign a heart attack in order to escape from it with any dignity. Gogol, Tolstoy and Dostoevsky are now the names of the conference rooms in the hotel's business centre. Only a few hundred yards from its glittering entrance there is a flight of steps where elderly women are offering a single shoe for sale, others hold out a paperback or a bottle of mineral water in the hope of ready cash. Many people are sleeping on rubbish dumps or round the railway stations; the rouble and full employment collapsed at about the same time as the Berlin Wall.

I had read, in the English papers, of rioting and anger in the streets, but I had to wait until a Sunday morning before I caught sight of any sort of demonstration. Perhaps two hundred people were standing on the steps of the Lenin Museum; some of the older women were carrying red flags on which the hammer and sickle still appeared. Other red flags, carried by similar ladies, bore the bearded face of Christ from a well-known icon. Some of them were shouting through loud hailers, but they were orderly enough. They had formed, it seemed, a strange alliance of old-time Communists and Christian monarchists: such a conjunction is unlikely to stand the tests of power.

'Oh, yes, the old Bolshevik women,' our friend Henrietta Dobryakova said. 'There are always a few of them holding up flags round the Lenin Museum.' She had been transferred from the Stanislavsky Museum to the house of Nemirovich-Danchenko. Nemirovich was a dramatist who, after a conversation in the Slavyanski Bazaar restaurant which lasted from lunch-time to breakfast the next day, founded the Moscow Arts Theatre with Stanislavsky. Nemirovich cared about writing; Stanislavsky was concerned with stage-effects and his somewhat tortuous methods of acting; but the Stanislavsky home is the mecca of many Americans, whereas Nemirovich's is a shrine hardly visited. Henrietta sits there unoccupied, occasionally emerging into the daylight for a quick drag on a cigarette. Her head tilted back on her short, round body, her wide eyes sometimes mocking but capable of tears on parting, her voice slow and precise, she passed judgement on the Moscow of the moment. 'No one here takes politicians seriously,' she said. 'We have many other things to think about. Personally I find watching the news worse than toothache.'

'Some English papers are talking about civil war in Russia.'

'Civil war!' Henrietta laughed. 'I don't really think we have enough energy for it.' Then she went on to talk about her home in Sebastopol and the real war, when every Russian family lost at least one member as the Germans invaded, and her father was killed when she was four years old. 'What do the Russians think of Yeltsin?' I asked her, after a silence.

'Oh, they like him because he gets drunk!' Henrietta laughed. 'When they see him in Parliament with his hair all over the place they say, "He's getting over a hard night. He's just like one of us." Probably you in the West think that it's either Boris or the gulag and the KGB. He does his best to encourage that.'

'And what do *you* think of him, Henrietta?' Her head tilted back as usual, she gave me a heavy-lidded smile from behind the smoke. 'To me, I'm afraid,' she said, 'Boris Yeltsin is a bit of a wanker.'

Emily was in Moscow with Tom, her boyfriend. They had acted Laertes and Gertrude in *Hamlet* at the Edinburgh Festival; growing younger, they were planning to become Hamlet and Ophelia when they got back to Oxford. Tom was about to do his finals and spent much time with the *Independent* crossword as a protest against last-minute revision. In the bar of the Metropol we met their friend from university, a girl who sang in a jazz club in the Arbat, who had just finished a love affair with a man uncomfortably close to the Mafia and who said she liked Russians because they were so honest, they made no secret of who they were: con-men, small-time crooks from the kiosks, poets or poetical drunks.

It was spring, but there was still snow on Chekhov's grave. Emily, a spectacularly thin girl, with the leather coat she had commandeered from me flapping round her, ran among the traffic, stopped cars at random and did quick deals with their drivers, causing them to change direction and take us wherever we wanted to go at far less than the rate for a taxi. In the Irish bar in the lower Arbat, where waiters in shamrock-green waistcoats pull pints of draught Guinness, we sat among Muscovites who have taken the place to their hearts. No doubt they have a great deal in common with the Irish; they love literature and strong drink, they can exert huge charm and suddenly become mad, bad and extremely dangerous to know. There we decided to give a party. So we went off shopping in the echoing halls of food, among banks of shining fruit, fresh eggs, vegetables and all sorts of cheeses, where old men offered us slivers of smoked ham held between a thumb and a sharp knife. The caviare counter was manned by two enthusiastic ladies, who travelled behind us wherever we went, offering us prices which fell like the Stock Exchange on Black Wednesday. It was all part of the free market economy, a market scarcely available to the ordinary Russian on a rouble salary.

The dark entrance to Emily's disintegrating apartment block was a refuge for Moscow's dogs and a huge man was asleep in one of the evil-smelling lifts. But as we crowded round the table, her living-room seemed warm and festive. Henrietta's husband Gennadi had been given no more children's films to direct since the fall of Communism, but he seemed in good spirits as he proposed a toast to 'Mr Mortimer, who has come a great distance to a strange country, in search of his daughter'. A middle-aged English woman, married to a Russian husband, said she had always voted Conservative in England so she regretted the old Communist days 'when you knew exactly where you were'. There was a successful actor there named Igor, one of whose films was playing on the huge television set that seemed to take up half the room. He was a gentle, loose-limbed man with an actor's wide eyes and a face of great mobility.

At the end of the evening Igor offered us a present of three mimes. They were entitled Drunk on the Metro, The One-armed Flautist and The Hunter in the Forest. For this last act, he stole cautiously into the room wearing a fur hat with flapping earpieces and carrying a non-existent but entirely visible shotgun. He was certainly in a forest, starting at every snapping twig, wheeling round to aim his gun at every shadow. Then, to his great disappointment, he was caught short and had to squat among the leaves. He had thoughtfully brought a sheet of newspaper for just such an emergency, but as he sat he became fascinated by some article or news item and missed the bird that came fluttering overhead. It was a long time since I had seen such immaculate acting.

*

British writers enjoy plenty of freedom and low esteem. A certain amount of disrespect is every writer's guarantee of independence and, although we're asked for instant views on every subject from open marriages to video nasties, no one takes our opinions, if given, particularly seriously. In Communist Russia writers were accorded high status and no freedom. Together with brain surgeons and ballet dancers they were the imprisoned aristocracy, given everything except what a writer needs most – the chance to bite the hand that feeds him. The Writers' Union in Moscow has always been a place of splendour and intellectual tyranny. It was once the palace Tolstoy used as a model for the Rostovs' home in *War and Peace*. We sat in a marbled hall at the foot of a great staircase, down which Nicholas, the last Tsar of All the Russias, after a heavy evening on the vodka, went tobogganing on a silver tray. Above us was the baronial balcony from which a self-appointed jury of servile hacks passed a sentence of expulsion on Pasternak. Now the Union didn't seem to be entirely devoted to writers; various entrepreneurs were sitting at the tables under the chandeliers and talking on portable phones. We were with Denis the poet, who had been pleased, three years before, to be crossing Red Square with Emily because her father had represented the Sex Pistols. Now he brought some poems he had written about her. They were in a magazine recently launched by a furniture manufacturer, a form of publishing Denis found bewilderingly new. On the whole, books of poetry no longer get published, although there is a huge market for the works of Stephen King. Denis went down to the basement of the ex-Rostov palace to look for peppered vodka from the Ukraine. 'Yeltsin?' he said when he got back. 'I feel I do not like him. I don't understand any of the politicians. Wasn't the USSR a better thing than Russia?' A few toasts later he said, 'I now think that censorship is the best thing for a writer. He should have something to fight against, and some stupid laws to get round by exercising his ingenuity.' Still later, we weren't tobogganing down the staircase but sharing toasts with a party of writers at another table.

A plump young man, with a pale face and shoulder-length hair, introduced himself as a Goethe Mannerist and his friends as the 'most talented in Moscow'. He recited a little Pushkin, we fought back with rather too much *Hamlet*; soon they were singing 'Moscow Nights' and we sang 'Jerusalem'. When we managed to collect our wits and go home, we left Denis a number of dollars to pay for the evening. Unhappily the cash was pinched by the most talented table next to us. 'The Writers' Union,' Denis said on the telephone the next day, 'is a very dishonest place.'

There was also the story of Emily's green jacket. She left it hanging on the back of her chair. The Goethe Mannerist, this time with the best of intentions, took it in order to keep it safely until he could give it back to her. Sadly when he got home, around four in the morning, he was met by a furious wife, who said she was sick to death of being married to a Goethe Mannerist who came back drunk in the small hours, probably slept with other women and made a pig of himself in the Writers' Union. 'You're entirely wrong, my darling,' the accused husband defended himself, 'I've been out searching for a present for you and I managed to buy this remarkably smart green jacket.' His wife went to bed mollified, but the next day Denis rang and told him he'd have to give my daughter her jacket back. So the poor Mannerist confessed all to his wife, who gave him such a hard time that he had to go out and get drunk at a friend's party, where, unfortunately, he left the green jacket which he had been seriously meaning to restore to its owner.

I went back to England and wrote a television story set in Moscow. There was a great deal in it about the Russian soul. When it was made, Emily played the part of the girl from a posh school, singing in a jazz club in the Arbat. The unit came to film in Moscow. Khasbulatov, the parliamentary speaker ('He wears high heels and pinches women in the canteen. No one takes him seriously,' one of Emily's friends had told us) and Rutskoi, once a hero of the Afghan war, had pushed Yeltsin beyond endurance.

Eventually he dismissed the parliament and our technicians, filming in Red Square, only found out what had happened when they rang their wives who had been watching television in England. Later the parliament building was fought over and destroyed. Yeltsin banned some newspapers and prepared for new elections with disastrous results. I don't know what happened to the Goethe Mannerist. Governments may come and go, but the spirit of Gogol and his absurd, sad, outrageous comedy will always stalk the streets of Moscow.

25

It had rained a great deal all the summer and for a long time, during the autumn, there was no frost. The leaves stayed on the trees far longer than usual. They turned yellow, red and russet; the maples seemed on fire and the beech woods on the hillside looked like cloth of gold. At long last the wind changed and blew icily, with flurries of snow, from Siberia. The leaves collapsed and fell, the trees made black patterns against the low and blinding sun. Another year was coming to an end.

At the midnight service the village church is packed out. There are new, fresh faces, sons and daughters, and the sons' and daughters' lovers, who are brought there to while away the long, soporific hours of a family holiday in a converted cottage. The few church-going regulars, elderly ladies, a retired schoolmaster, can scarcely find a seat. I'm also there paying my annual visit. I stand up for the Creed but I don't add my voice to the casual murmuring around me because I don't believe in God.

Lack of belief is also an act of faith; the one thing we can be sure of is uncertainty. The atheist longing for some deeper and more magical quality in living, and the religious man afraid he has devoted his life to a myth, have much in common. In 'Bishop Blougram's Apology' Browning wrote:

All we have gained then by our unbelief
Is a life of doubt diversified by faith,
For one of faith diversified by doubt:
We called the chess-board white, – we call it black.

My unbelief doesn't mean that I could do without churches. As
the slow queue shuffles up to the altar rails, Paul Nicolson says,
'You will be as much loved here whether or not you take Communion.' Whether that's true or not, I feel completely at home in
this church at Christmas. Even as an unbeliever, I am part of a
Christian civilization. Perhaps it's in its declining years, but
Christianity has been responsible for me. The poetry I value, the
art that is important to me, have existed in a Christian framework
and can't be understood without a reference to Christian beliefs,
even when they are rejected or used as a cover for more ancient
and pagan celebrations. The politics I have adopted come from
the Sermon on the Mount by way of Victorian Christian Socialists
and the preachers in Welsh chapels. For this reason, if for no other,
Christianity has to be treasured and learnt; without it we couldn't
understand Shakespeare or Milton. Without the Bible, in the form
it took before the new translation wrecked it, spoken English is
reduced to the meaningless waffle now heard in law courts and the
Houses of Parliament.

So should I be sitting, huddled in my overcoat, while others
kneel? Why shouldn't the ungodly pay their respects to this
superb invention, if that's what they believe it is? Voltaire said that
if God didn't exist it would be necessary to invent him. But does it
matter if God is man's creation and He is, like the Greek gods, a
supreme character in fiction? Fictional characters can influence
our lives, and from a jumble of myth and history there emerged
the revolutionary idea which has changed us all for the better: the
belief in the supreme importance of each individual soul. Ivan in
The Brothers Karamazov says that if human beings invented God
'the marvel is that such an idea . . . could enter the head of such a

savage, vicious beast as man'. So celebrating Christmas in the village church is at least as important as going in a procession to lay flowers on Shakespeare's grave.

This night began the year long before the people of the Angli were converted to Christ; they called it Mothers' Night and kept awake till dawn, in celebration, I suppose, of conception and birth. To the Victorians Christmas, with magical trees imported from Germany, wasn't an entirely religious occasion. For Dickens Christmas didn't mean the birth of a Son to redeem the sins of the world; it was about helping the poor and buying them a socking great turkey.

A Christmas Carol must be, outside the New Testament, the best-known Christmas story in the world and it asks us to believe, not so much in God as in ghosts. It is also a text of nineteenth-century humanism. The Dickens who wrote it was not the man at prayer but the committee man, the visitor to Samuel Starey's Field Lane Ragged School, and the chairman of a meeting of the Manchester Athenaeum, founded to bring culture and education to the 'labouring classes'. His concern wasn't with the stable birth centuries before but with the cry from the streets from the children of his day, who were 'condemned to tread, not what our great poet called "the primrose path to the eternal bonfire", but one of jagged flints and stones laid down by brute ignorance'. He contemplated writing a pamphlet called 'An Appeal to the People of England on Behalf of the Poor Man's Child'. Happily for us he changed his mind and wrote a fictional story. Does it really matter if the founders of the Christian religion did the same?

You could say Dickens's conception of Christmas was highly commercial, with the sale of huge birds, great puddings and plenty of port and brandy; but what's wrong with lights in Regent Street and people giving each other presents even if (and Christmas has to be a festival of tolerance) such presents consist of computer games and Lady Thatcher's memoirs? John Betjeman said that:

No loving fingers tying strings
Around those tissued fripperies,
   The sweet and silly Christmas things
Bath salts and inexpensive scent
And hideous tie so kindly meant,

No Love that in a family dwells,
   No Carolling in frosty air
Nor all the steeple-shaking bells
   Can with this simple Truth compare –
That God was Man in Palestine
And lives today in Bread and Wine.

Perhaps they can't, but it's no bad thing to have a day in the year
when family life, an institution much idealized by politicians who
are too busy sleeping with their researchers and attending all-night
sittings to have much time for it, consists of often warring, jealous,
quarrelling and closely related people doing their best to give each
other pleasure.

It's also important to have festivals, and their enhancement of
life doesn't depend at all on literal beliefs. The Roman centurion,
posted to Britain after the birth of Christ, may have started to
doubt the powers of the old gods, but he still paid his dues to
Vulcan and Mars, or wrote a curse to those who'd carried off his
girlfriend and recited it by the sacred spring of Minerva at Bath.
There could be nothing more depressing than modern or politically
correct festivals if we had to invent them, and there are already
signs of danger. There have been objections to an exhibition of
Women in Art because it contains paintings of the Virgin Mary
and the abduction of Helen to Troy. Women, it seems, must no
longer be seen as madonnas, or virgins, or the beauty who launched
a thousand ships and was hatched out from one of the eggs her
mother Leda laid after she had been seduced by Jupiter disguised
as a swan. These are not seen as suitable role models for women.

More sinister news comes from Australia, where some dotty

government commission has banned the singing of Christmas carols in kindergartens as they are 'culturally irrelevant' (regardless of the fact that Christianity is the basis of one of the world's greatest cultures). An equally dotty London borough has followed suit and banned nativity plays. The brave new world is threatening us in all its greyness, and its hideous attempt to impose a dictatorship on thought. The great advantage of the old gods, and the old religions, is that they sprang from life and cared nothing for political correctness.

The service is over, Paul Nicolson is shaking hands with everyone at the church door. The bells are ringing and the cold in the graveyard slaps us across the face. We go home to set out mince pies and glasses of wine to be consumed by a mythical figure even the youngest children can scarcely believe in.

All fiction, all plays, all detective stories, all parables, all fairy stories, myths and religions, are our attempt to provide an explanation for the haphazard events of our lives, or at least impose some order on them. We long for the logical patterns which poets and story-tellers provide so easily. So, depending on the time and place of our birth, we may decide that this cruel world is some sort of obstacle course on the way to heaven, or that quarrels among the gods are responsible for wars and shipwrecks, or that God was born of a virgin and executed to redeem our sins; or that, far from being merciful, God has decreed the death sentence for blaspheming against Him and His holy works.

'Literature is a luxury;' said Chesterton, 'fiction is a necessity.' Fiction is our excuse to play God, to create characters and set them in motion, to make them act out, at our command, what we hope, or believe, is the truth about existence. If only I were now writing a novel I could tie up all the loose ends of this book so that they pointed to a theme. I could explain these random encounters by some analysis of my character which would turn me into a credible and consistent work of fiction.

I have not been writing a novel, although once you decide what to leave out, or how you feel about an event that happened, or how you would like the reader to see it, you are on your way to inventing a myth. Politicians describing the economy, lawyers and judges describing a crime, every one of us re-inventing our pasts, are myth-makers to a greater or lesser degree. Fiction is what comes naturally to us.

All the writer, deprived of fiction's true freedom, can do is to try to remember, quite honestly, how things seemed at the time. This is how I felt then about the murderers and friends; the murderers who might have been momentary friends, and the friends, one friend at least, who became a murderer. It was not my business to reach a verdict on them and so there need be no summing-up. Summing-ups in court are, in any event, thinly disguised attempts to persuade twelve honest citizens to agree with you.

I have started having the dream again. I am running down the cold, marble corridors of the Law Courts to do some case I haven't prepared; in fact I know nothing whatever about it. Not only have I no idea what to say, I am inappropriately dressed. I am wearing a bright blue shirt, bought some years before for a summer holiday, and shorts, or I am in pyjamas. I turn up the collar of the shirt so that it may look as though it were of the stiff and stand-up variety. Someone I pass gives me a pair of crumpled white bands, which I try to tie round my neck, but I can't undo, or do up, the knot. I borrow a wig which I perch on my head. I haven't shaved for several days. When I get to the glass-panelled door of the courtroom it's locked and I rattle it uselessly. Inside I can see nothing but darkness.

One day, however, it will open and, I am assured, there will be a bright and blinding light. By that time will I have completely mastered my brief, or understood my instructions? Will I ever?